1—9
Question 9

P8 N/z ext
P8 8/ 1, 2, 3

Family Living

Family Living

Carol Leavenworth
Gay Hendricks
Kathlyn Gay
Lynda C. Harriman
Marlene Miller Kreinin

Prentice Hall   Needham, Massachusetts   Englewood Cliffs, New Jersey

CREDITS

Program Manager: **Marita A. Sullivan**
Art Director: **L. Christopher Valente**
Editor: **Margaret A. Sawyer**
Contributing Editor: **Pamela D. McCormick**
Contributing Writers: **Judith E. Harper**
Lynn Robbins
Suzanne J. Stark
Production Editors: **Suzanne M. Higgins**
Barbara A. Marchilonis
Design: **Shay J. Mayer**
Design Production: **Shay J. Mayer**
Design Production Assistants: **Katherine S. Diamond**
Michael A. Granger
Lisa-Jean Smith
Preparation Services Manager: **Martha E. Ballentine**
Senior Buyer: **Annie Puciloski**
Cover Design: **Martucci Studio**
Photo Research: **Pembroke Herbert/Picture**
Research Consultants

CONSULTANT

Yvonne S. Gentzler, PH.D.
Assistant Professor
Home Economics Education
University of Maryland
College Park, MD

ISBN: 0-13-301961-6
94 93 92 91 5 4 3

Prentice-Hall of Australia, Pty, Ltd., Sydney
Prentice-Hall Canada Inc., Toronto
Prentice-Hall Hispanoamericana, S.A., Mexico
Prentice-Hall of India Private Ltd., New Delhi
Prentice-Hall International (UK) Limited, London
Prentice-Hall of Japan, Inc., Tokyo
Prentice-Hall of Southeast Asia Pte. Ltd., Singapore
Editora Prentice-Hall Do Brasil Ltda., Rio de Janeiro

A Simon & Schuster Company

REVIEWERS

Joanne Bendall
Supervisor
South Bend School District
South Bend, Indiana

Linda M. Geary
Family Life Instructor
Sonoma Valley High School
Sonoma, CA 95404

Dr. Bettie Herring
Director of Vocational and Adult Education
Fort Worth Independent School District
Fort Worth, TX

Carol Maggioncalda
Department Chairperson/Teacher Home Economics
Family Living
Clearview High School
Mullica Hill, NJ 08062

Kristine E. Martin
Teacher of Home Economics
Rancocas Valley Regional High School
Mt. Holly, NJ 08060

Alma L. Payne
Home Economics Teacher
L. D. Bell High School
Hurst, TX 76053

Elaine K. Petach
Home Economics Supervisor
Long Branch High School
Long Branch, NJ

Jeanette Powell
Teacher—Department Chairperson
Olympic High School
Concord, CA 94520

Pat Stein
Assistant Professor
Department of Consumer & Family Studies
Georgia College
Milledgeville, GA 31061

Contents

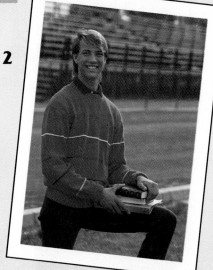

Features

Charts, Graphs, and Tables

1 Defining Yourself

As you read, think about:

- what two major factors affect human potential.
- how your identity is affected by your personal needs and roles.
- how Jean Piaget's stages of mental development affect your intellectual growth.
- how you learn to identify and communicate your emotions.
- how each stage in the life cycle presents a crisis to be resolved.

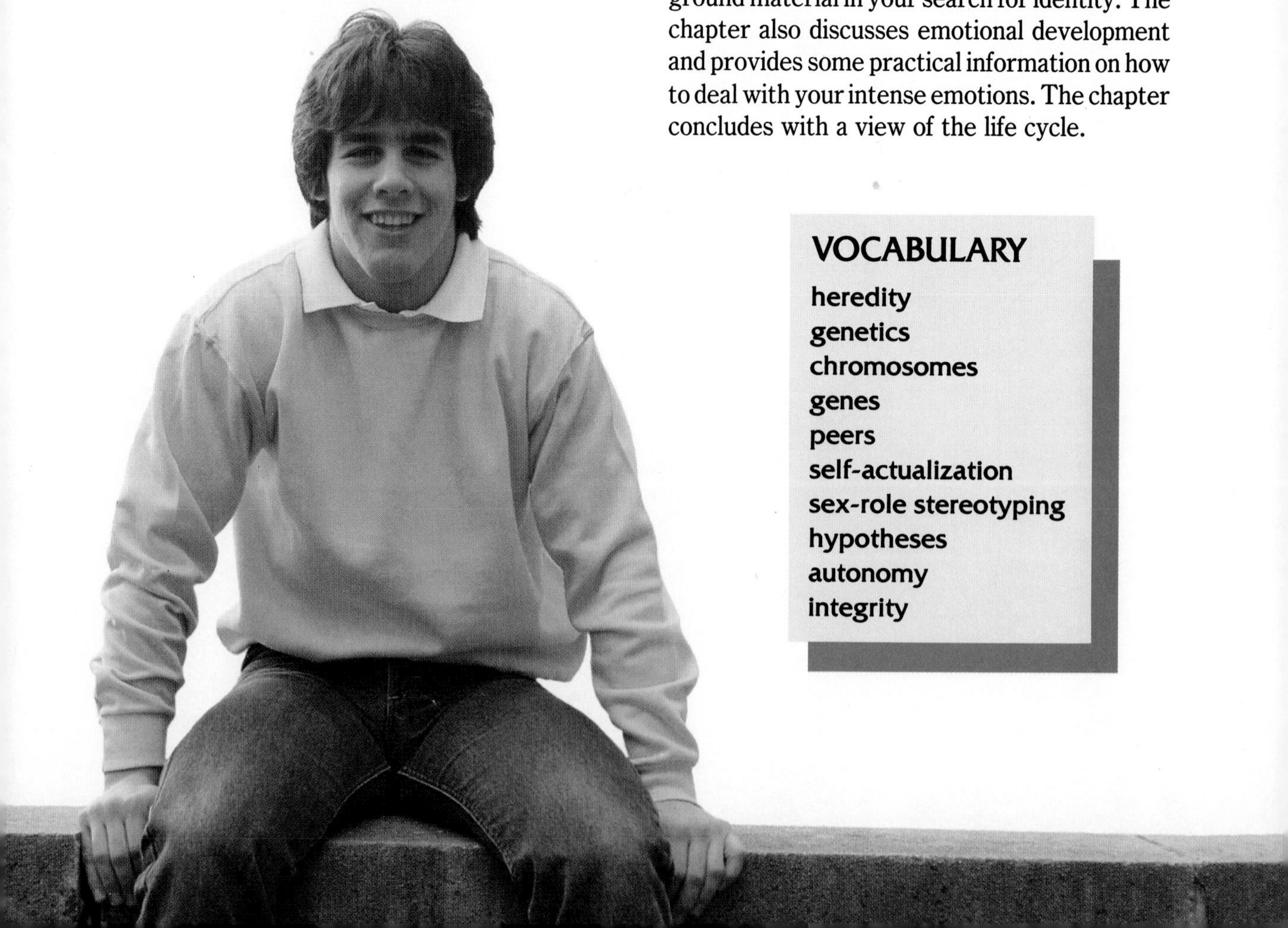

Solving the puzzles about your identity is a crucial task of adolescence. Before you enter adult life, you need to have a clear sense of who you are.

This chapter concentrates on the initial steps in the search for identity. First, there is an examination of heredity and environment and how these factors influence your development. Next, the chapter presents theories by various psychologists on human roles and needs. Facts about physical growth and theories about intellectual development provide you with background material in your search for identity. The chapter also discusses emotional development and provides some practical information on how to deal with your intense emotions. The chapter concludes with a view of the life cycle.

VOCABULARY

heredity
genetics
chromosomes
genes
peers
self-actualization
sex-role stereotyping
hypotheses
autonomy
integrity

Developing a secure sense of identity is one of the challenges of adolescence.

Identity

"What I am to be, I am now becoming." Life is dynamic and changes all the time. You also change every day. Adolescence is a time for moving forward to meet the challenges of the future. It also is a time to pause and examine the big questions that everyone faces at some time. "Who am I?" "What will I become?" "What do I want to do with my life?" Questions like these must be answered.

Searching for "The Real Me"

Libby, the heroine of the short story, "The Summer of Truth," pauses to ask herself some questions about her identity.

Who was I, anyway? I tried to count up the things that were real about the inside of me—the feeling, thinking Libby—and I couldn't find much. Was I, for example, the kind of girl who liked swimming? I didn't know. It had stopped being a simple thing between me and the water a long time ago. It was all mixed up with how I looked in my bathing suit and who would go with me to the pool and whether any boys would notice me there. . . .

Was I really the kind of girl who liked to go walking alone in the rain, or did I just say so because it sounded romantic? I hadn't actually ever done it. Would I rather dance than eat? Did I really like Dixieland music? *What was I?* A month earlier I could have given an easy "yes" or "no" to any of those questions. But now that I had time to think, I didn't know any of the answers. I had pretended to be so many different things to so many different people for such a long time that I couldn't find *me*.

The search for one's identity continues long past the teenage years and years of young adulthood. Nevertheless, it is during these years that people are most confused about who they really are. Adolescence is a troubling time, full of the turbulent search for identity. Like Libby, teenagers are looking to "find *me*."

In the passage from "The Summer of Truth," Libby reveals that she does not feel comfortable about her appearance because she is so self-conscious. She doesn't know in what direction she is "growing" because she isn't sure of her own likes and dislikes. Also, she has not received "recognition from those who count" in her estimation because she has been playing "pretend" games with others "for such a long time that I couldn't find *me*." Does this problem sound familiar? You, too, are probably involved in a search for identity. The situation may apply to you even if you haven't used the same words to describe it, and even if you haven't been asking yourself a lot of questions.

Getting a diploma can add to feelings of self-esteem and self-confidence.

The Sources of Your Potential

Everybody is born with the potential for mental achievement, just as a person is born with the capacity for friendship, love, physical activity, and career accomplishment. Recognizing your potential is a big step in the search for identity. Your next step is to consider what you intend to do with your potential. The decision depends on more than just circumstances and is not solely in your control.

The two main factors that affect the development of your potential are your heredity and your environment. Your **heredity** is the total package of traits and characteristics that you were born with, passed on to you by your parents and ancestors. Whether you are male or

female, short or tall, blue eyed or brown eyed, blonde or brunette is determined by your heredity. Your *environment* includes the wide range of life experiences everyone encounters — going to school, making friends and getting a job, to name a few. The language you speak and the way you express feelings are also a result of your environment. Today, most psychologists and social scientists agree that both heredity and environment are major influences on each individual and that both act together on the development of a person's personality and potential.

Heredity

If you look around, it is easy to see physical differences between people. Height, weight, skin, hair and eye color vary widely. These visible traits are hereditary, passed on through the years to new generations. Other traits, like blood type or color blindness, are not visible, but they are inherited. To understand how you inherited your unique characteristics, you need to become familiar with the basic concepts of **genetics,** "the science of heredity."

Genetics The nucleus of each cell in your body contains a master plan for your development. The plans are stored in **chromosomes,** structures that look like strings of beads. The beads are called **genes.** Humans have 23 pairs, or 46 chromosomes in every cell. Each of the thousands of genes in the chromosomes carries information about a single characteristic such as hair color, bone structure, or eye color. When the sperm cell of a male joins a female's egg cell, a new cell, a new life, is created that contains 46 chromosomes, 23 from the male and 23 from the female. This new set of chromosomes and the genes they contain create a unique blueprint, a new life.

Mendel's Laws of Genetics Between the years of 1856 and 1865, an Austrian monk named Gregor Mendel did simple experiments

Hair color is inherited; the gene for red hair is *recessive*.

on garden peas. The conclusions he reached have been proven to be typical of all living things. His findings include the following:

- The traits of parents are distributed to their offspring in a new combination when each offspring is formed. The combination in a particular offspring is determined by the laws of chance.

- Each trait inherited is controlled by a pair of genes, one from each parent.

- Each gene is either *dominant* or *recessive*.

Dominant and Recessive Genes As you know, genes occur in pairs. Mendel's genetic research proved that when two different characteristics occur in a pair of genes, one gene's effect will mask the other because it is dominant, or stronger. For example, if you have one gene for brown hair and one for blonde, you will have brown hair because the brown-haired gene is stronger than the blonde-haired gene. It is dominant and the gene for blonde hair is recessive.

In the same way that heredity determines hair color, it determines other visible traits like skin color, eye color, hair and facial features, and bone structure. There are dominant and recessive genes for these characteristics as well. For example, when two genes pair to determine eye color, brown is dominant; blue is recessive.

Culture and Environment

You now have an understanding about traits with which you were born. Other qualities are developed through interacting within your environment. Environmental influences include your family, peers, education and occupation. A look at each of these will begin to explain how they influence your process of development.

Family There is no such thing as a typical family. Individual differences are found among all homes. Whatever the differences, the family is an important cultural and environmental influence on personality development.

Enjoying leisure activities together contributes to a secure family environment.

The family is a child's main resource for healthy emotional, social and physical growth. The experiences a person has at home with family members will have lifelong effects. Without adequate love, attention, care and support from family members, children have an increased chance for having trouble in one or more stages of life.

The family is where children first learn socialization, or the basic rules of the culture. Children learn rules of discipline, as well as ways of behaving and expressing emotions from their parents. By observing and taking part in family interactions a child learns communication skills. The teachings and expectations of the family guide a person's decision-making process, especially during adolescence.

Peers Your **peers,** people in your age group, influence you in different ways throughout your life. When you were four or five years old, the adults in your life were your most influential role models. As you grew older and became an adolescent, the values, ideas, and actions of your friends took on more importance in your life. Now, in your peer group you frequently share information, attitudes, and values. Sometimes these are in conflict with what you learned in your family. Dealing with these conflicts is an important part of the formation of your character and your personality. Some people simply accept without question the values of their peers. Allowing decisions to be made for you can affect your self-esteem. It is important to have close friends, but it is equally important to keep the significance of your peers in perspective and to make your own decisions.

Education Your education is a very important factor in your environment. Because of the highly complex and technological society you live in, there is an emphasis on the value of a good education. The amount and quality of education you complete will affect your future in many ways, including your potential employment. Whether you plan to enter a profession, a trade, or a business, decisions about education must be made carefully. You might feel pressured by the expectations of your teachers and your parents as they encourage you to make the most out of your education. As you make decisions about school, now and in the future, it is important to consider your talents and abilities, your goals and your values. Talking about these issues with an adult you trust will help you face the challenges of education.

Occupation Since you will probably spend 40 hours a week working at some kind of job, your occupation is another influential factor in your environment. Your occupation has an effect on your self-esteem and on the degree of satisfaction with your life. The task of identifying the occupation that will be right for you is a

Although peers can influence attitudes and behavior, it is important to make decisions that are right for you.

difficult one. Talking with friends and family members who work at various jobs will help you with your selection of a career path. The information in Chapter 13 will also give you guidance and helpful suggestions for making this most important decision.

Sex Differences Your heredity determines whether you are male or female, but it is your environment that determines how you regard your sex. The expectations of the culture in which you live greatly influence the behavior of the sexes. Today, these expectations are in dispute. For example, some people claim that males and females have the same mental abilities and that they will behave in the same ways under the same circumstances. Others deny this claim.

Recent scientific evidence indicates that significant mental and behavioral differences between males and females do exist. In 1988, *U.S. News & World Report* compiled several recent research articles to conclude that differences between boys and girls "appear as early as six weeks after conception." These differences include the following:

■ Boys show signs of greater aggressiveness than girls and are more likely to be nearsighted, dyslexic, and left-handed.

■ Girls receive higher scores than boys on tests of verbal ability—a difference that appears during adolescence and increases throughout the high school years.

■ While boys and girls do about the same in arithmetic, boys score higher in mathematics and exhibit superior spatial skills.

Research in sex differences has resulted in the rejection of certain myths. For example, various studies have shown that the sexes do not differ in sociability, self-esteem, motivation to achieve, ability to memorize, or general analytic ability.

How does education affect the development of your potential?

Although it has yet to be proved, most experts believe that sex differences in human behavior result from environmental influences. Many parents tend to treat their male and female children differently, and a child tends to imitate the behavior, or role, of the parent of the same sex. Role is a major factor in the way boys and girls behave, and in the expectations they will have toward the opposite sex when they grow up.

For Review
1. What is heredity?
2. Name three ways in which you are influenced by your heredity.
3. Give examples of mental differences that exist between boys and girls.

Needs

One part of your search for identity involves identifying and evaluating the attributes and abilities that make you unique: a "gift" for this, a talent for that, a potential for something else, and so on. Another part of your search will lead you to consider the ways in which you are similar to other people, one of which is the needs people share. Following is one important theory of human needs.

Maslow's Pyramid of Human Needs

Psychologist Abraham Maslow studied human needs for many years. His work contributed the idea of a "pyramid," or hierarchy, of human needs to the field of psychology. Of major significance is his theory that the needs on the lower levels of the pyramid must be met before a person moves up to the next level. However, the theory takes into account the idea that people, as complex beings, usually operate on more than one level at a time. A person still has basic needs such as food and

safety even though he or she has moved to the level where self-esteem, or pride in oneself, for example, is the greatest need.

Starting at the bottom of Maslow's pyramid, you strive first to meet basic physical needs and the need for safety and security. Physical needs include food, water, shelter, and warmth. Security needs include freedom from financial worry and from the danger of attack.

If the basic needs at these levels are met satisfactorily, you can move up the pyramid to the need for love and a sense of belonging. You need to know that you are significant to others. Only when you feel secure and important as a person can you turn your attention to the need for esteem, including self-esteem.

You can develop self-esteem by asking yourself, "What can I do, or make, or what kind of person can I be that will give me a sense of pride?" Self-esteem is the sense of pride that comes from accomplishment. Striving for some type of mastery, and then seeking recognition for it, can occupy a lifetime. When the need for self-esteem is met, the process of self-actualization can begin.

Self-actualization means realizing your full potential. This is not the same as becoming a success in the eyes of the world. To achieve self-actualization you must discover who you really are, and you must continue to grow. According to Maslow, many people never fully attain this stage. Yet they continue to strive for it. In his own words, "In practically every human being there is an active will toward health, an impulse toward growth, or toward the actualization of human potentialities."

The Drive for Achievement

Maslow was optimistic about the ability of people to satisfy their needs. He believed that within each human being is an active will to achieve and to grow. As people approach self-actualization, they tend not only to face reality squarely, but to seek out problems to solve.

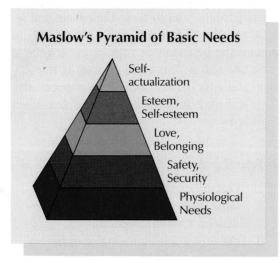

Maslow's Pyramid of Basic Needs

Self-actualization
Esteem, Self-esteem
Love, Belonging
Safety, Security
Physiological Needs

Source: A. H. Maslow, "A Theory of Human Motivation," Psychological Review, Vol. 50 (1943).

What is the main source of a person's drive for achievement?

Many creative ideas and accomplishments result from the personal search for ideals that derives from a positive inner drive.

Research confirms Maslow's idea that as people grow, they seek to achieve. Positive thinkers direct their attention mainly toward achieving success. Less confident people are more concerned about avoiding failure. One interesting finding is that people who are anxious about failure often pick very high or very low goals. They choose the latter to ensure at all cost that they will not fail. On the other hand, if they choose the high goal and fail, they rationalize that no one can blame them for failure.

Roles

A role is the behavior expected of a person because he or she occupies a particular position in a group — in the family, in school, or in society. All people play a variety of roles that vary in duration and complexity.

Types of Roles

Being a parent, a brother, or a sister involves a certain set of expectations. For example, in some homes older children may be expected to assume parental roles when parents are not at home. Other relatives — for example, grandparents, uncles, or cousins — play roles in the drama of family life, and each family position calls for certain kinds of behavior.

Roles involving people outside the family are based on circumstance. Friends fit into this category; the role of "friend" is usually less well-defined than "brother" or "son." You are free to choose friends and you probably base friendships on personal qualities rather than on social position. Sometimes, a friendship may become strained because each person has a different idea of what is involved in being a friend. This may be true whether friends are similar to you or different from you.

Occupational roles can be clearly defined. Firefighters, judges, and air traffic controllers all have specific tasks. Furthermore, each work role implies a certain type of relationship with the other people on the job. In a school, the teachers and the principal occupy positions that involve specified role differences.

Roles and Responsibilities

Roles make relationships possible. As you interact with people, your behavior alters with each role you play. These changes do not mean that you are wishy-washy, unpredictable, or unstable. Other people also modify their behavior as they interact with you and others.

On an ordinary day, you encounter different people and play different roles. You begin your day in the family group as a son or a daughter and probably as a brother or sister. Once in school, you assume the role of student, and with each teacher your behavior varies slightly as you adapt to their different personalities and demands. Later, at basketball practice, you assume still another role—that of a team player —and you interact with your teammates and your coach. After school, at your supermarket check-out job, you take on a work role. There you relate to customers, fellow employees, and the manager, each in different ways. This example clearly demonstrates the large number of interactions that can take place in one day. It also shows the complexity of relationships and roles that develops in a short period of time.

Sex Roles

In different societies and even in different families, the members do not view the roles of males and females in the same way. In one society, for example, males are active "doers" working outside the house; women are in charge of domestic affairs. In another society, the roles may be less clearly defined. You may have noticed that adults in different families hold various ideas about male and female roles.

Being a caring brother is one of many roles for this adolescent.

While there are still recognizable differences in boys' and girls' behavior in the United States, the roles of male and female are generally less rigidly defined today than they were in the past. Women were once viewed as one kind of people, while men were seen as a very different kind. Work and other activities that women performed were usually quite different from those that men performed. If people enjoyed activities inconsistent with their sex roles, they were considered inadequate or odd. The social pressure to maintain certain behaviors considered appropriate for men or appropriate for women is called **sex-role stereotyping.** Such stereotyping is still common throughout many parts of the world since most people accept the roles society sets for them.

Today, sex roles are different from what they were a generation ago, let alone a century ago. Some men and women believe that if they follow rigid sex roles, they may limit their potential. Others do not agree, and many men and women are still traditional in their attitudes toward sex roles. Even so, the lines between the sexes now are less clearly drawn than they were in the past.

Development

It has been said, wisely, that "adolescence is that time of life when you wake up one day with a new personality in the old body and on the next with a new body for the old personality." During this time of rapid physical growth and emotional change, you may feel, with good reason, that you are a different person each day. In the ongoing search for identity, you can benefit from learning about patterns of physical, mental, and emotional development. Knowing these patterns will help you feel comfortable with yourself and will lead you to understand what friends of the same age are experiencing.

Physical Development

The growth spurt that takes place during adolescence is one of the major characteristics of the teenage years. When children are around 10 years old, their bodies begin to grow more quickly. Between the ages of 10 and 13, girls gain from 10 to 12 pounds a year, and from 2 to 3 inches in height. The growth spurt for boys occurs slightly later than for girls, taking place when they are between 12 and 15 years old. However, boys tend to gain more weight and to grow taller — 12 to 14 pounds a year in weight

Today male and female roles are less rigidly defined than in the past.

and 4 to 5 inches in height. These figures are averages; many exceptions exist.

Proper care of the body ensures that the body will work for you, not against you. You must pay special attention to the areas of nutrition and exercise. If you eat properly, you will be more likely to have the energy you need to take part in activities you like. Exercise that is particularly suited to your body will keep your muscles toned up and your lungs and heart operating at maximum capacity. It will also provide other benefits that contribute to feeling good. In addition, it is important to learn healthy ways of handling tension, anxiety, sleeplessness, or other signs of stress.

People used to think of health as the absence of disease; people were considered healthy if they weren't sick. Now, physicians and other specialists in the field view health as an active feeling of well-being. One physical educator calls this state "high-level wellness."

Mental Development

From the moment you were born, your brain has been in charge of all your thoughts, emotions, and actions. Every human physical and mental activity—from the simple beating of the heart to the playing of a violin concerto — is the work of the brain and the nervous system.

Exercise is vital to healthy physical and mental development.

The brain stores highly complex information enabling humans to learn and to think. Receiving signals from the five senses, your brain interprets incoming information and combines it with memories already stored. It then directs your emotions and determines how your muscles respond.

Increasing Intelligence The physical growth spurt of adolescence is not matched by a corresponding growth of the brain, even though you may pride yourself on your academic accomplishments. When you were born, your brain contained all the brain cells it would ever have. Yet that fact does not mean your intelligence leveled off at the same time. It is difficult to judge the growth of intelligence because there is little scientific agreement on what intelligence is. However, experts agree that good physical and mental health, supportive people and circumstances, and strong motivation can extend one's capacity for intellectual growth.

Specialized tests measure different aspects of intelligence.

Measuring Intelligence Although there is no accepted definition of "intelligence," scientists agree that tests can measure some aspects of intelligence. You probably have taken an IQ (intelligence quotient) test one or more times during your school career. Your scores reflect how you compare with other students of your age.

Tests are designed according to psychologists' views of what constitutes intelligence. Some psychologists view intelligence as clusters of skills. They list seven primary mental skills: verbal comprehension, word fluency, arithmetic ability, space perception, rote memory, perception of similarities and differences, and general reasoning. There are tests to measure each skill. Few people would do well on all of these tests; most would score high in some areas and low in others. You probably already know what your greatest strengths are.

The original purpose of intelligence tests was to help place children in classes appropriate to their needs. The tests assume that intelligence changes with age in many ways. One theory states that intellect consists of 120 separate but related mental abilities, thus demonstrating the complexity of measurement. Knowing how to apply knowledge in life situations — to exercise good judgment — is an

Twins Raised Apart: Living Laboratories

Identical twins occur in about one out of 90 births each year. Identical twins are genetically alike; since they developed from the same fertilized egg, they have the same genes, or chromosome parts. The shared hereditary characteristics result in the same appearance, hair and eye color, blood type, and even brain wave patterns.

When raised in the same family, identical twins share environmental characteristics, too. However, what happens when twins are raised apart? Without shared experiences, how alike are identical twins, especially after reaching adulthood?

A research group at the University of Minnesota is currently studying twins who were separated at birth and raised by different families. When reunited as adults, these twins proved to be an extraordinary "living lab" in which to compare the effects of environment and heredity on human development. Both physical and psychological testing of reunited twins has revealed evidence supporting hereditary influence in areas previously thought of as primarily influenced by environment.

One pair of twins studied was raised in Ohio towns only 70 miles apart. When the two men met at age 39, they found they shared similar backgrounds and habits: both served part-time as deputy sheriffs, regularly vacationed in St. Petersburg, Florida, drove Chevrolets, and bit their nails. Both men had been named Jim, as children, had owned dogs named Toy, had married women named Linda, had divorced, had remarried women named Betty; one had named his son James Allan, the other James Alan. More significantly, their medical histories were similar: same blood pressure and sleep patterns, a sudden weight gain at the same age, and severe headaches starting at age 18.

Another set of twins raised apart was studied at age 47. Oskar was raised by his Catholic mother in Germany, while Jack had been brought up by his Jewish father in Israel. Although their lives growing up and in adulthood were very different, researchers learned that the two shared many common habits: both wore wire-rimmed glasses, sported mustaches, liked spicy foods, stored rubber bands on their wrists, and read magazines from back to front. Researchers found that the twins' mannerisms and temperaments were similar, even though they did not share the same language.

It is possible that the influence of genetics on the body's health is much greater than previously believed. The discovery that twins often have similar medical histories even when raised in separate environments may prove significant. Further findings may eventually help scientists identify and combat diseases caused by genetic tendencies.

According to studies, twins share much more than physical traits.

ability that tests seldom measure. Today, the purpose of most intelligence tests is to indicate strengths and weaknesses so that proper school or job placement can be made. By directing attention to those skill areas where a person needs improvement, tests can serve as valuable guides.

Split-Brain Research The brain has not yet begun to reveal all its mysteries, and scientists keep uncovering new areas for investigation. In recent years, much scientific research has centered on what is called the "split brain."

All people normally have a bridge, *the corpus callosum,* that connects the two hemispheres, or halves, of their brains. By studying accident victims whose bridges were severed, scientists discovered that each hemisphere controls different functions and responds to the environment in different ways.

The left hemisphere of the brain appears to be in charge of language and analytical abilities, such as logical thinking, language skills and mathematics. The right hemisphere appears to be the source of creativity — artistic and musical talents and that "sixth sense" known as intuition. Of course, the two halves usually work together, so that they attain a balance. For example, when a person looks at a picture of a dog, the left hemisphere of the brain, which handles language and analytic abilities, registers the word *dog* from a jumble of letters. The left side of the brain alone cannot identify the picture, however. Since the brain's right hemisphere handles spatial perception, this side identifies the picture as a dog, although it cannot register the word *dog.* The bridge between the two halves of the brain enables a person both to see a picture of a dog and to spell out the word.

The brain has two hemispheres connected by the *corpus callosum.* Each hemisphere handles different kinds of mental functions.

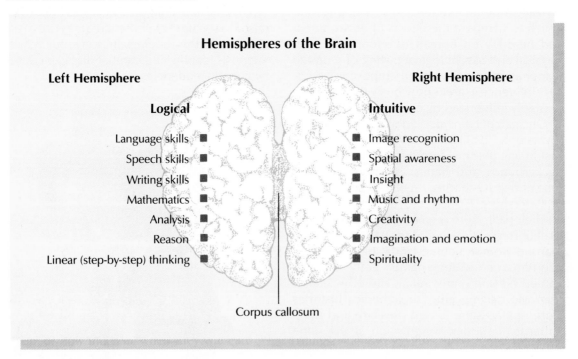

Hemispheres of the Brain

Left Hemisphere

Logical

Language skills
Speech skills
Writing skills
Mathematics
Analysis
Reason
Linear (step-by-step) thinking

Right Hemisphere

Intuitive

Image recognition
Spatial awareness
Insight
Music and rhythm
Creativity
Imagination and emotion
Spirituality

Corpus callosum

Sculpting is one of many outlets for creativity.

Creativity If the right half of the brain controls creativity, then being creative is not a special ability reserved for a relatively few, lucky individuals. Everyone can be creative. You may not have a talent for drawing, for composing music, or for designing clothes, but you have probably discovered some skill you can use creatively.

Creativity involves developing a fresh approach. As Abraham Maslow said, "A first-rate soup is more creative than a second-rate painting." What is important is the process. First, you observe the "problem"—what you have to work with and what goal you have in mind. You then play around with different ideas, no matter how unrealistic they seem. Sometimes, you reflect upon your thoughts; other times, you are hardly conscious of the various choices that come to mind. Finally, your ideas "click" and the solution flashes into your mind.

Research has shown that when people are encouraged to express their "far-out" creations or ideas, many original products result. You can make creativity part of your life by solving problems in unconventional ways. Self-expression is the key to creativity.

Piaget's Stages of Mental Development Thinking, or the end product of the human brain at work, has long been a fertile field for scientific research. One of the most renowned psychologists in this area was Jean Piaget. For many years, he and his coworkers tested children and adolescents. He found that as human beings grow, their thought processes go through four major stages of development.

Early in life (0 to 2 years), children pass through a stage in which they learn about the world through their senses and movements. When children are between 2 and 7 years old, they learn to think in symbols and to master language. At the beginning of this stage they are self-centered, but gradually they begin to consider the viewpoints of others. The third stage extends from about age 7 to age 11. During this stage, children use logic and reason but think very little about ideas. They mostly focus on things, people, and events in their immediate environment.

As a teenager, you are now in Piaget's final stage. You are able to deal with ideas and things beyond your immediate environment, and you can handle a time frame other than the present. You can think about the future, consider possibilities, and make **hypotheses** (hy-POTH-uh-seez), or educated guesses, based on past experiences and thoughts. However, while you are now equipped to think as an adult, you may not have yet completed your emotional development. Emotional maturity is hard to achieve, and you must work at it throughout your life.

Emotional Development

Adolescence brings a deepening of emotion as well as changes in mind and body. As a teenager, you are moving from spontaneous, quickly passing childhood feelings to the richer, steadier emotions of adulthood. You also may be experiencing feelings that you have never had before.

Learning to deal with intense feelings is one of the challenges of adolescence.

Basic emotions include anger, sadness, happiness, and excitement—feelings even small children experience. During adolescence, other emotions develop, such as feelings of romantic love. When you experience emotional growth, you learn to identify your feelings and to determine what triggers them. You also learn how to express your feelings effectively.

Dealing with Emotions   Some feelings are positive; others are negative. All feelings are important. Although negative feelings aren't pleasant, they often stimulate you to improve yourself in positive ways. Stage fright could be considered a negative feeling. Sweaty palms, "butterflies" in the stomach, shortness of breath, and a trembling voice are a few of the physical symptoms that accompany this unpleasant feeling. Stage fright results from a desire to please an audience along with a nagging doubt about whether it can be done. Although successful stage or public speaking experience is the best way to build necessary confidence, even experienced performers may feel nervous before going on stage, especially if their standards are high. This need not affect the quality of a performance; in fact, the extra tension may make it better.

Communicating Emotions   Dealing with emotions can be a problem for adolescents since they often seem to have a great many feelings, both negative and positive. If this is true of your experience, it doesn't mean that anything is wrong with you. It means simply that you must put extra energy into learning about your emotions and how to communicate them in satisfactory ways.

The way you express anger is a good gauge of emotional maturity. Sulking or throwing a temper tantrum usually doesn't work well because neither act conveys a clear message and both methods antagonize the person or persons to whom you are expressing yourself.

In order to communicate anger effectively, it is necessary to convey your message clearly. One person when angry says, "I'm angry." Another in the same situation says, "Don't you have any sense at all? What's wrong with you, anyway?" The first person communicates the feeling in a much clearer way than does the second. Let people know what they have done to trigger your feelings. This can help others alter their behavior toward you. It also can help clarify your own feelings if you are doubtful about how you really feel.

It is best to communicate anger in a nonthreatening way. Negative feelings almost always indicate that you are not receiving information or support from another person. If, for example, you are angry because your friend is losing interest in a project he or she agreed to share, you will want him or her to reassure you that this is not so. Even if your anger is justified, you will not help the situation by putting your friend on the defensive. All you want to know is where your friend stands. You can communicate your feelings effectively by stating in a nonthreatening way exactly how you feel and why you feel that way. You should then wait for your friend's response.

Emotional development, unlike the growth of the body and the intellect, doesn't follow a set of progressive stages. Learning to deal with your emotions and to express them to best advantage will be a challenge for you at every stage of life.

For Review

1. What are a person's basic needs according to Abraham Maslow?
2. Name some of the different roles you play in your everyday life.
3. What are some of the functions controlled by the left side of your brain?

Life Cycle

As people go through life, from birth to old age and death, they follow what is known as the life cycle. Psychologists and other researchers have studied each stage in the cycle: infancy, childhood, adolescence, young adulthood, middle age, and old age. Each stage has its own characteristics, problems, and potentials.

Erikson's Theory of Life Crises

One of the best-known theories about life stages and human development is that of psychologist Erik Erikson. He divides the life cycle into eight crises. To develop in the most satisfactory way, you must handle each crisis successfully.

Infancy Babies are concerned only with their own needs. When babies are hungry, they quickly and loudly make it known. Infants are also hungry for emotional attachment. A baby needs love, care, and reassurance. According to Erikson, it is during infancy that a person's first crisis occurs. If infants learn to trust other people, they face the future with confidence and hope. If they learn distrust, they approach life with suspicion and fear.

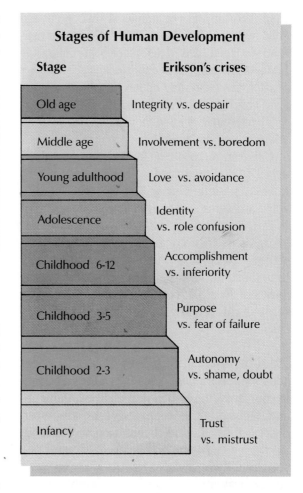

Stages of Human Development

Stage	Erikson's crises
Old age	Integrity vs. despair
Middle age	Involvement vs. boredom
Young adulthood	Love vs. avoidance
Adolescence	Identity vs. role confusion
Childhood 6-12	Accomplishment vs. inferiority
Childhood 3-5	Purpose vs. fear of failure
Childhood 2-3	Autonomy vs. shame, doubt
Infancy	Trust vs. mistrust

Childhood The years of childhood involve continuous learning and reaching for independence. Beginning in the second year of life, a child moves from complete reliance on others toward self-confidence. For example, a two-year-old child may say, "Me do it," when mother tries to help put on a coat. Erikson claims that when children have the chance to do things for themselves, they are more likely to develop **autonomy,** or independence. Failure to develop independence may result in a lack of self-control and an inability to make decisions.

Children between the ages of three and five gain a sense of purpose in what they do. They learn to start their own activities and to carry them through. For example, a three-year-old child may set the table with toy dishes and pretend to feed the dolls placed in chairs as "guests." If many play experiences are not successful, the child may be left with fears of failure. This fear in turn may lead to either a lessening of creativity or to showing off, to cover up a lack of self-confidence.

Children in middle childhood, from age 6 to age 12, are concerned with developing their talents and skills. During this time they learn to solve problems, and they acquire knowledge of their ever-expanding world. As their abilities grow, so do their confidence and a wholesome attitude toward self. It is important at this time that adults praise the budding accomplishments of a child. If the child does not develop a sense of competence, feelings of inferiority will result.

Adolescence As you know from experience, adolescence is a time of many changes, not only in your body, but also in your abilities, thoughts and feelings. The teenage years are often described as a period of confusion and turmoil. At the end of your adolescence, if you have successfully resolved confusions about your roles and relationships, you will be able to see yourself as a person with a unique identity. The various aspects of yourself will unify into a whole. If you do not master this stage, you may have difficulty becoming a successful adult.

Young Adulthood When you enter your twenties, you establish yourself in the world of work. Perhaps marriage and parenthood follow. According to Erikson, being a successful adult means having the ability to love and to commit

Erickson's theory of human development includes six stages: Left: (top) Infancy (middle) Childhood (bottom) Adolescence. Right: (top) Young Adulthood (middle) Middle Age (bottom) Old Age. Each stage of the life cycle presents a different crisis to be resolved.

yourself to others, while still maintaining your own identity. Developmental stages tend to blend, and there are degrees of success. Avoiding love or keeping distant from others could be signs of unresolved problems left over from adolescence.

Middle Age   Successful adjustment during middle age means broadening one's own interests to include the well-being of others and of society as a whole. During this stage, people often derive satisfaction from guiding youth and getting involved in community affairs. When middle-aged people remain creative and productive, they enjoy the benefits of a wide variety of life experiences. Those who do not handle this stage successfully experience bitterness and boredom.

Late Adulthood   Old age often is a more difficult stage than it should be. Older people must learn to accept their decreasing physical strength and perhaps to adjust to the deaths of friends and spouse. They may also face significant changes in lifestyle.

People who handle middle adulthood constructively have an advantage as they enter this final stage of life, old age. Looking back on their lives with contentment and with few regrets, they are able to look forward to the prospect of death without despair. Erikson calls this quality **integrity;** it is accompanied by faith in the meaning of life and by acceptance of its end.

For Review

1. According to Erikson, when does a person's first life crisis occur?
2. In your opinion, what is the most difficult aspect of adolescence?
3. What are some activities of people who are making successful adjustments to middle age?

1 Chapter Review

Summary

Adolescents need to develop a sense of identity, a task that is part of a lifelong process. While heredity and environment influence the development of one's abilities, people must recognize and decide how to use their abilities for their potential to be realized.

People play different roles during their lives, with each role demanding different behaviors. Learning to express emotions effectively is necessary to a person's emotional growth. Maslow's, Piaget's, and Erikson's theories chart the developmental stages people experience in their intellectual and emotional growth as they move through their life cycles.

Vocabulary

Match each of the vocabulary words with one of the definitions that follow.

autonomy
chromosomes
genes
genetics
heredity
hypotheses
integrity
peers
self-actualization
sex-role stereotyping

1. _____ social pressure to assume behavior considered appropriate for one's sex

2. _____ educated guesses
3. _____ chromosomal structure that carries information about an inherited trait
4. _____ Maslow's stage of development in which a person reaches his or her potential
5. _____ part of the nucleus that contains all the plans for making new cells
6. _____ people in one's own age group
7. _____ the "science of heredity"
8. _____ collection of traits a person inherits from parents
9. _____ independence
10. _____ quality that describes the life of an elderly person who looks back upon life with satisfaction

Chapter Questions

1. What structure in a cell's nucleus stores all of the genetic instructions for your development?
2. What environmental factors affect the development of an individual's potential?
3. How have your peers influenced your growth as a person?
4. Why is an adolescent's growth not matched by a similar growth of the brain?
5. Describe the steps that help a person develop maximum creativity.
6. What are the seven primary mental skills that constitute intelligence according to psychologists?

7. What is the purpose of most intelligence tests given today?
8. Give three examples of sex-role stereotyping in both family and work environments.
9. Describe your present level of intellectual development as Piaget has defined it.
10. Compare and contrast Maslow's concept of self-actualization with Erickson's concept of integrity.
11. How do methods of expressing anger relate to emotional maturity?
12. Why is it important to learn to communicate your emotions effectively?

Skill Activities

1. **Reading** Using your school or local library as a resource, read more about one of the topics discussed in this chapter. Consult encyclopedias, books, or other references to gather your information. Sample topics might include split-brain research, creativity, sex-role stereotyping, or the work of Jean Piaget, Abraham Maslow, or Erik Erikson. When you have finished your research and reading, discuss your findings in a brief written report.

2. **Communication** Create an illustrated autobiography that answers the question, "Who am I?" Think about the highlights of your life. What experiences, occasions, accomplishments, and people have been important to your development? You may want to include these in your autobiography. As you reveal your identity, express your personal characteristics, likes and dislikes, and dreams for the future. Do this by using written descriptions, magazine pictures, your own artwork, photographs, poems, and other materials.

3. **Critical Thinking** Have you ever felt pressure to behave in a certain way because of your sex? If so, write an essay in which you discuss the pressures and the situations that you have experienced. What did you learn about yourself and the other people who were involved? If a similar situation occurs again, how will you handle it? If you have not had this type of experience, discuss how social pressure has affected the sex role of someone you know (grandparent, parent, sibling, or friend).

4. **Communication** Write and produce a skit or short play with three or four of your classmates that demonstrates the different ways people express the same emotion. Select an emotion that can easily be expressed in a variety of ways. For example, one person might express anger with a violent outburst, someone else might burst into tears, and still another person might appear calm when he or she really is seething inside. Consider using typical social, work, family, or school situations for the setting of your production. Other emotions your group may decide to use as the focus of your skit are fear, jealousy, happiness, or love. Feel free to select another emotion.

2 Understanding Others

As you read, think about:

- what factors contribute to good relationships.
- what elements are essential in effective communication.
- how you can build a positive relationship with your parents.

From the moment of your birth and throughout your life, you need the emotional support of other people. All the people you meet, whether you like them or dislike them, have something to teach you about yourself. This chapter deals with the factors that bring people together and that maintain good relationships. It suggests ways of improving communication and discusses how to use these skills to build healthy relationships.

VOCABULARY

frame of reference
ambivalence
empathy
body language
verbal communication
listener feedback
modeling
rebellion
internalized

What Brings People Together?

Throughout your life, relationships with others will offer you opportunities to develop new interests and to learn new skills. When friends support you, you gain the confidence to try new activities. When they do not support you, you may discover that the fault lies within yourself. You may then take the appropriate steps toward self-improvement. Learning to understand others and to get along well with many different people forces you to consider ideas and attitudes that may conflict with your own. The ways in which you differ from others may prove painful to you at times. Nevertheless, differences also challenge you to grow into a mature person. Sociologists tell us that several factors are involved in forming good relationships.

Contact

In order to develop relationships with other people, you must first come into contact with them. You may see people every day whom you think you might like, but if you never get a chance to talk to them or to spend time with them, a relationship cannot develop. You will most likely make friends with the people you meet through your classes, after-school activities, job, or sports and hobbies. Once you meet someone, you have a chance to develop a friendship with that person.

Common Interests and Experiences

People who share a liking for repairing automobiles, playing volleyball, or running for school office have something to discuss that they enjoy. They may discover other common interests as well. It is easier to get to know more about a person if you have some impersonal topics to talk over together. Mutual interests can provide people with their first topic of

Common experiences, such as playing on the same football team, often bring people together in friendships.

conversation and make them want to know each other better.

Common experiences also can help bring people together. Surviving a tough class test together or working side by side on an absorbing project often mark the beginning of good friendships. Teammates may grow to be friends after spending a season learning to rely on one another on the playing field. Talking over old times can strengthen friendships that grow out of common experiences. Sharing experiences may lead you to discover that you share attitudes as well.

Similar Attitudes and Beliefs

You need to share some of your attitudes and beliefs with a person in order to enjoy being together, even though you may not always agree on all issues. Your closest friendships will probably be with those people who share your **frame of reference.** That is, you both view things in almost the same way and agree in most of your ideas and opinions. Of course, you can have good friends who are different from you, too. Most people, however, tend to feel more comfortable with other people who support their viewpoints.

Being in agreement with someone has advantages and disadvantages. The major advantage is that someone else who feels and thinks as you do can help you feel good about yourself. You have a chance to express ideas you might otherwise have kept to yourself. Another advantage is that when you discuss your thoughts and feelings, you also learn more about how you really think and feel. You gain a fresh perspective about even familiar ideas. By "comparing notes" with a friend, you are challenged to define and to express your own viewpoints clearly.

A disadvantage of associating only with people who share your point of view can be that you miss opportunities to grow. For example, a tourist who travels to a foreign country but eats only American food and stays only in American-run hotels misses the opportunity to live in a different way for a while and to savor the differences. People can learn from differences as well as from similarities. They need to achieve a balance between sameness and differences, between the familiar and the not-so-familiar.

You are now in a stage of life where your ideas, attitudes, and feelings, as well as those of your friends, may change rapidly. You may sometimes find yourself wishing that the important people in your life would always agree with you. However, if a friend always agreed with you, you might lose respect for his or her lack of individuality. You might suspect that your friend could not form opinions, or that he or she was dishonest. Fortunately, people do not always have to agree in order to have good relationships.

What Builds Good Relationships?

It is important to learn how to develop good relationships. To do this, you must first understand the important qualities that people look for in relationships.

Caring

People who care about each other want to know what has been happening in one another's life. They are interested in each other's thoughts and feelings, successes and failures. People like others who seem to be genuinely interested in them. On the other hand, people tend to avoid others who seem interested only in themselves. You probably know several people who want to talk about only their own activities, their own experiences, and their own point of view. They are not much fun to be with for very long.

Caring also means "being there" when friends need you. Many people hesitate to share their problems for fear of burdening their friends. However, if a friend you care about is having trouble with another friend or at school, you naturally hope that he or she will talk it over with you. While no one can solve another's problems, sometimes it helps your morale just to know that someone else will listen to you.

Respect and admiration are important factors in lasting relationships.

Stages of Friendship

Ages 3 – 7
Momentary Playmate

Cannot tell the difference between his or her viewpoint and the feelings of others. Best friends are those who have material goods — such as toys — that the other likes.

Ages 4 – 9
One-way Assistance

Knows that others have different viewpoints, but does not understand that give-and-take is necessary. Best friends are those who do whatever the other wants to do.

Ages 6 – 12
Two-way, Fair-weather Cooperation

Is concerned about what the other thinks about him or her. Best friends want reciprocal cooperation; the friendship must always serve both of their interests.

Ages 9 – 15
Mutual Sharing

Can evaluate a friendship objectively. Friends share secrets, agreements, feelings, and personal problems. Best friends are often exclusive, close, and possessive.

Ages 12 and older
Autonomy and interdependence

Recognizes that friendships are "complex, overlapping systems." Best friends give commitment of emotional and psychological support, but also give freedom to form other friendships.

Source: Reprinted from Psychology Today, copyright © 1979, American Psychological Association.

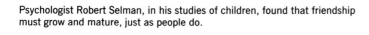
Psychologist Robert Selman, in his studies of children, found that friendship must grow and mature, just as people do.

Caring in a relationship means caring about yourself, too. There's a fine line between caring and being taken advantage of in a relationship. Sometimes real friendship means saying "No." When you suspect that someone is treating you unfairly, you should let the person know how you feel. It is better to face the problem than merely to avoid your friend or to make excuses for not getting together.

Trust

In order to enjoy being with people, you need to feel that you can trust them. If you plan to meet someone at a certain time and place, and the person does not show up, you will probably wonder whether to make similar plans in the future. Friends need to know that their agreements will be kept.

It is very important to be able to rely on friends in many ways. For example, you may expect your friends to keep their promises, to return items they have borrowed, or to help in emergencies. People who are not sure they can trust one another have a hard time becoming close friends.

Respect

Self-respect is an important human need. People may learn to respect themselves when they feel respected by others. People who believe in you, who appreciate you for yourself, and who admire your accomplishments and strengths are showing respect. People who demand the best from you and encourage you to develop your abilities are also showing respect.

Sometimes, you may be surprised to learn that others see in you a potential for achievement that you do not see yourself. New possibilities for growth, both for yourself and for others, can develop through expressions of respect and admiration.

Sharing

Most good relationships are based on sharing. You share not only your experiences and

Sharing your feelings is an important part of being a good friend.

material possessions, but also your thoughts and your feelings. Sharing means being willing to listen to another's hopes, dreams, and disappointments. Although many people hesitate to share because they fear others will reject or misunderstand them, the best relationships are strengthened by sharing.

It is not easy to share positive feelings and thoughts about others. Affection may sometimes be shown indirectly — through kidding and put-downs, and even through punching and wrestling. It takes courage to say, "I really appreciate your friendship."

Negative feelings are even more difficult to share. If a friend hurts you, you may not want to tell the person how you feel for fear of hurting the relationship. However, failure to show your feelings will rob you and your friend of a chance to learn and grow together.

Sharing thoughts and feelings helps you learn more about yourself. Everyone feels good or bad at times without knowing why. At times, you may experience **ambivalence,** or mixed feelings, which are even more difficult to explain. Sharing can lead to greater sensitivity to your own feelings and to the feelings of others.

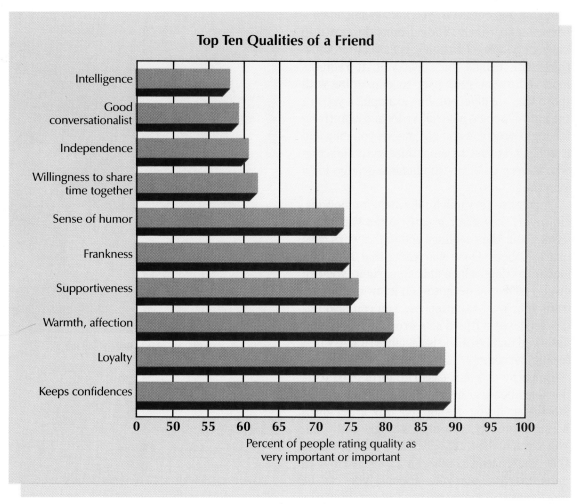

Top Ten Qualities of a Friend

Intelligence
Good conversationalist
Independence
Willingness to share time together
Sense of humor
Frankness
Supportiveness
Warmth, affection
Loyalty
Keeps confidences

0 50 55 60 65 70 75 80 85 90 95 100

Percent of people rating quality as
very important or important

Source: Adapted from Mary Brown Parlee and Psychology Today editors, "The Friendship Bond," Psychology Today, October 1979.

Increased self-awareness in turn helps develop the skills of decision making and problem solving.

Flexibility

A good relationship allows room for mistakes and differences. How much room there is depends on the flexibility of both people. Flexibility means that a person can accept and adapt to others. A flexible person can enjoy friends who have different opinions and ways of life without feeling pressured to imitate those friends.

People who are less secure in their own individuality may find themselves less able to accept as friends people who are different from themselves. Developing the ability to accept friends' differences and to adapt to them, when appropriate, challenges you to become more secure in your own identity.

Empathy

Empathy is the ability to put yourself in another person's place. In order to know how someone else feels and to understand another's thoughts and behavior, you must think and observe very carefully. You can empathize with all kinds of people, although it is easiest to empathize with people most like you. It requires more effort on your part to empathize with those who are different. For example, if you are the kind of person who talks a lot and has strong feelings that come and go quickly, you may find it difficult at first to empathize with someone who is very quiet or who holds a grudge for a long time.

People are very much alike in their emotions. However, they differ greatly in the ways they think about their feelings and in the ways they express them. Once you know that a certain look on a friend's face indicates fright, you can display empathy because you know about fear from your own experiences. You can also understand why a friend acts grouchy if you have observed that he or she is usually irritable when feeling nervous.

Empathy makes it easier to form good relationships because it prevents many misunderstandings. If you cannot tell why a person is acting strangely, you may wrongly think that you are somehow at fault. When you are aware that your friend's behavior is caused by his emotions, and not your actions, you can be more sensitive to that person's needs. Empathy is simply awareness and understanding of the signals others send you about the inner meaning of their words and actions and your response to those signals.

People with empathy are able to understand the feelings of others.

For Review

1. Name two factors that are involved in the beginning of a relationship.
2. Give an example from your own experience of how trust plays an important role in establishing a friendship.
3. How can the act of sharing build a more positive relationship?

Understanding the Elements of Communication

Everyone wants to have friends who will offer understanding, acceptance, and respect. The success or failure of a relationship depends upon whether or not these qualities are part of it. This process of give and take becomes possible through communication.

Communication is more than just talking. People communicate with one another through their personal appearance, facial expressions, and physical gestures as well. Since the process of communication involves receiving and understanding messages, as well as sending them, it is important to know how to be an effective listener. Understanding the various elements of communication will lead to a deeper understanding of people and will help you build better relationships.

What are these people expressing through their body language?

Nonverbal Communication

When you frown or point your finger at someone, you are using nonverbal communication, or **body language.** Psychologists report that people exchange 55% of their communication not with words, but with the use of body posture, eye contact, movement, and touch. Putting your hands on your hips could mean that you are taking a position of power. Crossing your arms or legs is like putting up a barrier between yourself and the person who is talking.

Some nonverbal messages are deliberate. When an enthusiastic speaker pounds a fist on the podium, she is emphasizing a point. Her words and her actions agree. Some nonverbal messages are unintentional and may conflict with what a person actually says. If someone says, "I want to be your friend," but looks down or turns away, the body language may be communicating one or more different messages. "I'm shy," "I'm lying," or "I'm afraid you'll reject me" are just a few of the possibilities. This person is sending a mixed message. The spoken words and the body language conflict.

Part of communicating clearly is making sure that verbal and nonverbal messages agree. You need to be consistent in what you say and do if you want other people to understand what you are saying. Otherwise, your nonverbal messages will confuse people or even cancel out your words. As the American philosopher Ralph Waldo Emerson warned, "What you are speaks so loudly I cannot hear what you say."

Another form of nonverbal communication is personal appearance. The way you dress and groom yourself gives others clues about your personality and your emotional state. Dressing

Being well-groomed communicates your feeling of well-being to others.

Listening is a vital part of the communication process.

Have you ever found yourself planning what you will say next while another person is talking? If so, you were not concentrating on the message and observing the nonverbal behavior of the speaker. One requirement of skillful listening is to make sure that you understand what the other person means before you respond with your own thoughts. You should ask questions if you do not understand. Ask what people mean when they use certain words. Ask them to rephrase what they have said so that you may better understand them.

When you listen skillfully, you let the other person know that you have heard and understood the message. Looking directly at a person when he or she is talking to you is a nonverbal way of letting that person know that you are listening. Responding verbally also helps another person feel that he or she is being heard. Repeating in your own words a part of what someone else has said is a way of confirming whether or not you really understood the speaker.

Poor listeners screen what they hear. They pick out what they want to hear and ignore the rest. Another bad listening habit is to read in, or add to the meaning of what someone is saying. Bad listening habits interfere with constructive conversations.

in a sloppy manner may suggest low self-esteem. Someone who is neat, clean, and well-dressed reflects a sense of pride and a positive outlook. Sometimes trying an outrageous hairstyle or wearing an unusual outfit is a person's way of saying "Notice me." People who use unconventional appearance to get attention do not seem to care if others' reactions to them are positive or negative.

Personal appearance plays an important role in your success at work. A salesperson, for example, must make a positive impression with his or her appearance, or the sales pitch will be ignored. Taking pride in your appearance indicates that you take your job seriously.

Listening

Skillful listening is an important element in the process of communication. When a person is attentive and responsive to what another is saying, communication flows freely between the speaker and the listener.

Practical Tip

To Be a Good Listener:

- Look directly at the speaker.

- Keep your mind on what the speaker is saying.

- Be an active listener. Repeat in your own words what the speaker has said.

- Do not change the topic of conversation.

- Try to respond to the feelings as well as to the words of the speaker.

Talk to Me — I'm Your Mother

I have always been envious of the mothers of children who talk. What an insight they must have into the personality of their child. What good times they must enjoy . . . the intimate laughter . . . the first blush of a shared secret.

[The relationship between my son and me] is a lot like the President and Congress.

"What's that hanging out of your notebook?"

(Shrug shoulders)

"You're having your school pictures taken tomorrow? And what's this one? An insurance form for football. What do you play? When do you play?"

(Grimace)

"Hey, here's one directed to my attention. They need someone to bake cakes for the ox roast. I think I could manage that."

"That's left over from last year."

"Oh, here's one. Memo to: Revolutionary Troops. Cross Potomac tonight at 7:30 P.M. Bring money. Signed George Washington. Thought I'd toss in a little humor there."

(Sigh)

"Look here. You're having an Open House. I think I'll go."

(Moan)

Now if you think things at home are painful for the mother of a nonverbal child, you should try enduring Open House. . . .

My son's teacher put a hand on my arm. "I want to talk about your son's problem," she said.

So! It wasn't me. It was definitely a case of a poor, shy boy who couldn't express himself, so he lived in a world of silence.

"Your son can't seem to keep his mouth shut," she said. "He talks incessantly during class, shouts out the answer before there are questions, and is known to his classmates as 'Elastic Mouth.'"

Erma Bombeck, I Lost Everything in the Post-Natal Depression (New York: Fawcett Crest Books, 1973).

Can you identify aspects of both verbal and nonverbal communication in this exchange?

Verbal Communication

Listening carefully and being aware of nonverbal messages are only two parts of the communication process. Another key part of the communication process is verbal communication.

Verbal communication is the use of spoken or written words, signs, or sounds to express ideas or emotions. Verbal communication includes *sign language*. Sign language is a system of hand gestures used primarily by people who are deaf. Verbal communication can also take the form of *braille*, which is a system of writing for the blind. In braille, letters and numbers are represented by raised dots. These can be identified and understood through the sense of touch.

Sometimes verbal messages are sent without words. A cry of surprise or delight, a deep, long yawn, and other such sounds are forms of verbal communication. In other words, they are ways of communicating our thoughts, emotions, and feelings.

Communicating Well with Words

Knowing how to express who you are and what you want can help you in every aspect of your life. To help make sure that your message is received, be particularly careful about your tone, your mood, and your eye contact with listeners.

Tone Your tone may vary with your message and your audience, but in general you want your tone to be either neutral or friendly. Your voice usually doesn't have to be loud to be heard. Similarly, almost no message requires anger or impatience to be received.

Mood Approach a conversation with an open mind. Don't begin a conversation when you are angry. Don't let your emotions interfere with what you say. Strong feelings can block communication. If you're not feeling stable emotionally, it may be best to wait to send your message.

Eye Contact Make and maintain eye contact as you talk. This is polite to your listener, who will want to see your expressions and hear you clearly. When a speaker looks away or down, the listener could interpret it as fear, insecurity, insincerity, or even hostility. Whether these emotions are present or not, if the listener thinks they are there, the message might not be received.

Listener Feedback

When a message is sent, the communication process doesn't end. The listener has to interpret the message. The speaker has to listen for and look for feedback. **Listener feedback** is the response or answer the receiver of the message gives.

An example of feedback is a clear statement such as, "I agree with you on that point." Another example of feedback is a nonverbal response such as a glance at a watch. A third example of feedback is a question or request to repeat something or make it clearer.

Good communicators are always using feedback as they speak or sign. Listener feedback tells a speaker what to repeat, what to gloss over, what to clarify, and what to leave out. Parts of a message that bring a smile, a look of interest, appropriate laughter, or an appropriately serious expression are parts of a message that have been received.

For Review

1. Give two examples of nonverbal communication.
2. How can you be a more effective listener?
3. What is listener feedback?
4. What should you remember about tone and eye contact during verbal communication?

How Can Communications Be Improved?

Many of the problems that occur between individuals, groups, and even nations, are a result of a breakdown in the communication process. Learning to use skills that improve communication and promote understanding will improve your relationships with others. Being honest, and sending clear messages will help you master the art of successful communication.

Being Open in Communication

When you learned good manners as a child, you probably learned that there are some things you should not say to people. Most parents are embarrassed if their child says, "How did you get so fat?" to an overweight neighbor or if the child asks the baker for a cookie. Children soon

Honesty and clarity in presenting one's opinions, plus good listening skills, contribute to effective communication.

learn that they should not always say what they really think or feel. It is also important to take time to think before you speak. Arguments often begin when one person reacts too quickly with words.

Many adults hide their real reactions to people and events out of politeness or from fear of rejection. Learning to be open and honest in communication means regaining a child's freedom of expression and combining it with adult consideration for others' feelings and an awareness of how your words fit the occasion. "Never say anything that will not improve on silence." is the advice of the long-time American politician Edmund Muskie.

Sending "I" Messages

A good way to tell people what you really think without being abrasive or tactless is by sending "I" messages. It may take some practice to learn how to do this, but you will probably find that it is an effective way to express feelings and opinions. "I" messages begin with the word "I" and convey an opinion without making a judgment on someone else. For example, if you say, "I don't feel good about lending you money because you still owe me five dollars from last month," you can be open and honest with a friend without labeling him or her irresponsible.

"I" messages are both easier to hear and less open to argument because they are not judgmental. If you say to your friend, "I'm not lending you any money because you are irresponsible," you aren't sending an "I" message even though you begin with "I", the first-person pronoun. Expressing a feeling in this way usually puts the other person on the defensive. Your friend is likely to respond, "I am not irresponsible!" and then you have an argument on your hands. You may even lose a friend. If you share your own feelings and describe other people's behavior factually, you can maintain honest relationships without turning people against you.

"I" statements help you to be responsible for your feelings. Recognizing and taking charge of your feelings is the first step toward dealing with them. If you say to someone, "You make me angry!" you have lost a chance to accept responsibility for your own feelings. It is better to say, "I get angry when you are late." Clarify the message by being specific. You can then move toward solving the problem and away from feeling angry.

Sending Clear Messages

How many times have you come away from a conversation wondering what the other person meant, or if you got your point across? Feelings of confusion can signal that there has been a problem in communication. Many misunderstandings would not occur if people said what they really meant completely and clearly.

One way to clarify your messages is to stop asking questions that hide statements. "What are you doing tonight?" can mean many things. The hidden statement might be any of the following:

- "I'm curious about how you spend your time."

- "I'd like to get together with you."

- "I want to know if there is a party tonight."

- "I am upset about something and would like to talk it over with you."

Probably 90 percent of the information we try to convey in questions would come across more clearly as statements.

Another way to improve your communication is to ask direct questions. This advice is not as simple as it sounds. Sometimes you may avoid asking for what you want because to ask means to risk rejection. On the other hand, not asking means to risk not communicating. Although it is sometimes effective to hint at your wants and needs, this indirect approach more

Teenagers and their parents get along much better when they have learned to communicate effectively.

often results in mutual frustration. You are not satisfied with the response you receive and the other person is uneasy because the message was not clear. You can meet your needs most effectively by asking for things directly and by encouraging others to do so as well.

What Builds Good Relationships with Parents?

The principles of good communication and effective problem solving apply to all relationships, those with acquaintances, friends, parents, brothers and sisters and other relatives. At this stage in your life, there are some special factors in your relationship with your parents that you must think about carefully. During adolescence, you are changing rapidly from a child whose parents were the center of your life into an independent adult. These years are a time of emotional and intellectual preparation for leaving home. You need more and more freedom to make your own decisions and to learn from your successes and failures. You need to learn about your strengths and weaknesses and to develop the skills that will enable you to succeed on your own.

Differences Between Generations

Both adolescents and their parents have mixed feelings about the "growing-up" years.

You probably feel excited about what you are doing part of the time and depressed or anxious at other times. Parents, too, are pleased that their teenagers are growing up, but they may also be fearful at the same time.

Parents of teenagers have many mixed feelings because they want their children to grow into happy adults, and yet they are afraid of the pitfalls that may await their children during adolescence. As a teenager, you may find that your parents want to protect you from the pain you will feel when things don't go well for you, just as they always tried to protect you when you were younger. Most parents know that this protection is impossible to give. They may react to your efforts at independence by being disapproving and critical. They may seem overprotective even when what they want is to support and to help you. Many parents experience an inner conflict between their desire to protect you and their wish to express love, trust, and confidence in you as a growing person.

As their children approach adulthood, parents reach a new stage in their own lives. The task of supporting and caring for a family begins to change. Their own parents are growing older and may require help or care. In some cases, their parents may have died, and they, in midlife, are reevaluating their lives. Most parents are able to realize that a new stage of life can be rich in possibilities for growth and change. As an older teenager, you can help by understanding your parents' special needs and by supporting their efforts at adjustment.

Modeling and Rebellion

You may be able to see some of the problems your friends' parents are facing, but often it is harder to notice what is happening in your own family. The reason is that your feelings are very closely involved with those of your parents.

When you were younger, it seemed that your parents had the power to make you feel good or bad about yourself. It became very important for you to please them and to make them proud of you. At times, you wanted to be just like them in every possible way. You may have dressed up in their clothes, imitated their voices and mannerisms or played games based on your notions of what they said and did. This kind of behavior is called **modeling** — patterning your ideas, viewpoints, and behavior according to the way someone else lives and the things he or she tells you.

You probably can remember other times when you said to yourself, "I'll never do that the way my parents do." You could see traits in your parents that you disliked. You may have promised yourself that you would always act differently from the way your parents acted in certain situations. This kind of behavior is called **rebellion** — taking on ideas, attitudes, and behaviors opposite to those that other people close to you display.

Both modeling and rebellion are important in the process of becoming your own person. Everyone begins to grow toward independence within the framework of his or her own family. Your parents' ways of seeing and doing things have been the most powerful influences on your development. Their influence is still very powerful when you are an adolescent, not only because you see them every day, but also because their teachings and expectations still influence the decisions you make.

The Parent Inside You

At an early age, your conscience developed according to things your parents told you and experiences you had. Later, as you grew intellectually, you became better able to think things over and to make up your own mind about whether the voices in your conscience at a given time were helpful. At some point, for example, you decided for yourself that it was permissible to light matches under appropriate conditions and that you could touch the stove without burning yourself.

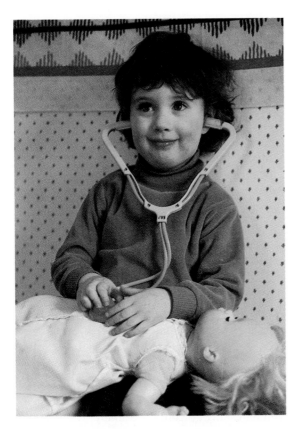
Children often imitate the behavior of important role models in their lives.

Many of your beliefs about the kind of person you are, what others are like, and how the world works are ideas you picked up from your own parents and then **internalized**, or made part of you. During adolescence, you are not only dealing with the rules and wishes of your parents as they are today, but you are also testing the do's and don't's of your childhood. How you resolve these questions will have a lot to do with how you choose to live your life and what kind of relationship you have with your parents, now and in the future.

Understanding Guilt

Guilt is the feeling you have when you have broken an inner rule. Other people may try to make you feel guilty, but they are unable to do so unless you yourself feel that you have done something wrong. Many times, people also feel angry or anxious when they feel guilty. They fear rejection, punishment, or humiliation. They feel angry because they want other people to accept what they have done without question. They believe they would not feel so uncomfortably guilty if it were not for the attitudes of others. Usually, this belief is not true. It is simply more comfortable to believe that others are responsible for the way you feel.

Living with Your Parents

Considering the changes a family faces as teenagers grow toward independence, it is no wonder that many problems arise in the family members' relationships with each other. Differences over school work, clothes, money, social activities, companions, curfews — in fact, nearly everything — are likely to occur at this time. How you and your parents handle these differences will be important for all of you.

It sometimes may be hard for your parents to accept that their children can assume greater responsibility for themselves. At the same time, you are gradually moving toward the time when you will take charge of your own life. Your movement is less like a straight line and more like a line with peaks and valleys. Sometimes the need for independence pushes you forward. At other times the security of depending on your parents pulls you back. Even so, agreement is possible if everyone involved works at finding solutions to problems as they occur. It is easier to solve problems when everyone can discuss them openly and without anger.

For Review

1. Give an example of an "I" message.
2. What are some of the special needs of the parents of adolescents?
3. What is meant by internalized beliefs?

2 Chapter Review

Summary

Contact, common interests, and similar experiences, attitudes, and beliefs bring people together in relationships. Good relationships depend upon mutual caring, trust, respect, sharing, flexibility, and empathy.

Effective communication helps to build relationships. Openness, the sending of "I" messages, skillful listening, and agreement between verbal and nonverbal messages improve communication in relationships. Using feedback provided by the listener helps people to send clear messages.

Teenagers may model themselves after their parents, or they may rebel. They can build positive relationships with their parents through clear communication, understanding their parents' needs, and resolving any differences as they occur.

Vocabulary

Use the following vocabulary words to complete the paragraphs below.

- ambivalence
- body language
- empathy
- frame of reference
- internalized
- listener feedback
- modeling
- rebellion
- verbal communication

People are most likely to form relationships with those who share their __1__. __2__ is an important quality in relationships because it enables people to understand the feelings and actions of others. This quality also helps people to understand those who are experiencing mixed feelings, a state known as __3__. While effective verbal communication is essential to any relationship, interpreting the __4__ of others also provides important clues about the messages others send.

__5__ is the use of spoken or written words, signs, or sounds to express ideas or emotions. To improve communication, speakers should think about their tone and mood, as well as their eye contact. Finally, they should pay close attention to and use the signals they receive in the form of __6__.

All human beings have __7__ their beliefs about themselves and the world from their parents. At times adolescents pattern their behavior and opinions after those of their parents, which is called __8__. At other times, adolescents act and think in ways contrary to their parents, which is called __9__.

Chapter Questions

1. What are the factors that contribute to the formation of good relationships?
2. Which of the six qualities that are important to relationships do you value the most and why?
3. What are the essentials of being a skilled listener of others?

4. Give an example in which a person's non-verbal communication interferes with the message he or she is trying to convey.

5. What is the difference between empathizing with someone and merely feeling sorry for him or her?

6. Name three forms that verbal communication can take.

7. Give two examples of listener feedback. Then discuss ways for the speaker to use each in order to improve his or her communication.

8. How can a person communicate openly and honestly without alienating others?

9. Discuss some of the ways you have modeled your parents and some ways you have rebelled against them.

Skill Activities

1. Critical Thinking All people have experienced ambivalent feelings at some time in their lives. When people feel ambivalent, they have "mixed" or conflicting feelings. They may feel both happy and angry about something that happens, or both jealous and proud. For example, Liza and her best friend, Zoe, applied for two job openings at a local restaurant. When the manager called to tell Liza she had the job, she was ecstatic. Then Liza learned that Zoe had not been hired. Liza felt immediately sad and disappointed that her friend would not be working with her. Deep down, however, Liza still felt happy that she had the job. Her sad feelings mingled with her happiness, which caused her to have ambivalent feelings about taking the job. Think back to a time when you felt ambivalent about something that happened to you. In two or three paragraphs, describe the situation that left you feeling ambivalent. What were your conflicting feelings? How did these feelings affect you and the outcome of the situation?

2. Communication At a family party, your older brother (father, sister) relates a story about you that you had told him in confidence. Naturally, you are embarrassed and furious with your brother. What is the best way to communicate your feelings? What are some less effective ways you could let him know? Write an imaginary dialogue in which you openly communicate your feelings about this incident to your brother. Remember to speak honestly, send "I" messages, and ask direct questions.

3. Social Studies With your classmates, conduct a poll among the students in your school to determine the qualities of a friend that they feel are most important. You may use the list of qualities shown on the graph on page 27, or compile your own list.

Try using some scientific polling methods to make your poll a more valid measure. First, define the population to be surveyed. Second, construct a sample (representative cross-section of the school's student population). Third, prepare specific questions. Fourth, select the way in which you will take the poll, and fifth, analyze and report your results.

3 Loving Relationships

As you read, think about:

- how a loving relationship begins.
- what dating teaches you about relationships.
- how many different kinds of love you can experience.
- how the myths of love are inconsistent with real experience.
- why people in love should retain their individuality.
- how love brings challenges into one's life.

Love is probably the human emotion most talked about, written about and sung about. People will always try to define love according to their own personal experiences.

This chapter deals with how many loving relationships begin, and the different kinds of love people feel. The chapter goes on to discuss several ideas about love that are popular in this society. You will be able to test them against your own awareness and experience. The chapter concludes with a description of the important qualities in a relationship.

VOCABULARY

unromantic love
infatuation
myth
essence
ultimate

How a Relationship Begins

The previous chapter discussed how a friendship between two people develops. Sharing common interests, experiences and similar attitudes and beliefs stimulates not only the growth of friendship but of loving relationships as well. In fact, many relationships that result in marriage begin as friendships.

A loving relationship is always changing. One of the first steps in the development of a serious, or lasting, relationship, is dating.

Different Styles of Dating

Dating is a training ground for dealing with members of the opposite sex. Dating helps you learn how to relate to other people on different emotional levels. When you have a variety of dating experiences, you are more able to make good decisions about personal commitments.

Group Dating   The most informal type of dating takes place in groups. Sporting events, club meetings, concerts and movies allow groups of people to spend time together in a relaxed way. The focus is on having a good time with several people you enjoy. Group dating allows people to get to know each other in a relaxed atmosphere.

Dating as a Couple   When people begin dating as a couple, there is more of an opportunity to learn about an individual's personality, values and goals. By spending time alone together, as well as seeing movies, dining out, going to concerts, a couple's relationship may develop more dimensions than in casual dating arrangements. Usually teenagers and young adults date a variety of people before making a permanent commitment to another person.

Serious Dating   Serious dating usually means that a couple is making a commitment to each other and to the relationship. This type of

Whether you are dating seriously or dating on a casual basis, relationships can teach you a great deal about yourself.

What are the advantages of group dating?

dating may or may not result in marriage, but it is definitely a way of testing your ability to maintain a loving relationship with someone.

Think about how your environment and your family affect this process of testing out a relationship. The models that you have for relationships, especially your parents, influence how you might treat someone else, and how you express your feelings toward that person.

Whether in large groups, or couples, as casual arrangements or serious commitments, dating adds to a person's understanding of self and others.

Different Kinds of Love

At times the notion of love can be confusing. Probably the fact that there are many kinds of love adds to the confusion. You might feel a protective love for your brother, a love based on loyalty for your friend, and an overwhelming love for your girlfriend or boyfriend. Experience in recognizing the different forms of love will help you deal realistically with your current and future relationships.

Unromantic Love The love you feel for a friend, a brother or sister, a grandparent or a parent is an example of **unromantic love.** It is a strong and lasting love, but it is different from the love between a husband and wife.

- ■ PARENT-CHILD   There is a unique loving relationship between parents and their children. This type of love is based on the bond that was formed when the child was an infant. As a child's needs for attention, discipline, and care change, so does the loving relationship. Parents sometimes feel disappointed in their children, and children often rebel against their parents. However complicated and difficult the relationship between a parent and child may become, feelings of love are still present.

- ■ SIBLING   Brothers and sisters share a loving bond that is often marked by jealousy and competition. Even though sibling relationships can be stormy, especially during childhood and adolescence, loving feelings survive because of shared experience and family loyalty.

- ■ LOVE FOR FRIENDS   The love you feel for a friend might be described as a safe, relaxed kind of love. There are few barriers involved in friendship. Friends can share feelings and thoughts without feeling threatened by negative reactions. Some of the elements of friendship are also found in romantic love.

For a better understanding of unromantic love, think about the relationships you have with your friends, parents, siblings, and grandparents. The love you feel for your mother is different from the love you feel for your best friend. However, both are examples of unromantic love.

Romantic Love Romantic love is a combination of tender feelings and physical attraction. In another section of this chapter, many dimensions of romantic love will be discussed. When you feel romantic love for another person you often feel vulnerable and confused. Love can be exciting and painful at the same time.

Love vs. Infatuation Infatuation is often mistaken for love, especially when strong feelings of attraction and admiration for someone occur for the first time in your life. In a relationship based on infatuation, feelings surge quickly, and they seem explosive and passionate. Focusing on one characteristic of the other person is often a sign of infatuation. You may be attracted to another person's appearance, sense of humor, or particular skill. In contrast to infatuation, lasting love is based on an attraction to and acceptance of the total person, not just one part. Loving feelings are steady and secure. Infatuation is limited, hasty, and may end as quickly as it begins. Overwhelming feelings of infatuation may blind you to the reality that love is not present. Over time, unhappiness can follow.

Falling in love with a role or an image is a sign of infatuation. How does infatuation differ from other loving relationships?

Love and Jealousy When one partner in a loving relationship becomes overly possessive, or jealous, he or she makes unrealistic demands of the other partner's time and loyalty. Jealousy sometimes indicates that a person is immature and/or insecure. A mature person is not easily threatened when his or her partner spends time with friends or pursues activities that take time away from the loving relationship.

Myths About Love

Since you were a child, you have been absorbing **myths,** or legends, about love from popular music, movies, television, and books. The myths persist because they are often comfortable illusions for people who do not choose to face reality. Myths offer an escape from the dull routine of daily life. Unlike scientific theories, you cannot prove or disprove them. However, because myths are often repeated, many people accept them as true.

Myth: "Someday I Will Find The Perfect Partner for Me."

The fairy tale of Cinderella and the prince is an excellent example of the myth of "the perfect partner." It carries the message that some day you will find your prince or princess, the perfect partner, the one destined for you and you alone. When you meet, the moment will be magic. You will fall in love and from that time forward, life will be a series of magic moments as you live happily ever after.

The idea of perfection is the basis for the concept of romantic love. Because falling in love is a very exciting emotional experience, a person at first will tend to view the other person as perfect and to think of the shared feelings as ideal. Two people in love seem to complete one another. They need only to be together to achieve total happiness.

Believing the myths about love can set you up for disappointment. There is no such thing as a perfect relationship.

When the first rush of excitement gives way to other feelings, some of them negative, people feel tricked. If two people discover that one has a nasty temper and that the other is habitually late, they both might wonder if they were wrong about each other in the first place. Becoming aware of imperfections, however, need not be a calamity, even though both people may have been misled by the myth of "the perfect partner." When two people in love begin to discover their mutual differences, they need to view the differences as challenges in building a relationship. Learning to handle negative feelings toward one another and to reach workable solutions to problems that arise can help to strengthen loving feelings. Partners may become irritated even in the very best relationships. In every relationship, there will be times of anger as well as times of joy.

Myth: "True Love Happens Only Once in a Lifetime."

The myth of "true love" states that "true love" is not "infatuation" or "affection" or "a springtime romance." Even if you believe the myth, you may not be able to distinguish between feelings of "true love" and other feelings when you experience them. Only when the feelings have passed might you say, "Oh, it wasn't true love at all. It was only infatuation." After one or two such experiences, you may begin to wonder whether you can trust your own feelings at all.

All the loving feelings people have are real. Love is just love – neither true nor false. Love simply *is*. One reason for the confusion between "true love" and other love is that "true love" supposedly occurs just once in a lifetime. Thus, according to the myth, people have only one chance to find "true love." Fortunately, love is not that rare. Moreover, while love is important for a lasting relationship, it is not the only factor that helps a relationship survive and grow.

Myth: "Love Never Changes."

When people fall in love, they expect the intense feelings that fuel the start of a relationship to last forever. A conversation between two people under the spell of the myth of unchanging love might go something like this:

"The best thing about our relationship is that we love each other."

"Oh yes, and that will *never* change."

Actually, love is among the most fragile of feelings; it can and does change. Although feelings of love are always present inside, anger, worry, or even a bad headache can displace them. Preparing for an important exam can cause love to disappear temporarily. Anxiety and stress also take their toll on affectionate feelings.

How partners feel about themselves and about their loved ones may affect their feelings of love toward each other. Angers, fears, and irritations that go unshared can build up inside and may sometimes destroy love. However, problems faced honestly and resolved can lead to deeper and richer feelings of love.

Feelings of love are always changing. The most vital relationships include periods when both people's feelings are not warm or excited. Sometimes, love feels soft and tender, sometimes, passionate and exciting, and sometimes, sad or angry. As the individuals in a relationship grow, love also may deepen and grow. The most interesting fact about love is that it never stays the same.

Myth: "Others Cause Love to Happen."

The source of your feelings of love is inside yourself. Most people do not believe this. When you fall in love, it may seem as if the person you love has caused you to feel terrific. You may believe that his or her lovable qualities have almost forced you to fall in love. This is not the case; love is an inner experience. Writer Stewart Emery has explained that you open up to the love inside you when you are close to someone with qualities you think are lovable.

When we say we are in love with someone else, what is happening is that when we are around that person we have an experience of our own **essence** [essential self]. And we fall in love with that experience, because that experience *is* love.

Unfortunately, we put the cause of the experience over on other people, rather than realizing that what we love is ourselves around them. Something about them inspires us . . . into a direct experience of our own beauty. We really fall in love with our **ultimate** [most real] self. It is an experience of freedom and release.

Myth: "Love Solves All Problems."

"If you *really* loved me," Karen told Paul, "you would call when you aren't going to show up." This conversation is only the latest in a series of complaints. Karen has a list of things she feels Paul should do because he loves her. Paul, too, has a list. Both people believe the myth that merely loving each other a little more or a little better will solve their mutual problems. Both make an effort, but they find that they are not as interested in seeing each other as they used to be. Loving a person does not mean that conflicts will be easily resolved.

Love does not solve problems. In fact, it is likely to create new problems. On the other hand, love offers people challenging opportunities to grow. Since people grow by facing and solving problems, love provides ample potential for growth.

People who believe the myth that love solves problems might become upset about problems that arise with loved ones. They might begin to

The Knight and the Lady — Then and Now

Romantic love — we all recognize it when we see it, read about it, or feel it. Nevertheless, it often seems confusing and full of contradictions, both too wonderful and too painful for the everyday world. Did you ever wonder where the myths and customs of romantic love originated?

Historians believe that the concept of romantic love began in the Middle Ages. The code of honor and courtesy that guided a medieval knight was called *chivalry*. It involved religious fervor, protectiveness toward the weak, and tender love of a lady.

Songs of the period often told of a knight's adoration of and service to a beautiful lady. Typically, the knight would have an idealized image of his lady, and love her from afar. This worshipful attitude was known as courtly love. Most often, the knight and lady could not marry because of the social rules of that time period. Thus, courtly love involved longing and pain. Suffering for love was a common theme of medieval songs as it is of many songs today.

Rescuing "a damsel in distress" was an opportunity for the knight to show his protectiveness. He defended his lady against dragons, sorcerers, or other threats. Updated versions of this rescue story — in movies with settings ranging from the Old West to the distant future — are still popular today.

On occasions when the lady did not need to be rescued, the knight could still show his bravery and unselfish service to her by performing "love tests," or feats designed to impress her. In return, the lady would give him tokens of encouragement and devotion. For example, a knight would participate in a *joust* (a contest of battle skills) or ride off to war wearing his lady's veil or scarf. Tokens ex-changed today are very different. They may include a loved one's bracelet, ring, special jacket or varsity sweater, yet the feelings are much the same.

Because the medieval knight and lady loved only from a distance, their illusions about each other could remain intact. Even today, many people view the one they love in idealized terms, and develop impossible expectations of their romantic relationships. No one — male or female — can live up to the knight-in-shining-armor ideal; no single "rescuer" can solve all of life's problems. As males and females become friends and equals — studying, working, and competing with each other — some of the romance may go out of their relationships. On the other hand, if these relationships are based on realistic expectations, they are more likely to have a happy ending than the often tragic medieval romance.

Ladies in medieval times were often loved from afar.

Source: "May" page of Brevario Grimani, Biblioteca Marciana, Venice.

think less of themselves or of the one they love, and they might even wonder whether they are really in love at all. Paul and Karen have not fallen out of love. Rather, neither has learned to consider the needs of the other. The love they feel can help them solve problems, but only after they recognize each other's needs. Loving someone is a strong motivation for problem solving. While love itself cannot provide solutions, it may stimulate partners to think over and discuss and solve their problems.

Myth: "The Best Love is Unselfish Love."

Love is neither selfish nor unselfish. However, people can behave either selfishly or unselfishly toward those they love. Behavior is different from feelings, and the feeling of love may get mixed up with many other feelings. People in love also can feel afraid of their loving feelings. They may become angry if the loved one does not act in a certain way. A big difference exists between feeling love for someone and being able to treat that person in a loving way. How people in love act toward one another indicates whether they will be able to have a good relationship. Being willing to give your partner freedom and being respectful of his or her individuality are examples of behavior for making relationships work successfully. For love to grow, each of the two people needs to respect the other's feelings and recognize him or her as a complete and separate identity.

For Review

1. Describe three kinds of loving relationships.
2. Why is the idea that "Love solves all problems" a myth?
3. What is inaccurate about the statement that "Love happens only once in a lifetime"?

A Loving Relationship

Falling in love with someone who is in love with you is simply the beginning of what can be one of life's great adventures. Love merely releases the potential for a good relationship. It doesn't ensure that you will live happily ever after, like Cinderella and Prince Charming. Love helps make you capable of doing some very difficult tasks. Being patient through lengthy arguments or handling loneliness when you are separated from the one you love are examples of difficulties you might encounter. Even though you think that love should always be easy and joyful, you realize that it is often painful and demanding.

Falling in love is very easy to do; however, having a loving relationship requires a great deal of effort. You need to develop communication skills that will help you meet the challenges of the relationship. You also must handle the feelings of anger, fear, and loneliness that emerge from time to time. Mature individuals who share a loving relationship can manage such emotions with ease and confidence. Some people never learn to deal with their emotions.

Perfect Love for Imperfect People

Psychologist Abraham Maslow, who devised the "pyramid" of human needs (Chapter 1), found that the love relationships of self-actualized people were quite different from those of most people. Self-actualizers are people who have reached their fullest potential as human beings, usually in the second half of life. In studying their love relationships, Maslow revealed that self-actualized people do not feel the need to be on guard with one another or to impress one another. Further, they do not need to hide their thoughts and feelings or to maintain an aura of mystery. They feel free to be either independent or dependent whenever they want. Their relationships display trust, creativity, admiration, fun, wonder, respect, mutual acceptance, and an ever-deepening joy in one another's company. Although Maslow's theory may seem to create still another myth about love, Maslow believed that an almost perfect love can exist between self-actualized people.

Maslow's studies may be inspirational to people who have not yet attained the elevated state of self-actualization. His findings reveal that it is possible to attain a love relationship that is both desirable and reassuring. Love need not die or become less exciting over time. People do not need to settle for dreary but "secure" relationships, or move from one love to another to maintain a sense of excitement.

Maslow's research also shows that the ability to feel good about oneself while being free to be open with another person keeps love relationships alive. Many relationships die from anger or boredom because the two people involved stop trying to learn both how to be themselves and how to accept one another. Love, like friendship, needs sharing, respect, acceptance, and flexibility.

Equality

In healthy, growing love relationships, the two people are committed to establishing and maintaining equality in the relationship. Equality means that the ideas and feelings of both people are important whenever they must make a decision that will affect the relationship. If one person makes all the decisions, that person may soon begin to feel pressured, while the other person may feel left out and resentful.

Equality in a relationship avoids misunderstandings and enhances feelings of security and trust.

Love is not a blending of personalities but a healthy acceptance and appreciation of differences between two people.

In the relationship between Jack and Laura, one person appears to make all the decisions. Jack always drives the car when he and Laura go out to dinner, and he usually chooses the restaurant. Laura makes sure she is available when Jack calls each evening. Couples like Jack and Laura do not question their roles in a relationship because they probably feel comfortable with their arrangements. Laura could be a person who cannot handle conflicts. Agreeing with Jack all the time is a way of avoiding disagreements. Nevertheless, it might be more convenient for Laura to phone Jack sometimes. In fact, both people might enjoy the change if, from time to time, Laura made the plans for their dates.

A couple selects whatever arrangement works for both of them. If both have a say in decisions about all parts of their relationship, from their social activities to the handling of joint problems, the relationship may be more fun. It may become more secure, too, for neither partner feels that he or she must give up an important idea or feeling in order to be part of the couple.

Practical Tip

To insure that a good relationship stays that way, consider these reminders:

- Take it slow. Give a relationship time to grow and change.

- Maintain your own interests and friendships. Do not let your love life monopolize your time.

- Communicate. Do not expect your partner to read your mind. Share your feelings. Do not hesitate to report negative as well as positive feelings.

- Do not always try to have your own way.

- Compromise whenever possible.

Individuality

People in love must take special care to maintain their own individuality in the face of the intense feelings they have for one another. Many people think that people in love should become one unit, thinking and feeling the same way and doing everything together. Since it is not possible for two people to be identical in every way, an attempt to bring this about may actually destroy loving feelings. Relationships may die from boredom or from resentment. It is not very interesting for partners to talk things over if they always think alike or always agree. Further, partners may begin to feel uncomfortable if they think they have to agree with everything the other person says.

Couples who have many things in common sometimes begin to speak for one another. The partners may have begun to believe that all the thoughts and feelings they share are the same. However, people rarely agree on everything. Even if two people do agree on many things, one would not enjoy having the other partner tell people how "we" think or believe. Speaking for oneself means taking responsibility for one's own ideas. It helps both members of a couple maintain their individuality.

A sense of being separate from each other is important in a relationship. It confirms that each partner is a free person. They spend time together because they want to, not because they need to be together to feel good or because they have nothing better to do. Having separate interests, activities, and friends, as well as those they share, is important. Both people then have interesting things to talk about and bring renewed energy to the relationship. The benefits of being together are multiplied when both people are as enthusiastic about the part of their lives spent apart as the part spent together.

When people first fall in love, they often want to spend most of their time together, getting to know one another better. Sooner or later in a

Whatever the reason for the breakup of a relationship, both people are left with some sad feelings.

healthy relationship, the time will come when both people need "space" to follow their own interests. This is a good sign. People who do not pursue independent activities may end up overly dependent on one another. Their love will not grow, and thus will not survive.

Endings

No matter how good a relationship has been, the two of you may drift apart or may develop problems that drive you apart. Sometimes, it is hard to know just why a relationship is ending, at other times, it is very clear. In either case, it is painful to break up with someone you have cared about.

Some people spend a great deal of energy hoping that things will change or blaming the other person. These are negative ways to handle the sadness and anger most people feel after a breakup. Relief at getting out of a bad situation will be mixed with other feelings such as loneliness and disappointment. All these emotions must be felt and accepted so that you will soon be ready to enjoy new relationships. It takes time for this adjustment process to ease a person's turbulent feelings. When it is clear that love is over, there is really no positive choice but to go on with your life.

For Review

1. Describe some of the difficult tasks of being in a loving relationship.
2. Why is it important for people in love to spend time apart?
3. Why might a relationship die from anger or boredom?

Homework

3 Chapter Review

Summary

Love is one of the most talked about but least understood human experiences. Loving relationships grow for many of the same reasons friendships develop. Dating gives young couples the opportunity to learn about each other's personality, values, and goals. While there are many different kinds of love that people can share, a lasting love relationship between two people is steady and involves a total acceptance of the other person.

Many popular myths about love obscure the reality that it is imperfect, always changing, and can be difficult, although well worth the challenge. Loving relationships grow when both partners communicate, express their emotions, accept their differences, value equality, and work out arrangements that allow them to grow as individuals. Love, whether it continues or ends, has painful as well as joyous moments. Endings may be easier to accept if you remember that each relationship gives you the opportunity to grow.

Vocabulary

Complete each of the following sentences with one of the vocabulary words below.

essence
infatuation
myth
ultimate
unromantic love

1. According to writer Stewart Emery, when a person falls in love, he or she has an experience of his or her essential self, or _____ .
2. The type of love people feel toward their parents, brothers and sisters, friends, and other relatives is called _____ .
3. A _____ is a legend or popular belief that provides an illusion of reality.
4. Often confused with love, _____ occurs when a person experiences sudden overwhelming feelings of attraction and admiration for another person.
5. Emery states that when people love another person, they reexperience their own beauty and their _____ selves.

Chapter Questions

1. What can be learned about another person through dating?
2. How does jealousy affect a relationship?
3. Why is it important to date a variety of people before making a commitment to only one person?
4. Compare the love you feel for a friend with the love you feel for a relative (brother, sister, parent, grandparent).
5. What do you think the difference is between love and infatuation?
6. What is inaccurate about the myth that states, "Love never changes"?
7. Which of the six myths about love do you think could affect a couple's relationship the most? Why do you think so?

Facing Complex Decisions

You are just beginning to make choices that help you define who you are, what you want, and where you are going with your life. Such choices often create tension, since a variety of factors play a part in decision making. It is important for you to understand how certain factors help or hinder you in making choices that are right for you.

Factors Affecting Decision Making

People do not make decisions in a vacuum. Your family, friends, classmates, and your own needs and desires affect what your choices will be. Many decisions involve the roles people play and the expectations people have. You are also influenced by your environment and the teachings and expectations of community and religious groups.

Peer Pressure Perhaps you have just moved to a new school and you have joined a group that is involved in team sports. You might prefer being with musicians or artists. However, you go along with the sports crowd because you want to make friends. If your choice pleases everyone except yourself, it is probably a result of **peer pressure,** a need to be accepted by people in your age group.

In some cases, peer pressure can be harmful to you. For example, you might decide to smoke just because everyone else does it, rather than consider the health risks involved. When you think for yourself, you are more likely to make decisions that are truly your own.

Parental Expectations Some parents urge their children to learn a family trade or to carry on a family business. Other parents may expect their children to follow their footsteps into politics, acting careers, or social service. Many parents also want their children to marry, raise families, and maintain family traditions.

Friends can influence the decisions you make. Consider different viewpoints, then make decisions that are right for you.

As you develop within your family, you become aware of what your parents or other family members expect of you. Family expectations often have a positive influence on the types of choices you make. In other instances parental expectations may be too rigid or not in line with the hopes and dreams of their children. As a result, some young people rebel. Being able to communicate effectively can help family members resolve such conflicts.

Self-Image The choices you make are often based on your self-image. If you see yourself as shy, or if you can't stand rejection, you may fear the unknown and decide to pursue only familiar activities. Some people have such poor self-esteem that they find it difficult to make decisions of any kind. Those who have inflated ideas about themselves sometimes choose to accept challenges that are beyond their talents or skills.

People need realistic images of who they are in order to make effective decisions. By honestly seeking to know yourself, you can identify your assets and priorities. Then you can set up realistic goals, make effective choices, and

A positive self-image is an important factor that affects the decision-making process.

commit your energy to them. Making decisions on the basis of who and what you really are gives you power over your life.

Society's Expectations "What will the neighbors (or family or friends) think?" That question is often raised by people who seek approval for their actions from those around them. As you make your own decisions, you may not consciously worry about others' opinions, but like most people you will probably be influenced by the larger society's expectations. That is, you may choose actions that reflect the values of the general society. For example, you will probably obey laws and try to be a productive citizen.

There may be times when you will have to decide whether you should choose a course of action different from what the general society expects. For example, you might wonder about becoming an activist for an unpopular cause. The steps in decision making can help you make choices best suited to your needs and goals.

How Decisions Are Made

When you make a choice, you may choose from two or more alternatives. Perhaps you have had to decide between two events scheduled for the same time, such as a party or big game. If you go to one event, you'll miss the other. In order to come to a decision, you may have to weigh the cost (how much you are giving up) against the benefit (how much you are getting). This process is called a **trade-off**—an exchange of what you are getting for what you are giving up.

An important decision may also involve related decisions. For example, if you decide to buy a stereo, you may have to give up special events that cost money, or delay the purchase of new clothing. Thinking through and rejecting alternatives helps you make wise decisions.

Steps In Decision Making Effective decision making usually involves eight steps.

1. Identify the decision to be made.
2. Know your goal.
3. Check available resources; consult authorities if needed.
4. Decide what choices are possible; consider the likely results of each choice.
5. Select the best choice for you and determine the procedures you must follow to reach your goal.
6. Act on your plan.
7. Evaluate the results and change your procedures if they don't work.
8. Take responsibility for your decision.

Using the Decision-Making Steps You do not need to use all the decision-making steps each time you make an important decision, and in some situations, steps may overlap. Suppose that you want to go on with your education after high school. As a first step you might ask: "What school should I attend?" Such a question identifies what must be decided.

Think about the last time you shopped for clothes. Can you identify the steps involved in making a decision?

Even if you follow the steps described here, sometimes factors beyond your control can complicate your decision-making process. Sometimes other people can severely limit or change your choices. Long-term illness, death, divorce, and unemployment in a family are just a few factors that can alter the original choices you might have made. Changing circumstances may require you to start over again with the decision-making process.

For Review

1. What are the major factors that influence your decision making?
2. How does peer pressure affect the decisions you make?
3. Describe the decision-making process.

Perhaps your goal (step 2) is to become a commercial artist. You may determine (using steps 3 and 4) that you could attend a state university about 100 miles from your home, a nearby private college, or a two-year technical school located downtown. Each school could provide the basic courses you need to become a commercial artist.

Using step 5, you decide that tuition at the two-year technical school is within your budget, you can travel to the school by train or car and you can take most of the graphic arts courses you would like. So (step 6) you enroll in the technical school.

After the first semester, you evaluate (step 7) and decide that you would like to expand your studies beyond the graphic arts available at the school. You accept (step 8) that you made the best decision for you at the time and will complete the year since you need the courses. Then you'll consider transferring to the state university for more general courses along with your art major.

Decisions About Drugs

You probably know people who take pills for the most minor ailments, or who drink alcohol or smoke to fit in socially. The misuse of over-the-counter and prescription drugs, including inhalants, and the use of illegal drugs are critical issues facing our country today. In this section, the term drugs includes prescrip-

Some medical experts believe that Americans overuse or misuse medications.

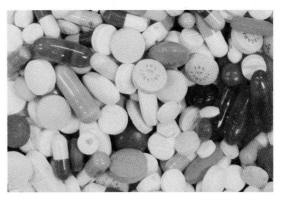

tion and over-the-counter medications, alcohol, nicotine, and illegal substances.

The widespread habit of taking pills to ease pain or to relax may be one factor that leads people to consider using **mind-altering substances** such as alcohol and illegal drugs. Reality-altering substances change the way a person experiences or perceives life. Frequent use of any of these substances causes more pain than enjoyment, since many have harmful side effects. Why, then, do people use drugs? Peer pressure, or pressure from society at large, and family problems are some of the most common motivations for drug use and abuse.

Pressure from Peers

In spite of the possibility of addiction, many people decide to use alcohol and other drugs. Surveys show that one high school senior out of 10 has used cocaine, and one in 20 uses marijuana daily.

Young people are often influenced by their friends and classmates, as described earlier in this chapter. The pressure to go along with the crowd can be intense and can affect even elementary school children. Reports from schools across the nation show that a large number of grade school and junior high school students are afraid they will be offered alcohol or other drugs and will not be strong enough to say no. As you will see in the next few sections, there are very good reasons why you should not take drugs.

Family Problems

Some people decide to use reality-altering substances because they want to escape problems at home. Perhaps there is a lot of tension in the household, a parent is abusive, or the effects of poverty are ever present. Some adults in a household may be setting a poor example by using and abusing alcohol and other drugs themselves.

Lack of communication among family members can also be a factor in drug use. Sometimes young people in a family are unable to talk to the adults in their households about their problems or the pressures they face every day. In some cases, parents may ignore or be unaware of signs of alcohol or other drug abuse. Thus, families not only have to learn to communicate, but also need to become educated about the effects of reality-altering substances.

Pressures from Society

Television, magazine, and billboard ads may encourage people to use medications, alcohol and tobacco products. The images of well-being and glamor associated with drug products are designed to motivate people to buy. It is important to weigh the influence of advertising if you are faced with decisions about any kind of drug use.

Many young people model their behavior after their favorite performers or sports figures. If the famous flaunt their use of alcohol and illicit drugs, their life styles may be seen as the way to fun and success. Yet, people who know themselves usually choose to live by their own values.

Do not let advertisements for cigarettes and alcohol persuade you to smoke and drink.

Effects of Drug Use

The abuse of drugs has become epidemic in our nation. Both legal and illegal substances are abused. Up to 2.4 million Americans take anti-anxiety drugs, or tranquilizers, on a regular basis. Countless more Americans misuse other prescription drugs and over-the-counter medications to help them feel better, to aid sleep, or to be stimulated. Some misuse inhalants, while others illegally use or overuse alcohol. These are forms of drug abuse.

The U.S. Drug Enforcement Administration classifies these substances into five major groups: Narcotics (such as heroin and morphine), **Stimulants** (such as cocaine), **Depressants** (such as tranquilizers like Valium),

Hallucinogens (such as LSD), and Cannabis (Marijuana and Hashish from Canabis sativa plants).

Health practitioners often use broader groupings, categorizing drugs by the effects they produce: depressants, stimulants, and hallucinogens. Depressants, or "downers," decrease the activity of the central nervous system. Stimulants, or "uppers," have just the opposite effect. Hallucinogens alter the chemistry of the brain.

Marijuana

Marijuana, or "grass," has been called a "gateway drug," since many young people start with smoking marijuana and then go on to using stronger drugs such as heroin and cocaine.

Source: National Institue on Drug Abuse.

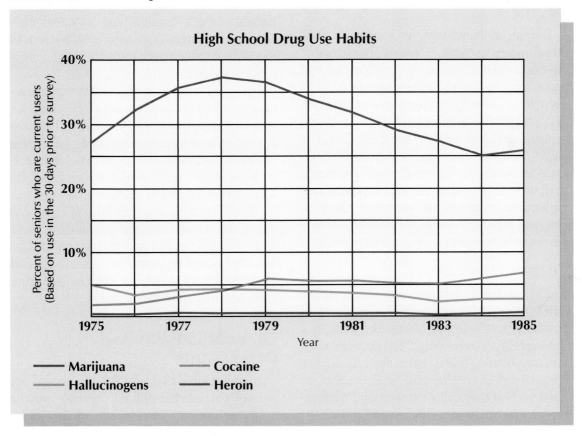

Symptoms experienced by marijuana users depend on the dose taken and the setting in which it is used. Marijuana frequently gives the user a false sense of well-being. Nevertheless, it can cloud judgment, and it actually distorts a person's perception.

Several studies have connected marijuana with increased danger when driving. There is an even higher risk of automobile accidents when drivers use marijuana along with alcohol. The combination severely impairs reflexes and reaction time.

Another danger of marijuana use is its damaging effect on the lungs. Marijuana cigarettes are never filtered and are usually smoked to the end. In terms of tar and gases released, the effect of smoking one marijuana cigarette is equivalent to smoking a far greater number of regular cigarettes.

Heroin

Heroin, a depressant, is known by such street names as "junk," "smack," or "horse." Heroin powder is sniffed into the nostrils or in liquid form is injected into a muscle or vein. Users often take heroin to relieve anxiety, anger, or pain. Because worries, fears, and tensions seem to fade away by using the drug, it is easy to become dependent on it. Increased use leads to addiction. Heroin dependency means that without the drug an addict experiences withdrawal symptoms such as chills, aching muscles, and abdominal pains. An overdose of heroin can result in a coma, or convulsions and death.

Cocaine and Crack

The National Institute on Drug Abuse (NIDA) says that the stimulant cocaine, a white powder from the leaves of the coca plant, is a "powerfully addictive drug." It is usually sniffed into the nostrils. At least one million Americans are addicted to cocaine and "so dependent on the drug that they cannot stop using it no matter how destructive it is to their health," NIDA officials say.

Many schools sponsor drug information fairs as a way to make accurate information available to students.

Cocaine users take the drug to feel self-confident and exhilarated. The drug appears to banish fatigue and hunger. However, shortly after consumption, a cocaine user may feel more tired and anxious than before. A person addicted to cocaine may prefer the drug over all other activities.

Frequent cocaine sniffers often experience damage to their nasal passages. Bleeding and cold-like symptoms result. Abusers may also have permanent hoarseness, fuzzy vision, and impaired breathing. When cocaine interferes with the brain's respiratory control center, the lungs fill with fluid and death results.

"Crack" is a more potent form of cocaine. It is prepared for smoking and gets into the bloodstream within ten seconds. It is not only faster, but more potent and thus more addictive. Crack can be highly toxic and users risk lung damage, brain seizures and heart attacks.

Other Stimulants and Depressants

Amphetamines (am-**FET**-uh-meenz) are a drug that stimulates the central nervous system. Like marijuana, amphetamines can give the user a false sense of well-being.

Some Commonly Abused Drugs

Drug*	Physical, Social, and Legal Risks and Dangers
Hallucinogens	
Marijuana *Street names:* grass, pot, weed, hash, smoke, reefer, tea, joint, Acapulco gold	Alters brain chemistry, perceptions; affects memory and judgment; affects reproductive system; damages lungs to a greater degree than tobacco smoke; lessens motivation, concentration, and attention; overdose can result in fatigue, paranoia, possible psychosis; affects vision, judgment, and physical skills needed for driving; relationships with family and friends, and job performance may suffer; arrests, fines, and jail terms resulting from use can be costly.
Stimulants	
Cocaine *Street names:* coke, blow, flake, snow, crack, rock, nose candy, stardust, C, heaven, dust, paradise	Raises blood pressure, heart, and breathing rates; depresses appetite and increases alertness; as "high" wears off, user feels tired, anxious, depressed; highly addictive; can cause damage to brain, lungs, liver, nose; risk of AIDS and infections from sharing needles; major problems for unborn babies of addicted mothers; small amounts can cause coma and death; can destroy relationships with family and friends and harm school and job performance; users risk arrests, fines, jail terms; crimes of violence committed to secure drug; the most addictive substance in the drug realm.
Crack	Same effects as cocaine, but more rapid and deadly, with marked increase in violent behavior by users.
Amphetamines Benzedrine, Dexedrine, Methadrine, Delcobase, Desoxyn	Create false sense of well-being; reduce appetite; may cause dizziness, insomnia; overdose can result in hallucinations, coma, convulsions, death.
Depressants	
Alcohol beer, wine, "hard liquor," and cordials; also used in over-the-counter medications and prescriptions	Reduces control of thought processes, reflexes, and physical skills; may cause addiction; damages brain, liver, other organs; may cause blackouts, coma, even death with prolonged large doses; endangers unborn children when used by pregnant women; a major factor in many divorces, family, school, and job problems; greatest cause of auto accidents; often a factor in crimes and violence, resulting in millions of arrests annually.
Inhalants	
Solvents, aerosols paint thinner, glue, gasoline; chemicals (gases) used in spray cans	Can cause permanent damage to nervous system, lungs, kidneys, other organs; cause confusion, dizziness, mood swings, delusions or hallucinations; endanger unborn children when used by pregnant women; overdose may result in convulsions, coma, and death.
Tobacco	Prolonged inhalation of tobacco smoke: a major factor in the development of lung cancer and in cancers of larynx, mouth, esophagus; a leading cause of death from lung cancer; a factor in cancers of bladder, pancreas, and kidney; restricted in many private homes and public places.

*Danger of abuse from over-the-counter and prescription drugs occurs mainly from misuse or failure to follow cautions listed on label.

Amphetamines are also used to curb appetite and lose weight. Overuse of the drugs creates psychological addiction, and can result in high blood pressure, abnormal heart rate, and mental confusion.

Barbiturates such as Phenobarbital are depressants used to relax muscles, induce sleep, or reduce anxiety. Such drugs can cause slurred speech and poor coordination, and overuse may result in physical and psychological addiction. An overdose of barbiturates can cause coma and death.

Other Hallucinogens

LSD (d-lysergic acid diethylamide-25), an experimental substance first developed in liquid form, and PCP (phencyclidine), a tranquilizer for animals, are hallucinogens, or drugs that alter perceptions. The abuse of these drugs has caused "bad trips"—hallucinations that lead to panic. Studies show that LSD may cause genetic damage; thus, it is not as popular a drug as it was in the 1960s and 1970s. LSD users have sometimes turned to PCP. However, long-term use of PCP may lead to uncontrollable seizures, brain damage, or respiratory arrest.

Several new "designer drugs" have appeared recently. They are being manufactured from chemicals that are readily available. Prepared in illegal underground factories, these hallucinogens have mind-altering effects similar to LSD. Use of these synthetic drugs may lead to permanent brain damage.

For Review

1. What usually motivates people to use drugs?
2. What is the greatest danger related to cocaine use?
3. What is the difference between a stimulant and a depressant?
4. What are "designer drugs"?

Dealing with Alcohol

Up until a certain age, drinking of alcoholic beverages is illegal. Each state determines a legal drinking age. The drinking of alcohol is legally restricted, because alcohol is a dangerous drug. Its use and abuse lead to countless automobile accidents, acts of violence, and other tragedies each year.

It is important to obey liquor laws, not to drive after drinking, and not to get drunk. Being responsible also means respecting the decisions of those who choose not to drink.

Effects of Alcohol

Alcohol is mainly used as a form of escape. Some people are able to drink alcoholic beverages on occasion without harmful effects. However, alcohol is the number-one drug problem in the United States, with an estimated nine to ten million persons considered *alcoholics,* or people addicted to alcohol. Alcohol abuse can be a major factor in divorce, physical violence, and loss of employment. Alcohol is also responsible for 50 percent of all fatal automobile accidents.

Contrary to popular belief, alcohol is a depressant, not a stimulant. If you drink a glass of beer, 20 percent of the alcohol is absorbed instantly into the bloodstream. Eighty percent is carried at a slightly slower rate to the brain. As the concentration of alcohol in the bloodstream increases, it depresses the cerebral cortex, which controls memory, reasoning, and muscle coordination. Further intake of alcohol depresses deeper parts of the brain, and normal control of speech and movement disappears. All types of alcoholic beverages, even beer and wine have these dramatic effects on the human body.

If a person continues to consume alcohol, it can penetrate the inner brain. Dulled perception and impaired judgment can result. Finally, a person who drinks excessively may lose

HEALTH & SAFETY

Conquering Alcoholism

If anyone you live with or care about has a problem with alcohol, it also affects you. Action must be taken to help solve the problem. However, it is very difficult to fight addiction alone. The alcoholic must first want to help himself or herself before others can help.

The first step is recognizing the problem. Any of the following characteristics could mean that a person may have a problem with alcohol and should seek help:

- hiding the amount of drinking from family and friends
- experiencing a loss of memory after drinking
- getting drunk at least once a month
- feeling ashamed for getting drunk
- arguing or fighting with family or friends when drinking
- regretting things said or done when drunk
- centering most social activities around drinking or partying
- driving while drunk
- drinking to gain courage or self-confidence

Organizations provide counseling for people who have a drinking problem. If the alcoholic is willing, professional help can be found at local health centers, clinics, and family service agencies. Check the yellow pages of your telephone directory under the heading "Alcoholism information and Treatment Centers" if you need to find an outside resource in your area.

The largest self-help group on alcoholism, Alcoholics Anonymous (A.A.) has had great success in working with alcoholics of all ages. A.A. believes that alcoholism is a disease that can be arrested but not cured. They maintain that the only way to arrest the disease is to refrain from drinking any alcohol.

A.A. differs from most organizations in several ways. There are no membership fees, no application to complete, and few formal rules. The only requirement for membership is a desire to stop drinking. A.A. has hundreds of small groups that meet regularly. No one outside the group knows who its members are. They take no pledge to stop drinking forever, but concentrate on staying sober for the next twenty-four hours. Members have found that in helping each other, individuals solve their own drinking problems.

People interested in finding out more about A.A. can contact a school counselor, local social service agency, or call A.A. directly. Some people may prefer to talk with a doctor or psychologist. No one should feel forced to fight the battle against alcoholism alone.

Help can be as close as a telephone directory. Calling for help is an important first step in conquering a drinking problem.

There are many enjoyable and meaningful ways to spend leisure time. Involvement, in sports, hobbies, volunteer work, or part-time work provides pleasure, and satisfaction and promotes self-esteem.

consciousness. Prolonged drinking can lead to "acute alcohol poisoning" and death.

The progressive effects of alcohol hold true for all people, but individual responses to alcohol differ. What is safe for one person may not be safe for another. For example, a small person drinking the same amount of liquor at the same rate as a large person will get a higher concentration of alcohol. Also, alcohol can have different effects on the same person under different circumstances. If a drinker is ill, nervous, or tired, the alcohol may cause more intense reactions at a faster rate.

Although alcohol has rapid effects on the body, it is slow to leave the bloodstream. Cold showers and black coffee may make a person feel more alert, but they do not affect the alcohol level in the bloodstream. However, the presence of food in the stomach can slow down the absorption of alcohol into the bloodstream.

Alcoholism

Today medical experts define **alcoholism** as "controlled and uncontrolled use of drugs." Not all people who are alcoholics drink. Some alcoholics learn to control their drinking because they know they have the disease of alcoholism and will be in trouble if they drink or use drugs.

An alcoholic can be anyone from any walk of life. An alcoholic is usually preoccupied with drinking or getting high, may gulp drinks or sneak drugs, drink alone, and be dependent on alcohol or drugs to alleviate stress or anxiety.

The total cause of alcoholism is unknown, but experts believe the disease can be inherited. It is also partly due to the lack of a chemical called **endorphin** in the brain. The lack of endorphin often causes alcoholics to feel depressed. When alcoholics drink, the missing chemical is replaced and they feel better. Drinking, though, leads to uncontrolled use of alcohol, since alcoholics lose the ability to stop drinking.

Health Problems of Alcoholics

Uncontrolled alcoholics are subject to chronic health problems. Long-term use of alcohol can lead to increased acidity in the stomach, which in turn can cause painful ulcers. The pancreas can also be affected. Damage to the pancreas can be life-threatening.

Ninety percent of alcohol consumed is processed by the liver. Since alcohol is toxic, the liver must detoxify it. Too much alcohol used over a long period of time causes the liver to become inflamed, swollen, and tender. If the condition continues, cirrhosis of the liver can result, and death may follow. Thus, alcohol abuse is not only a cause of ill health, but is also life-threatening.

Children of Alcoholics

The alcoholic isn't the only person who suffers when there is a drinking problem. Researchers now believe that the alcoholism of one family member is an illness that affects the whole family. Children of alcoholics (COAs) suffer the effects of their parent's illness not only as children but also as adults. Information on help for children of alcoholics can be obtained through local chapters of Al-Anon.

Drinking and Driving

One of the most life-threatening situations occurs when a person drives a vehicle after consuming alcohol. To drive safely, a person should have good coordination, vision, judgment, and the ability to react quickly. These skills are impaired when alcohol is consumed before driving. In fact, statistics support the slogan "Alcohol and driving don't mix." Nearly half of the deaths from alcohol-related crashes involves people between the ages of 16 and 24.

People need to know the facts when it comes to alcohol abuse.

Citizen Activists A number of citizen action groups have formed in recent years to lobby for tougher laws against drunk drivers and to educate the public on the dangers of drinking and then driving. These include RID and MADD.

RID (Remove Intoxicated Drivers) was the first national organization to try to fight the drunk-driving epidemic in the nation. Founded in 1978, RID now has chapters in over 30 states and has successfully pressured legislators to pass tougher laws against drunk driving. One important law in New York mandates that the judge take away the driver's license of a second-offense drunk-driver until the court case is settled.

Mothers Against Drunk Driving (MADD) was founded in 1980 by Candy Lightner of Fair Oaks, California. Candy's 13-year-old daughter, Cari, was walking to a church picnic when a drunk driver struck her from behind and killed her. The driver had been convicted of drunk-driving on two previous occasions; he had been arrested a third time for the same offense and was out on bail.

Many citizens involved in MADD groups are just that — angry because of the senseless slaughter of innocent victims by drunk drivers. Some have called the killings "socially accepted murder," since in many states vehicular homicide is a misdemeanor that usually carries a fine of only $200–300 and a sentence that is often suspended.

Teens who learn the facts about alcohol now will be able to make responsible decisions later.

Using Tobacco

Tobacco is grown and prepared for smoking, chewing and inhaling in powdered form (snuff), but smoking is the most common use of tobacco. Smoking is on the increase worldwide. Over a billion people smoke nearly five trillion cigarettes a year.

Americans, however, are changing some of their smoking habits. Young people begin smoking later in life and overall are not as likely as previous generations to choose to smoke. Americans, though, have increased their use of chewing tobacco, under the mistaken notion that "smokeless" tobacco is less hazardous to health than cigarettes. Chewing tobacco is in fact strongly linked to oral cancer.

Why People Use Tobacco

As with those who use alcohol and other drugs, tobacco smokers often make their first decisions to smoke because their friends do it. Young children who begin smoking may do so to imitate older brothers or sisters or parents who smoke. Many shy people choose smoking as a way to gain confidence in social situations; by smoking they feel they are in control. Ads for cigarettes often show smokers who are glamorous or prosperous. These ads convey the idea that smoking will enhance well-being. Such implied messages can influence young people to smoke.

How Tobacco Affects Health

Studies show that tobacco kills thirteen times more Americans than hard drugs and eight times more Americans than automobile accidents. First, smoking affects the respiratory tract, which is covered with a film of mucous to which inhaled dust and other impurities stick. Ordinarily, the **cilia,** tiny hairlike projections in the lining of the bronchial tubes, sweep away undesirable elements. The gases and tar in the inhaled smoke paralyze the cilia and thus interfere with the self-cleansing action of the respiratory system. Smokers, therefore, have a much higher incidence of chronic bronchitis, emphysema, and lung cancer than do nonsmokers.

However, nonsmokers who breathe in other people's smoke ("passive smokers") are also at risk for some of the same health problems. They may be three times more likely to die of lung cancer than they would be if not constantly exposed to tobacco smoke.

Teens often say that they smoke because their friends do. Have you ever felt this kind of peer pressure?

Practical Tip

To avoid having to breathe someone else's smoke, try saying the following to a smoker:

- The circulation is poor in here, would you mind not smoking?
- I'm allergic to smoke!
- Let's move to the no-smoking section.

Second, smoking is responsible for between 15 and 30 percent of all heart attacks in the United States. The nicotine drug in tobacco increases the work the heart must do. This increase causes a rise in both heart rate and blood pressure. Since the heart muscle must work harder, it needs more oxygen. Oxygen is carried to all the tissues by hemoglobin, an iron and protein compound in red blood cells. From 3 to 7 percent of smokers' hemoglobin is usually saturated with carbon monoxide: thus, the amount of oxygen available to the heart muscle is significantly decreased.

Smoking also affects unborn children. Pregnant women who smoke generally have more complications with childbirth and their children are more often born prematurely than children of nonsmokers. Premature babies have low birth weights, which often lead to serious health problems early in life.

How to Stop Smoking

The risks to health prompt some smokers to quit. However, it is often difficult to stop smok-

It's not easy to quit smoking. Supportive friends can help someone kick the smoking habit.

ing. Tobacco can be so addictive that 75 percent of those who stop smoking start again, usually within six months.

To help people quit the habit, classes are available in many communities across the nation. The U.S. Public Health Service also provides ideas and information for those who have quit and do not want to start smoking again.

Many people who have given up smoking found it easier to stop when they were physically active and had many interests. Quitting is also easier when a friend who has already quit agrees to give encouragement or when a friend who does smoke agrees to stop smoking at the same time. Having a definite plan for spending the money saved by not smoking can be another strong motivating force.

Physical endurance increases when a person quits smoking.

For Review

1. What three functions of the brain are affected by alcohol consumption?
2. Describe three health problems of alcoholics.
3. How does nicotine affect the heart?

Making Social Decisions

As Chapter 3 pointed out, building a loving relationship requires a lot of effort. Part of that effort may involve making difficult decisions about sex. Young people make these decisions based on the teachings and expectations of family, community and religion. Developing a loving relationship means being responsible for your actions and understanding how your actions can affect the lives of others.

Sexual Relationships

When two people are "in love," they experience deep emotions and strong feelings of attraction. Quite often, there is a desire to express feelings of intimacy. These are normal feelings that often lead to questions about sexual intercourse. Sexual intercourse should be reserved until marriage. This act of love consummates a marriage.

Becoming Informed Ideally, your sex education begins at home, and studies show that most young people prefer that their parents provide sex information. However, some parents may be uncomfortable talking about sex. In such cases, family, school, or religious counselors may be able to provide books or pamphlets that answer some of the questions young people have.

Decisions about relationships have to begin with identifying what you are looking for. Maybe you want attention, affection, and the feeling of being close to someone. These desires do not necessarily mean engaging in sex.

Some young people feel pressured into having sexual relationships before marriage. Perhaps their peers brand them as being "goody-goody" or childish for not indulging in sex. Some fear that they won't get dates if they say no to sex.

Many young people decide that sex outside marriage is not for them and do not yield to peer pressure. In fact, decisions about sexual relationships are personal and not the business of classmates or a group of friends.

Understanding How Premarital Sex Affects a Relationship For many young people, premarital sex can create more worry than enjoyment. There may be concerns about whether the relationship is based on sex only, rather than on love and respect for one another. The fear of pregnancy or of contracting a sexually transmitted disease (STD) may contribute to anxiety and tension in a relationship.

Contraception The most effective and universally accepted method for avoiding pregnancy is **abstinence** — that is, not having sexual relationships. Many young people do make

Developing a loving relationship means being responsible for your actions. Sexuality is only one part of a marriage relationship.

Sexually Transmitted Diseases

Disease	Cause & Effects	Symptoms	Treatment
Gonorrhea	Bacteria (Can lead to sterility, nerve disorders, blindness in newborns.)	M: Puslike discharge from penis; painful urination. F: Most affected areas have no symptoms; lower abdominal pain; discharge; burning during urination.	Penicillin or antibiotics; sexual partner needs treatment.
Syphilis	Bacteria (Can lead to brain damage, insanity, paralysis, heart disease.)	1st stage: Pimple, blister, or sore; heals in 1–5 weeks. 2nd stage: Rash or mucus patches (highly infectious), spotty hair loss, swollen glands, and fever.	Long-acting penicillin; sexual partner needs treatment.
Herpes	Virus (Linked to cervical cancer; can infect newborns.)	Painful blisters on genitals and rectal area, around mouth; painful urination, swollen glands, and fever.	No known cure; treatment relieves symptoms.
Chlamydia	Bacteria (Can cause pelvic inflammation that leads to infertility; can infect newborns and cause eye infections.)	M: Discharge from penis, painful urination. No symptoms in some cases. F: Vaginal discharge, painful urination, spotting between menstrual periods, lower abdominal pain.	Tetracycline or erythromycin.
Veneral Warts	Virus (Linked to cervical cancer.)	Local itching and wartlike growth on genitals, anus, or throat.	No known cure. May require cauterization, freezing, or surgical removal.
AIDS (Acquired Immune Deficiency Syndrome)	Virus (Leads to death. Can infect newborns.)	(Note: Other diseases may have similar symptoms) Enlarged lymph glands, weight loss, diarrhea, night sweats, fatigue, white spots or blemishes in the mouth.	No known cure. Treatment focuses on secondary illnesses.

this choice based on the teachings and expectations of their family, community and religion. Others may consider using some type of **contraception** or birth control (see page 72). Birth control practices are inconsistent with the teachings of certain social and religious groups.

If a person decides to use birth control, a physician should be consulted.

Avoiding STDs Thousands of high school students miss school each day because of sexually transmitted diseases. Learning how to avoid these diseases is the first step in prevention. The only completely effective method for avoiding these STDs is abstinence. Another effective preventative against STDs is the condom. The chart in this chapter shows the causes, symptoms, and effects of STDs and the treatment for these diseases.

Premarital Pregnancy The United States leads other developed nations in pregnancy rates for girls aged 15 to 19. In France, for example, the rate is 43 pregnancies per 1000 teens, while the Canadian rate is 44 per 1000. In the United States, 96 out of 1000 girls in the 15–19 age group get pregnant.

Teenage pregnancy often carries health risks to both the mother and the baby. Death rates from complications during pregnancy are much higher among teen mothers than those in their twenties. Babies born to teen mothers often have low birth weights, which may result in mental retardation, and such physical problems as underdeveloped lungs and heart.

Options for Pregnant Teens

When an unmarried teenage girl becomes pregnant, she and the boy are faced with some very difficult decisions. Should they marry?

If a teen thinks she is pregnant, she should seek medical attention immediately.

An unmarried pregnant teen must face many crucial decisions. Planning for the future is difficult.

Should they decide against marriage, have the child, and give it up for adoption? Should she try to raise the child on her own? These and other questions can involve much soul-searching and may require the help of a professional counselor or someone who can objectively present the available options.

Adoption One option for unwed parents may be to give up their children for adoption. This decision is not an easy one. Both the father and mother may face emotional turmoil. However, it is usually the mother who must deal with the conflicts and traumas associated with such a decision. It is not unusual for teen mothers to feel depression, remorse, guilt, or a sense of loss when they choose to give up a child for adoption.

Yet, for some unwed mothers, adoption may be the best possible choice to make for a child. Counselors are often able to help mothers see that placing a child with an adoptive family can be a responsible decision. Such an act could be selfless, truly in a child's best interests.

Birth Control Methods

The only totally effective method of birth control is abstinence.

Method	Description	Possible Problems	Effectiveness
Abstinence	No sexual intercourse.		100%
Natural Family Planning	Woman determines fertile periods by charting body temperature and mucus discharge during monthly cycle.	Illness or emotional problems could alter temperature and mucus readings. Medical consultations often needed.	86–99%
Condom	Thin rubber sheath; fits over penis.	Could tear or be punctured. Should be lubricated with water-based jelly, not petroleum-based products.	90–97%
Vaginal Foam	Foam, cream, or jelly with chemicals that act as barriers to sperm.	Could lose effectiveness if inserted more than 20 minutes before intercourse.	90–97%
Vaginal Sponge	Small polyurethane sponge with spermicide to immobolize sperm.	May be difficult to learn insertion technique, thus decreasing effectiveness.	83–91%
Diaphragm	Soft rubber cup over cervix—the opening to vagina; must be fitted by medical personnel.	Improper fit because of changes in weight, surgery, or childbirth; must be refitted.	83–97%
IUD (Intra-uterine Device)	Plastic devices in various shapes inserted by trained medical personnel.	Could cause side-effects such as cramping, painful urination, discharge, or heavy menstrual flow.	95–99%
Birth Control Pill	Two synthetic hormones in pill form prescribed by qualified medical personnel; taken orally at the same time every day.	Could cause side-effects such as swelling, headaches, visual disturbances, depression, and weight gain; not recommended for women over age 35.	98–99.7%

Abortion The controversy surrounding *abortion*, the termination of an unwanted pregnancy, has become heated in recent years. Because of the precepts of some religious and social groups, many individuals believe abortion should be made illegal. Others believe that legal abortion is one option among others that a woman should be able to consider when faced with an unwanted pregnancy. Still others believe that abortion is only acceptable for medically therapeutic reasons.

Family members and religious or professional counselors may be able to help a person make a decision about abortion. The teachings and expectations of one's family, community and religion will guide the decision-making process. If a woman chooses to have a legal abortion, she needs professional medical advice.

Single Parenting In the past, families often pressured unwed mothers to give up their children for adoption. Today, however, many

A single teenaged mother can feel overwhelmed by the responsibilities of caring for an infant by herself.

single parents choose to keep their children, although they may make such a decision for immature reasons. For example, they may see having a child as a way to get a home of their own or as an excuse to drop out of school or quit a job. A mother might hope to find a closeness and emotional attachment with her baby that she herself did not receive as a child. However, a baby is hardly a solution to such problems.

In order to be effective single parents, teen mothers need knowledge about family living and child care. Parenting classes—for both fathers and mothers—are available in many schools across the nation. Such classes often include information on money management, health and nutrition, and child development. Single parents may need help to continue with their education, get good jobs, and provide for their families. Some government programs provide financial assistance for single parents.

Choosing Marriage A pregnancy may prompt some teens to consider marriage. Contrary to popular belief, many unwed fathers want to take responsibility for their children, and marriage may be one way to accomplish this goal. Choosing marriage because of pregnancy may not allow a couple to experience the engagement and wedding rituals described in the next section. However, the methods for making adjustments in marriage, ideas on family management, and other aspects of family living covered in this text can be helpful to teen parents.

For Review

1. Discuss the ways in which premarital sex affects a relationship.
2. Name the STDs that cause burning or painful urination.
3. What STDs have no known cure?
4. Discuss some of the options that are available to a pregnant teenager.

4 Chapter Review

Summary

Adolescents face many critical personal and social decisions. The choices they make are based on the teachings and expectations of the family, religion and the community. Decisions are sometimes influenced by self-image and peers, as well. Decision-making techniques can help a person to make wise choices.

Pressure from family problems, peers, and society motivate people to use mind-altering substances. Depressants, stimulants, and hallucinogens powerfully affect the body. Smoking tobacco harms the respiratory tract, heart, and other organs.

Decisions about sexual relationships also confront adolescents. The possibility of pregnancy and STDs are serious considerations when beginning a sexual relationship. A knowledge of contraceptives and methods of avoiding infection are important, yet abstinence is the only certain method of protection. When a teenage girl becomes pregnant, the couple faces some difficult decisions.

Vocabulary

Match each of the vocabulary words with one of the definitions that follow.

alcoholism
amphetamines
barbiturates
cilia
abstinence

contraception
depressant
endorphin
hallucinogen
peer pressure
mind-altering substance
stimulant
trade-off

1. _____ tiny hairs that cover the lining of the bronchial tubes
2. _____ decision-making process in which one thing is given up in exchange for something else
3. _____ drugs that decrease the activity of the central nervous system
4. _____ disease characterized by uncontrolled alcohol consumption
5. _____ methods of avoiding pregnancy
6. _____ substances that change the chemistry of the brain and produce mind-altering effects
7. _____ stimulants or "pep pills"
8. _____ influence or force exerted on a person by members of his or her age group
9. _____ drugs or other materials that change the way a person experiences or perceives life
10. _____ drugs that increase the activity of the central nervous system
11. _____ the lack of this chemical in the brain is believed to contribute to alcoholism
12. _____ depressants or "downers"
13. _____ not having sexual intercourse

Chapter Questions

1. Which of the factors affecting decision making has the strongest impact on you and why?
2. Relate an example from your own experience in which you made a trade-off to arrive at a decision. Identify the costs and benefits of the trade-off you made.
3. What are the physical and mental effects of smoking marijuana?
4. What is cocaine?
5. In your opinion, which factor most strongly motivates young people to use substances that have mind-altering effects? Why?
6. What do you think the penalty for drunk driving should be and why?
7. How does smoking affect the action of cilia in the respiratory tract? Why is this dangerous?
8. Why do smokers have a decreased amount of oxygen circulating in their blood? How does this affect the heart?
9. What risks does teenage pregnancy have for both mother and child?
10. What is the most effective method of contraception?

Skill Activities

1. **Decision Making** Review the decision-making steps listed on page 56. Then think of a decision that you are facing now, or will be in the next few years (choice of career, education, summer employment, friends). Use the decision-making steps to help you begin making a decision. Fold a piece of paper in half lengthwise. On one side list the eight decision-making steps, leaving spaces beneath each one. Next to each step on the opposite side of the paper, write the specific action you must take to complete that part of your decision making.

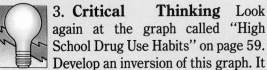

2. **Communication** Design a poster that will teach others about one mind-altering substance discussed in this chapter. Research information about your topic in your school or local library. Locate or make your own drawings, graphs, photographs, and charts to illustrate the facts you present. Organize your poster in an attractive way; include a caption or a brief written description with each visual that explains its significance.

3. **Critical Thinking** Look again at the graph called "High School Drug Use Habits" on page 59. Develop an inversion of this graph. It should show the changing percentages of *nonusers* for each drug on the graph. Then conduct interviews to probe the reasons why people say no to the use of prescription and over-the-counter drugs, including inhalants, as well as illegal drugs, such as alcohol and tobacco. Before you begin interviewing, create questions that will encourage people to speak in depth. After the interviews, compile the information you have gathered. On a sheet of paper, summarize your findings in essay form.

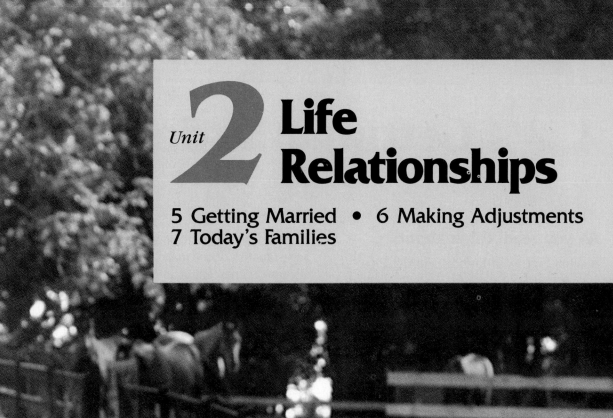

Unit 2 Life Relationships

5 Getting Married

As you read, think about:

- what factors influence one's choice of a marriage partner.
- what functions the engagement period serves.
- what some of the legal requirements for marriage are.
- what components make up a wedding ceremony.

Marriage is here to stay. Despite the alarming statistics about marriage, separation, and divorce, 95 percent of all Americans are or will be married at some time in their lives. Further, at least 60 percent of those who divorce will remarry.

Today, the ways of courtship and marriage are changing. Studies reveal that more persons say they are marrying to achieve personal happiness than say they view marriage as a duty to their families or to society. This chapter explores the choice of a marriage partner, engagement, and wedding rituals.

VOCABULARY

complement
betrothal
officiant

The Marriage Partner

Imagine that you line up a group of people of the opposite sex and then look them over carefully to find a person whose appearance appeals to you. You interview each person to learn whose financial potential and personal viewpoints come closest to your "ideal." Finally, you select for marriage the one you rate the "best."

In many Eastern countries, parents make just such judgments when they arrange marriages for their children. These parents are also careful to select a mate who they believe will benefit the entire family. In the Western world, however, and in the United States in particular, love is expected to be the basis for choice of spouse. Still, whether or not you realize it, many other factors will influence your selection of husband or wife.

Similarities

Studies made by sociologists over the past few decades show that most people select mates similar to themselves. This finding does not mean that to be happily married you and your future partner must be alike in all or most of your personal characteristics. Rather, it means that you and your spouse will tend to have similar educational and occupational backgrounds and will probably belong to the same religious, national, or ethnic group. You are likely to be close to each other in age and to have lived in the same neighborhood in a city, or within a few miles of each other in a small town or rural area. Since you and your partner will have shared a number of common experiences, your attitudes, interests, and philosophies of living may well have developed in similar ways. Usually, these similarities help form the basis for a successful marriage.

People in the United States are free to marry whomever they choose. However, they often experience pressure to marry within their own group, whether the group is defined by religion,

Finding a suitable mate can be a complicated matter. Sharing similar interests and values with someone is a first step toward building a lasting relationship.

What do you consider important characteristics to look for in a marriage partner?

nationality, race, or occupation. Family, friends, acquaintances, and society as a whole may exert these pressures. For example, families with strong religious beliefs may become alarmed if a member wants to "pull away" and marry someone of another faith.

Differences

It is not unusual for two people to fall in love because they **complement** each other. To complement means to complete. In marriage, this means that while one partner has personal traits quite different from those of the other partner, these different traits complete the couple, that is, they make each person feel whole. Have you ever met two people like Ellen and Larry, who are becoming serious about each other?

Ellen and Larry are a couple. Ellen likes to be around people and has been active in local political groups as a volunteer. She enjoys fund-raising activities for causes she supports. Larry is quiet and studious. He has a keen interest in political science, but seldom discusses his interest with anyone other than Ellen. The two often share their ideas, his from books and observations, hers from practical experience. Larry gains new information about politics from the experiences that Ellen shares. Even though Larry prefers to stay in the background while Ellen likes to mingle and be out among people, the two complement each other.

Many types of complementary traits may enter into the process of mate selection. You may not even be completely aware of the qualities missing in yourself that you seek in someone else. Maybe you are somewhat shy and need a mate who is more aggressive. Maybe you are driven to achieve constantly, while your partner has a more relaxed attitude. Maybe your mate likes detail, while you prefer to look at the total picture. A complementary relationship can make you both feel more comfortable and secure.

Seeking a Suitable Mate

Because of increased mobility among today's young people through changing jobs and changing locations, people more frequently select mates from groups other than their own. More people are now selecting marriage partners on the basis of personal qualities rather than for similar social or ethnic background. As a result, in recent years there has been greater emphasis on the individual characteristics that people expect to find in their life partners.

Being similar to your partner, having complementary traits, or a combination of both can

Some couples find that their personalities and interests are different, but complementary.

The Engagement

There is no specific test to determine whether a couple is ready to make a commitment to marriage or not. Individual couples make these decisions in their own ways. Some couples date for several years before deciding to marry. Others become engaged after only a few months. *Fiancé(e)* is the word used to describe either member of the engaged couple.

"You are engaged as soon as you decide to marry and receive your parents' blessings," according to the *Bride's Book of Etiquette,* compiled by the editors of *Bride's Magazine.* However, you probably know couples who do not formally announce their engagement or seek family approval. These couples simply come to an "understanding" while dating that they will marry at some future time. The woman may or may not wear a ring as a symbol of the pledge to marry.

In earlier times, such informal engagements would have been highly unusual, if not impossible. The engagement, called the **betrothal** was a legal contract. As such, it often carried with it the right of ownership to land, possibly a place in a family business, or an exchange of money between families. A betrothal was almost the same as a marriage except for the formal wedding ceremony. If you broke an engagement, you would be legally responsible for breaking the contract.

Some states still have laws permitting legal action if a promise to marry has been broken, but such cases are seldom brought to court. Most Americans regard the engagement as a time for becoming better acquainted with a partner, even "testing" the relationship. During this time, if you and the person you had intended to marry find that you are not suited to each other, you can call off the wedding. There is much less distress and unhappiness in a broken engagement than there is in a marriage that ends in divorce.

help make a harmonious marriage. It is unusual, however, for a couple to remain together when one person does all the taking at the expense of the other. Resentment often develops if the relationship is not one of give-and-take.

Seeking a suitable mate and attaining a satisfactory relationship can be a complicated matter. Striving for balance serves as a function of the engagement period, the step that usually follows the decision of two people to marry.

For Review

1. How has the increased mobility of young people changed the mate-selection process?
2. What are some of the personal characteristics people usually seek in a spouse?
3. What is meant by the statement that a couple has complementary traits?

What kinds of issues can couples deal with in pre-marital counseling sessions?

Comparing Attitudes

During the engagement, you and your fiancé(e) can examine your respective attitudes about many issues that will affect your lives together. One major issue many couples discuss is that of starting a family. Before marrying, both partners should make their positions clear on whether or not they want children, how many children they want, and how soon they want to have them. They should also discuss related issues such as parenting styles, education of children, and religion.

Friction arising from disagreements over the way money is earned and spent is one of many possible sources of unhappiness and discord in a marriage, especially when a couple hasn't discussed finances earlier. It might be wise for you to discuss some of the following money-related issues with your partner:

- Do we agree about the work roles of men and women?

- Will the wife have a job outside the home?

- Whose salary will pay what bills?

- Should there be a budget? Who will handle it?

- Should a certain amount of money be put in the bank each week, no matter what?

- Is there agreement on the importance of vacations and how much they should cost?

Answers to all kinds of questions related to money matters reflect a person's viewpoints on money. One partner might consider the other extravagant. One's emphasis on money as a way to gain power and prestige might rub a less ambitious partner the wrong way. Also, tastes and interests may vary. If you want a record collection and your partner feels that wall-to-wall carpeting is more important, squabbles could easily result. Or perhaps you think it is absolutely essential to have a new car but your fiancé(e) believes that a married couple must first have a complete set of furniture for their home. Both people may have to examine the situation, compromise, and decide on what they really need for everyday survival as opposed to what they merely want for convenience, or fun.

Dealing with Conflict

No one can possibly anticipate all the issues that will arise in a marriage. How flexible are you? How well do you communicate your complaints? How do you and your partner arrive at decisions or compromises?

In any relationship, there are possibilities for conflict. A couple needs to look at some of these potential difficulties and try to resolve them before the marriage. Each partner needs to learn how to express his or her feelings honestly, but without causing undue hurt to the

The transition between single and married life includes experiences such as shopping for rings and talking over plans for the future.

other. For some, this process can take several months or more. The length of time you spend is not as important as the recognition that you need to deal with and look realistically at both yourself and the person you intend to marry. Since people change, even this effort will not guarantee a lasting, happy relationship. However, good communication skills and an unselfish approach to each other can make a successful marriage much more likely. Community mental health centers, private therapists, and religious organizations can provide premarital counseling for engaged couples. These sessions give the partners a chance to identify aspects of their relationship that could cause trouble in the marriage. The counselor helps the couple begin to work out ways to communicate effectively as husband and wife. Potential conflicts generated by different family backgrounds, different religions, different role expectations or misunderstood values can all be handled before they ruin a marriage.

Getting to Know Friends and Relatives

Besides using the engagement period for examining personal beliefs and attitudes, you can use this time to relate to the larger community as a couple and to make preparations for the wedding. You can also use the engagement period to look carefully at relationships with your future in-laws. Sometimes, even your partner's close friends and business or work associates may be important to your future together. Many engaged persons insist, "I'm not marrying a family or friends; I'm marrying an individual!" Nevertheless, the kind of life a person leads can be greatly influenced by those with whom he or she has close ties. Each partner might ask, "Do I feel comfortable with my fiancé(e)'s time commitments to friends and relatives?"

What happens, for example, if you like to go out every weekend, while your future husband

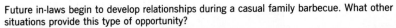

Future in-laws begin to develop relationships during a casual family barbecue. What other situations provide this type of opportunity?

or wife prefers to stay at home? Friction might also arise because you have grown up within a small family and you feel smothered by your partner's large, affectionate family gatherings. You must then consider whether you can adjust to a situation where many relatives offer advice or join in your activities.

It is well to consider both your own and your partner's adaptability in general. Again, it is important for a couple to consider the following questions: How flexible are you? How well do you communicate your complaints? How do you and your partner arrive at decisions or compromises?

Sharing a Household

"Should we live together before we get married?" This is a question some couples deal with once a relationship has become serious. Couples base this decision on the teachings and expectations of their family, community and religion. Couples who live together before marriage claim that they do so to increase their understanding of their potential mate. Living together forces people to share the difficult, as well as the pleasant tasks of everyday life. While this experience can help you make decisions about marriage, living together before marriage can also have its disadvantages.

Living together without the benefit of marriage can put a strain on the relationship. The question of whether or not there is a future for the couple is a constant source of tension. This uncertainty affects many different aspects of the couple's life, from questions of faithfulness to finances. If the relationship does not succeed, recovering from the breakup is much more difficult if it involves the disruption of a shared household.

Waiting until after marriage to live together can bring stability to the relationship. Making a public commitment to one another gives a couple the added support of families and friends.

Breaking an Engagement

Sometimes, couples decide to call off their wedding plans. Often, they give different reasons for these broken engagements. Perhaps one or both of the partners loses interest.

Two people may find that they mature at different rates, grow apart, and are no longer the same as they were before in their interests and attitudes. In such cases, compatibility also can disappear. That is, the two people no longer have the same approach to life.

Cultural differences or disapproval of the marriage by family and friends can also cause broken engagements. Perhaps one of the partners is too dependent on his or her family. Would you want to go ahead with a marriage if your intended mate was not accepted within your family circle? You might feel that the marriage relationship just would not hold up against a great deal of hostility from relatives. You might feel guilty about distressing your family.

It is not unusual for many couples engaged for the first time to decide not to marry each other. According to various studies, from one-half to two-thirds of engaged couples are likely to break their engagements. This can be an upsetting experience, but it is still preferable to an unhappy marriage. The engagement period, then, serves a very important function in helping you determine whether a successful marriage is possible.

For Review

1. What is the basic purpose of the engagement period?
2. What are some issues a couple should discuss during their engagement?
3. What are some of the potential conflicts between an engaged person and his or her future in-laws?

Marriage Laws

In some cultures marriages are arranged without the participation or consent of the bride and groom. People in the United States have freedom of choice as to whom they marry, but to marry legally, they need the consent of the state government. Thus, the marriage is a civil contract for all couples, as well as an emotional commitment for most. Each state has its own set of marriage laws that follows similar patterns nationwide. These include requirements for having a marriage license, taking blood tests and being of legal age.

License

All states require a couple to apply for a license before they can marry. In issuing a marriage license, the state government grants a couple the privilege of marrying. An **officiant** (a member of the clergy or a civic official) authorized by the state must conduct the ceremony and sign the license.

There are some exceptions to the officiant requirement. Certain religious groups like the Quakers, or Society of Friends, are allowed to marry without an officiant. According to religious custom, the Quaker couple stands before a congregation and announces their intention to marry. After hearing the pledges, the guests sign a wedding certificate, which makes the marriage legal in any state.

More than half the states require couples who apply for a marriage license to wait several days from the date of application until the license can be issued. In a few states, marriage laws specify a waiting period of from one to five days after the license is issued before the ceremony can take place. The purpose of a waiting period is to prevent both hasty marriages and those undertaken simply as "fun and games" adventures.

Some states recognize common-law marriages. A couple may be considered legally married if the two people have lived together as husband and wife, and their community accepts them as a married couple. Usually, the couple has to have lived together as husband and wife for a specified number of years. In the pioneer days of the United States, many couples had common-law marriages. During this time, couples lived in isolated areas and had to wait months or even years for traveling judges or ministers to perform a formal ceremony.

Health Requirements

All states prohibit marriages between close blood relatives such as brother and sister, parent and child, aunt and nephew, or first cousins because of the health risks to the offspring of such a couple. Another health-related law requires couples to have a blood test to determine whether they are free of venereal disease. This test is mandatory in most states since it not only helps prevent the spread of disease but also protects unborn children, who can be infected by a mother with syphilis. There are also laws in some states to prevent people from marrying if they have certain other communicable diseases, or if they are judged mentally incompetent or retarded.

Age Requirements

All states have a minimum age at which people can marry. Age requirements are set primarily to prevent marriages of people who are either considered too young to support families or are not mature enough for marriage. Statistics show that teenage marriages are twice as likely to end in divorce as are marriages that occur when the man and woman are in their twenties.

A fairly large number of states allows marriage at age 16, with the consent of parents. In one or two states, however, a girl may be as young as 12 years old and marry with parental and state consent, especially in cases of pregnancy. Most states require a person to be 18 years old before he or she can marry without the consent of parent or guardian.

Planning a Wedding

Whether you have an elaborate wedding or the simplest ceremony at home, careful planning, budgeting, and scheduling is vital. Otherwise, everybody at the wedding has a wonderful time except the frazzled bride and groom.

The bride and groom should decide on the kind of wedding they both want. List all the items in a notebook: where the ceremony and the reception will take place; how many people will be invited, who the attendants will be, what kind of invitations and/or announcements will be sent. Before you set the date, be sure the facilities you choose are available. Check that family members and close friends can come on the appointed date.

Now you are ready to begin making a budget, which you can revise as you go along. Write down who is going to pay for what. Traditionally, the bride's parents pay most of the wedding expenses: the rental of the church, snyagogue, or hall, the wedding music, most of the flowers, transportation of the bridal party, and—the largest expense of all—the entire cost of the reception.

The groom traditionally pays for the license, the bride's ring, the bride's bouquet, the fee for the clergyman or other person who performs the ceremony, and the honeymoon. His family picks up the bill for the rehearsal dinner.

Today, the bridal couple can work out wedding costs in a way that is appropriate to their life style. They may pay for everything themselves. Their friends may also share costs by offering such services as preparing food for the reception, providing music, or offering their home for the reception.

Whatever your financial arrangements are, you need to budget all the costs. You may find that your original plans are a little too grand for your budget. Decide which items you can eliminate and how you can reduce the price of others. Do some comparative shopping, as prices may vary a great deal. For example, you may decide to have a simple buffet meal instead of a sit-down lunch or dinner. This saves costs of renting chairs and tables and a lot of dishes. Perhaps you will decide to bake the wedding cake and make some of the refreshments yourselves. You can use tape decks instead of live music for dancing. Perhaps a photographer friend can take the wedding photographs. There are many books and magazines at your local library that will help you plan and budget your wedding.

Once your budget is organized, make a schedule. Allow enough time for invitations to be printed and mailed. Schedule the time needed for clothes to be ordered and fitted. Also time the events of the wedding day. How long will it take to transport guests to the reception? What time do you plan to leave the reception?

Detailed planning is a lot of work, but it means that on the day of your wedding you and your new spouse can relax and celebrate. You will not be busy trying to remember if you ordered glasses for the reception or forgot to invite your favorite aunt.

When planning a budget for a wedding, couples have to decide how much they want to spend on wedding rings.

The Wedding

Long before marriage was governed by civil laws, the wedding served as an announcement to the community and to society at large that two people have become husband and wife. That purpose has remained constant over the centuries. It is a public ceremony in which a couple pledges and willingly agrees to accept the responsibilities of marriage. Many couples consider the wedding a religious commitment.

Traditional Ceremonies

Do you think that you will follow the long-standing tradition of marrying in a religious ceremony? Today, most couples follow tradition. The standard American wedding includes the wedding march, the wedding party in formal attire, flowers and candles for decorations, an exchange of rings, the presentation of the new husband and wife to the audience, a reception for their guests, and, finally, a shower of rice or confetti over the married couple.

Symbols used in the wedding ceremony add to and strengthen the purposes of the wedding itself. The use of wedding rings, for example, is an ancient custom for sealing a pledge or promise. In Egyptian hieroglyphics, or picture writing, the circle represents eternity. In the marriage ceremony, the wedding ring is often called "a symbol of the unbroken or eternal ties of matrimony"—a pledge of faithfulness to one another.

Some couples light two candles separately and then a third one together in a ritual that publicly symbolizes two people uniting with spiritual as well as physical bonds, yet remaining individuals. Many other parts of the ceremony dramatize and state for witnesses that the two now belong to each other.

Within this standard form, however, different ethnic groups in the United States have added customs, rituals, and symbols that reflect their particular religion or culture.

When Lise and Jacob were married according to Jewish traditions, they stood beneath a canopy supported by four poles, which symbolized their new home. During the ceremony, the bride and groom shared a goblet of wine, which represented joy and sorrow. Their sharing of the wine also symbolized that they were prepared to accept both the good and the bad in their life together. After the rabbi pronounced them married, Jacob crushed a glass under his foot. This broken glass was to remind everyone of the destruction of the Temple of Jerusalem, and that there can be great tragedy amidst great joy. Another interpretation is that just as the smashing of the glass is permanent, the marriage also will last forever.

Some ceremonies include customs from different parts of the world. Church bells might ring for the celebration of the marriage, as they have done in England for centuries. The bride could follow the ancient custom of wearing something old, something new, something

Practical Tip

To plan a successful formal wedding an engaged couple should begin working on the following tasks at least six months before the wedding:

- Decide on the site of the wedding and the reception.
- Meet with clergymember or judge.
- Plan details of the wedding and the reception.
- Order bridal gown.
- Meet with the florist and the caterer.
- Order wedding rings.
- Make honeymoon plans.
- Mail invitations.

Wedding ceremonies reflect the beliefs, interests and personalities of both the bride and the groom.

borrowed, and something blue. National dances and traditional foods that have long been part of weddings in other countries might be carried over to wedding receptions in the United States today.

Other Ceremonies

Although most couples follow customs and traditional rituals in their weddings, some prefer to "personalize" their ceremony. These couples feel that they want to do more than just say the "usual" words. Sometimes, they create their own marriage ceremonies, using a combination of poetry, Biblical passages, and music to express their own intentions and beliefs.

The wedding ceremony might be held in a place that has particular meaning for a couple. A beach, a forest preserve, a mountain retreat, or other outdoor setting might reflect a couple's feelings about the importance of nature and the earth's beauty.

A private home, social hall, or public building such as an art museum might be used because the setting is pleasing to the couple or because it has a special significance for them. Places where people work or spend a lot of time together might also become wedding sites. Members of the clergy who have officiated at weddings in unusual locations report that the site need not detract from the seriousness and deep commitment inherent in the ceremony. The place chosen for the wedding may help the couple express their most personal feelings, hopes, and plans for their future together.

The Honeymoon, or the Glow Period

If you have given serious thought to your own wedding, you probably have had some ideas about how you want to spend your honeymoon. Possibly, your plans include a trip to a faraway place and a blissful week or two of privacy with your new spouse. Like most couples, you probably have high expectations for enjoying the excitement of the event without the obligations of daily chores, the work routine, and the demands of family or friends.

One of the broad functions of the honeymoon is to allow a newly married couple the freedom to learn more about each other without pressures. Even if a couple has had a long engagement and the two have known each other for some time, the honeymoon may still mean learning about one another as total human beings. Thus, planning for the honeymoon should include time to be alone together for rest and relaxation, particularly if the wedding was large and taxing. On the other hand, being completely isolated can be a strain. Honeymoon time should also include time for recreation and activities with other people.

The honeymoon provides each partner an opportunity to begin to think and act as part of a married couple. More than when the couple was just "going together," they now begin to speak in terms of what "we" do, rather than primarily of what each does as an individual. Couples learn to adjust to and cooperate in the little things that will carry over into the day-to-day pattern of married life. For example, suppose one spouse leaves the caps off tubes of toothpaste and shampoo or places bottles and jars of toilet articles in disarray on a bureau. The other spouse may have neater and more orderly habits. During the honeymoon, the two begin to work out a way to live with both types of traits; or, one person may decide to change out of consideration for the other. In countless ways, they begin to alter habits and patterns as they learn to live with a spouse.

Many couples expect to find satisfactory sexual adjustment during the honeymoon. Yet both the husband and the wife should realize that it may take weeks or even months to learn about each other's needs. The honeymoon can be a

A wedding can be an exhausting experience. The honeymoon can give a couple time to relax and enjoy each other.

time to begin sharing feelings about intimacy and personal privacy. Most couples have very high expectations for their honeymoon. They anticipate a blissful time period, free from any stress. The blissful time does occur, but usually after a brief encounter with a feeling of let-down. After the high excitement of the wedding preparation and the ceremony itself, couples are extremely tired and spend the first part of their honeymoon wondering why all they feel is fatigue and even a sense of emptiness.

Money is a consideration for most new-lyweds when they are planning their honey-moon. If they make their plans with a worry-about-the-bills-later attitude, they may manage money that way during their entire married life. Honeymoon plans should be talked over well in advance with an eye toward determining finan-cial obligations.

Not all newlyweds can afford a honeymoon, either financially or in time taken off from work. However, for many couples a honeymoon is not necessary to the process of adjusting to each other. They are able to make the transition into the daily routine of marriage with just the prep-aration period of the engagement. Sometimes, merely acknowledging that they are going to marry is enough. They recognize that marriage is not all sweetness and harmony, nor is it con-tinuous discord. They realize the need to coop-erate on a daily basis and learn what to expect from one another. They are aware that they must adjust time and time again. In a growing, creative relationship, they discover that their roles and tasks in marriage change over a life-time so that both partners' needs and expecta-tions can be met.

For Review

1. Explain the origin of common-law mar-riages in the United States.
2. What are some of the components of a traditional wedding ceremony?
3. In what ways can a honeymoon fall short of a couple's expectations?

5 Chapter Review

Summary

Research shows that almost everyone will be married at some time in his or her life. Although many people choose marriage partners who are similar to themselves, others select mates on the basis of complementary traits.

The engagement period gives a couple the opportunity to learn to communicate effectively with each other and to determine if a successful marriage is possible.

Because marriage is a civil contract as well as a personal commitment to another person, each state has established several requirements that must be met before a couple can obtain a marriage license. The wedding, whether a traditional or a civil ceremony, announces to the community that the couple pledges to accept the responsibilities of marriage. The honeymoon provides a time for the newly married couple to adjust to each other's habits and to learn about fulfilling each other's needs.

Vocabulary

Use the following vocabulary words to complete the paragraphs below.

betrothal
complement
officiant

A number of factors influence a person's selection of his or her marriage partner. While most people choose mates who are similar to themselves, others select partners who __1__ them. Years ago, a couple's engagement was formalized by a legal contract known as a __2__ . Today, however, there are no legalities binding couples who wish to marry.

Wedding ceremonies are conducted by either a member of the clergy or a civic official, who is known as an __3__ . He or she is responsible for signing the marriage license.

Chapter Questions

1. Based on your own observations, do you agree with sociological findings which show that most people select mates who are similar to themselves? Why or why not? In discussing your answer, consider the educational, occupational, religious, ethnic, and national backgrounds of the couples you have known.
2. What qualities might you seek in a mate to complement you?
3. How did the betrothal of earlier times differ from the engagement period today?
4. Name at least four issues and attitudes a couple can examine during the period of their engagement.
5. If a couple experiences difficulties, how might premarital counseling be helpful during their engagement?
6. What are the advantages and disadvantages of a couple's living together before they are married?
7. What strategies would you suggest a couple use to help them become acquainted with each other's relatives and friends?

8. What are the legal obligations a couple must fulfill before they can marry?

9. What is the purpose of the wedding ceremony, whether traditional or civil?

10. What are three functions of the honeymoon?

Skill Activities

1. **Math** Research the cost of a wedding. With a partner, interview owners of a bridal and tuxedo shop, a photographer's studio, a jewelry store, a bakery, a florist, a reception hall, a printing company, and a travel agency to learn the types of goods and services purchased by most engaged couples. Then, determine the price range of materials and/or services offered by each place. Finally, compute the cost of an inexpensive, moderately expensive, and very expensive wedding. As part of your cost analysis for each wedding, include a brief written description that details the content of each type of wedding.

2. **Reading** Use your school or local library resources to research the marriage customs of one nation or area of the world. Investigate the wedding ceremonies and other rituals associated with the wedding day. Have there been adaptations or changes to the rituals or ceremonies? If so, why? Once you have gathered and organized your information, write a report in which you describe the nation's wedding customs, their purposes, and origins.

3. **Human Relations** Organize a panel discussion with five or six other students on the positive and negative aspects of marriage between people of different backgrounds. As you and the other panel members prepare background information and topics to be discussed, consider the following questions to help you organize your discussion. How might differences in religion, ethnic heritage, values, and interests affect a married couple? How might two people with diverse backgrounds have a stronger relationship than a couple with similar backgrounds? What strategies might a couple use to prevent differences from threatening their relationship? What is the most important variable for a couple to share and why? If a couple has children, how might they be affected by differences in their parents' backgrounds? You may choose to create case examples of couples to refer to in your panel discussion.

4. **Social Studies** Investigate the marriage laws that exist in your state by calling or visiting the local government official who is responsible for enforcing state marriage laws. During your interview, obtain a complete list of these requirements and the reasons for them. Have there been any recent changes in the laws? If so, why? If all your questions have not been answered by the end of the interview, locate the missing information in your local library. Once you have organized your information, prepare a brief written or oral report to give to your class.

6 Making Adjustments

As you read, think about:

- how couples view their roles in marriage.
- how attitudes and preferences affect money management in a marriage.
- how marital differences between married couples can be resolved.
- how a couple adjusts to each other's relatives and friends.

VOCABULARY

marital roles
reciprocal
role making
dual-earner family
budget

No marriage manual can provide advice on how to have a successful marriage that will fulfill everyone's needs. Each man and woman brings into marriage different beliefs, attitudes, and ways of relating to others. Some of these traits are difficult to change, while others are not. It is most important, however, to recognize that marital adjustments are necessary.

No couple gets along perfectly all the time; but change, though inevitable, is not necessarily bad. As married couples experience changes in their relationships with each other, with their families, with friends, and in their jobs, they can continue to grow as individuals while developing as a couple. Even though their experiences differ, most couples do develop in their relationships according to predictable patterns.

Assigning Roles and Tasks

The terms husband and wife imply a set of roles. If a marriage is to succeed, a couple must agree on what they expect of themselves and each other in the roles of husband and wife.

Role Perceptions

In the traditional view of **marital roles,** certain traits and tasks are assigned to the husband and wife. Various studies show that many couples still view their roles in traditional terms. Unmarried people, too, often express their desire to divide household tasks along traditional lines when they marry, with women caring for the home and children, and men taking on the financial responsibilities.

The majority of people surveyed in recent years regarding their views on marital roles, however, believe that women should not be restricted to the home and that men should share the responsibility for managing the home. The view that women can perform most jobs, except those requiring great physical strength, as capably as men has gained in acceptance. A number of national polls and surveys conducted during the 1970s indicate that a majority of husbands now feel less pressure to be the all-powerful, all-knowing authority figure in the home and that they perform many household tasks. More and more people are coming to believe that both husband and wife should contribute both money and household labor to the support of a family.

The kinds of roles and task assignments husband and wife accept in any given marriage depend on a variety of factors. Most people are influenced by their parents' marriage. They often follow the role model of the parent of the same sex and look for a mate similar to the parent of the opposite sex. For example, suppose your mother works outside the home and your father does dishes and puts children to bed. You might, as a female, expect to have a

How have the roles of husband and wife changed in recent years? Why?

career yourself and expect your husband to help out with household chores. As a male, you probably would look for a mate who would share in earning the family income, and you would take doing laundry for granted.

Couples may also see their roles and those of their spouses according to their personal ideals of what a husband and wife should or should not do. These ideals can stem from the couple's cultural background or from the images of self they have developed. For example, a young woman might see herself as a "good wife" because she is not only helping her husband get a college education by working as a librarian, but also intends to keep working afterwards. The husband, however, may be thinking of a "good wife" in other terms. He may imagine that his wife will stay home after he gets his degree, allowing him sole responsibility for the family income.

Couples may find that sharing responsibilities and working together on tasks strengthen their marriage.

Today, couples face many choices in their marriages, and more and more often they deal with them jointly using open and honest communication. Cooperative mates can discuss decisions about careers—having them, changing them, or leaving them. Together they can choose where and how to live, and what kinds of friends and activities to enjoy. Freedom to express a variety of emotions and to pursue a number of different interests is increasingly available. If couples prefer to accept traditional roles, they are free to choose them. Yet most couples do not feel bound to accept traditional patterns. They aim for mutually satisfying, or **reciprocal** roles. In the following paragraph family expert Evelyn Duvall explains her theory of give and take in a marriage:

Each partner has rights and responsibilities that are necessary for the continuation of the marriage. Reciprocity is based on an exchange in which each spouse receives from and gives to the other.

Effects of Role Expectations

As two people in a marriage begin to accept their particular roles, changes occur in the ways they relate to one another. During courtship and in the early stages of marriage, the couple may concentrate on their similarities and shrug off differences in attitudes, beliefs, or habits— then, suddenly, "the honeymoon is over." The partners realize that they do not have the same ideas about what it means to be a husband or a wife, or about what each partner is like as a person.

The highest percentage of divorces occurs during the second or third year of marriage, according to the Bureau of the Census. Many couples divorce because they cannot cope with the realities of their relationship. They buckle under the strain of trying to adjust to their separate and combined marital roles.

Competition Some couples cope with their differences by competing with each other. Both

How Much Are a Homemaker's Services Worth?

In purely economic terms, what is the value of a homemaker's services? Homemakers receive no income for the goods and services produced for their families. They also do not receive benefits such as social security, insurance, retirement income, sick leave, and holiday and vacation pay.

The following chart shows the jobs done by a typical housewife in a family with two children. Hourly rates for each job are based on estimates taken from average wages compiled by the U.S. Department of Labor in 1986.

Service	Hours per/wk.	Wages per/hr.	Total
Child-care workers (6 hours per day, 7 days)	42	$ 4.00	$168.00
Cook	14	10.00	140.00
Bus driver (or chauffeur)	5	9.00	45.00
Laundry worker (washing and ironing)	5	3.35	16.75
Dishwasher	7	3.35	23.45
House cleaner	14	3.35	46.90
Professional shopper	4	10.00	40.00
Bookkeeper	1	8.00	8.00
Totals	92		$488.10

Yearly total— $25,381.20

This chart estimates a homemaker's weekly hours at 92 hours per week. Since most of these jobs on the open market would pay overtime after the first 40 hours, weekly pay for 52 overtime hours would be much higher than the wages listed on the chart. Even if all the jobs paid only the minimum wage of $3.35 per hour, at time-and-a-half, 52 overtime hours would amount to an additional $174.20. This brings total wages to $662.30 per week or $34,439.60 per year.

Furthermore, in addition to the jobs listed, a typical homemaker may spend time on jobs such as the following:

Service	Wages per hour
Plumber	$15.00
Carpenter	15.00
Teacher	12.00
Counselor	14.00
Nurse	11.00
Garment worker (sewing and mending clothes)	4.00
Gardener	5.00
Decorator	12.00

The financial worth of a homemaker's services quickly adds up.

Doing laundry is but one of many tasks involved in maintaining a home.

may argue about issues, try to be best at a given task, or attempt to have the final say in various matters. If partners are always opponents, they may eventually become enemies and be well on the way to separation or divorce.

Compromise Most couples learn to cope with their problems through compromise. In various ways, they come to accept the realities of living as husband and wife. A couple can achieve compromise constructively, according to one psychologist, if each can give in on points that are not essential to her or his own needs. Partners should consider what is most important to each other. If compromise proves impossible and a couple cannot reach an agreement, they at least may agree to disagree. They can tolerate each other's views or behavior without becoming angry.

Cooperation Marriage means dedicating yourself to a relationship where you grow in understanding, loving, and encouraging your mate to achieve his or her goals. When a couple can cooperate, learning to give and take and work together to achieve common goals, they have a good chance for a successful marriage.

In cooperation, each person usually acknowledges the other's strong points and weaknesses, and both partners determine their roles according to their own abilities. The wife might be better at bookkeeping and money management, so she pays all the household bills, sets aside the savings, and gives out "spending money." The husband might be an excellent cook, so he prepares many of the family meals. The wife does the yardwork because the husband hates it. Perhaps the husband takes care of the mechanical failures around the home because he likes to fix things.

If one partner is ill, absent, or unable to perform a task for some reason, the other can take over or arrange to have the work done. Neither resents the other or refuses to fill in because it is "his job" to put gas in the car or "her responsibility" to buy all the groceries. If couples can clarify marital roles early in marriage, they can usually adapt well to changes in the years ahead.

What role does communication play in learning how to make compromises?

Role Making

In recent years, some couples have engaged in **role making.** They have written contracts to define clearly what their roles will be in their marriages, and to designate who will perform certain tasks. Often, these marriage contracts are designed to spell out the rights and duties of each spouse. There might be an entire section on housework, for example, with specific chores listed.

- Wife does the laundry at home.
- Husband takes clothes to cleaners.
- Wife cleans home one Saturday.
- Husband cleans the next.
- Wife does cooking for daily meals.
- Husband washes the dishes.

Some marriage contracts are not written down, but are made after the partners discuss their various responsibilities. Duties to discuss may include not only work around the house, but also bill payments if both partners have jobs.

Dual-earner Families

In 1940, only 30 percent of the women who worked were married. By the 1970s, the percentage had nearly doubled. According to the United States Department of Labor, the total number of all working women is now more than three times what it was before World War II.

With so many wives and mothers now in the work force, a new kind of family has emerged, which some call the **dual-earner family** or the "two-paycheck marriage." In this type of family, both partners hold full- or part-time jobs. For some couples this is a personal choice, but for many couples becoming a dual-earner family is a necessity in order to meet monthly expenses. Usually, a working couple makes some attempt to divide the household chores fairly. However, various studies show that many

Why are dual-earner families growing in number?

working wives still have the major responsibilities for home care. Further, the wives' careers have secondary status as compared to those of their husbands.

If you become part of a dual-earner family, you may face some role conflicts that sociologists, family counselors, and others are just beginning to analyze. As a member of a two-job family, you might ask the following questions:

- Who will do household chores?
- Can we afford a housekeeper or cleaning service?
- What about transportation costs?
- Is it worth the expense and strain for both of us to travel to different jobs each day?

These are just a few of the difficult decisions that must be made when both partners work, but the advantages to having two paychecks make many couples choose this course of action. One obvious benefit in having both partners work is increased family income. Extra money can help improve the standard of living and the overall morale of the family. Research also indicates that women who choose to have jobs, rather than work because they need to help make ends meet, seem to be happier individuals. The satisfaction they feel can make them better company for their families.

Agreements about family responsibilities, whether formally stated or informally decided, are part of the process of determining roles of the husband and wife in the dual-earner marriage. Yet other questions about marital roles and tasks may arise. With few guidelines, how can a couple deal with other family members who might expect more traditional behavior from the married pair? What if one partner decides that career or personal fulfillment is more important than his or her development as part of a couple? Will the couple remain married when few restrictions direct their individual pursuits? In democratic marriages, who has authority? Is it possible to share decision making on all issues? Each couple will need to work out the answers for themselves in constructive ways.

The number of women in the paid labor force has steadily increased since the 1950s.

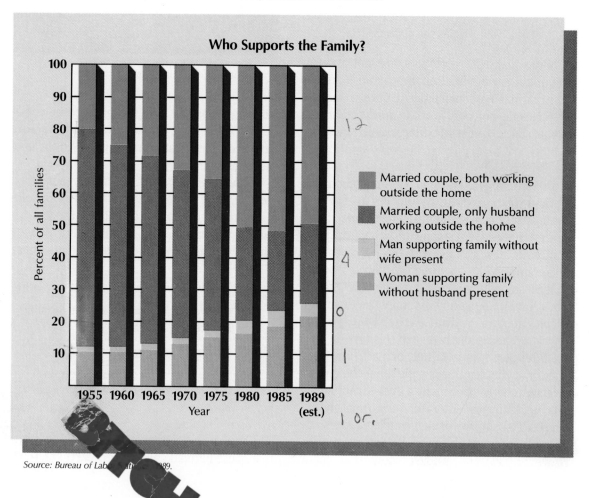

Source: Bureau of Labor Statistics, 1989.

Conflict in a marriage arises when there is disagreement about how money should be spent.

Resolving Financial Conflicts

Family finances are often a focal point for conflicts and an area in which many married couples have adjustment problems. Studies show that money matters can be the basis for disagreements in all stages of marriage.

Attitudes Toward Money

Each partner brings his or her own viewpoints and attitudes into a marriage. While society as a whole may emphasize possession of money and material goods as a goal, there are many different attitudes toward money. Some people consider money to be "the root of all evil." They do not want more than what is needed for the basic necessities of life. Others satisfy their drives for power and prestige by accumulating large amounts of money.

Poverty, or the lack of money, can create considerable personal and social problems. It can have a damaging effect on marriages and on families. On the other hand, poverty might act to motivate people to strive harder to overcome their financial disadvantages.

Preferences and Needs

The way a person uses money reflects his or her preferences and needs. Some people spend money on goods that indicate high status in the community. Buying a big or expensive sports car, a home in an exclusive neighborhood, and stylish clothes may be one person's way of saying, "Look how important I am." On the other hand, a thrifty person who carefully saves money may need the feeling of security that having money in the bank can bring.

Today, it is not unusual for some people to spend money to satisfy their immediate desires. They use it as a means of self-fulfillment, and give little thought to the future. "Money is to spend, to make life worth living" is the common attitude in such instances.

If two people in a marriage differ on the use of money, problems might easily result. One who saves money would have difficulty accepting a spendthrift partner. A person who believes that the accumulation of money is a corrupting influence will have conflicts with a partner who constantly strives for financial advancement. A couple should discuss certain money-related issues before they become big problems.

- How much money will we need for a satisfactory standard of living?

- How much time should we spend in the pursuit of money?

- Which of us should earn the income and determine how it is managed? Should we both do this?

- How and where will our money be earned?

Any or all of these aspects of money matters can be a source of friction in marriage. However, they may also serve as a unifying force.

Money Management

A couple must decide not only what money means to them, but also who is to take responsibility for financial decisions. If the husband alone has a paying job, he may believe that he should decide what to do with the income. Yet, the wife may indirectly have helped to produce that income or expanded its use. Her management skills, such as wise shopping, may have provided both a productive and healthy environment for the family and more material goods. In fact, some home managers can add more to the family income by providing services than would be possible through outside employment.

Consider the situation, however, where both partners earn money and the wife manages their income. If the husband has no feelings of inferiority about turning over a paycheck to his wife, there probably will be harmony in this area of their relationship. The opposite would be true if the husband felt threatened or inadequate by not taking charge of the household expenses.

In dual-earner families, decisions must be made about how to spend the two paychecks. A couple may decide that one will make the car payments, while the other pays the rent. One may agree to buy the groceries and the other to pay for their clothing needs. Nevertheless, if this type of system is to work successfully, the

When a couple works together to manage their finances they are more able to save money for major purchases.

partners also need to think in terms of "our" money, "our" car, and "our" home.

A **budget,** or a plan for managing income, often helps couples deal jointly with family finances. Keeping a budget is not in itself a way to solve differences. Rather, it is a way for couples to discuss money matters *before* they become problems.

No financial plan is right for every couple in every month or year. Needs vary with individuals and change throughout life. A budget that works for one couple might be a very detailed list of expenditures. Another couple might simply agree that a certain amount of money should be put aside for food, shelter, clothing, entertainment, travel, savings, and miscellaneous needs. Some people budget every week, depending on variations in income and expenses, some budget from paycheck to paycheck, and some from year to year. Making up a budget is discussed in more detail in Chapter 14, Balancing Needs and Resources.

People who want to learn to manage their money responsibly can refer to countless books and magazines. Still, the major adjustment in money matters usually concerns individual attitudes and preferences. When a couple can reach an agreement about the meaning of money in their lives together, they usually can agree on how to spend it. Reaching agreements, or even compromises, on money-related issues means hard work for a couple. Resolving differences on these matters requires effective communication and that takes a great deal of effort.

For Review

1. Describe some nontraditional roles for husbands and wives.
2. Explain why the highest percentage of divorces occurs during the second or third year of marriage.
3. What are some of the role conflicts that dual-earner couples must resolve?
4. What is one of the major sources of financial conflicts in a marriage?

Resolving Marital Differences

No marriage relationship can exist without some type of conflict. A disagreement may be as trivial as an argument over whether one partner should read the paper at the breakfast table when the other wants to talk, or it may be as serious as an argument over attitudes and beliefs. Sometimes, one partner in a marriage may have conflicting ideals and needs. These may erupt and cause problems in the relationship. Not all conflicts occur because individuals want or believe different things. A conflict can arise when one partner is disappointed in the behavior of another.

The success of a marriage depends on how couples handle their differences. Couples can try to avoid conflicts, or they can work hard to resolve them. Since working out differences takes so much practice, patience and energy, some couples try not to confront each other with their differences.

Conflict: Avoidance

Many people believe that they should avoid conflict at all costs. They may have carried over this idea from childhood experiences when stern discipline insured peace and quiet in the household. Anxieties, frustrations, and even physical illnesses sometimes can result when people are denied the opportunity to express differences. Yet to handle conflicts so that there is growth in the marriage, a couple first must acknowledge that conflict is a natural part of a marriage relationship. Couples who cannot handle the expression of negative feelings deal with their differences by ignoring them. Other disagreements may be so slight and easy to resolve that the husband and wife do not think of them as "conflicts" at all. To understand each other successfully, couples need to talk about their problems and differences. This way, both partners can recognize and deal with conflict as it occurs.

Conflict: Resolution

Many marriage counselors point out that a vital marriage needs a certain amount of arguing. However, the methods used in arguing or dealing with conflicts can determine whether a relationship will grow, or whether it will end in divorce, separation, or a lifetime of disinterest.

Having angry feelings does not mean that love has disappeared. As counselors point out, anger and love are "natural companions" and not direct opposites. You needn't be afraid of anger if it stems from shattered hopes as you recognize that your partner is a human being with less than perfect traits. As your disappointment fades, so does your anger.

It is normal for conflict to arise in every marriage. Dealing with problems as they arise can be helpful.

Practical Tip

To promote successful marital communication:

- Do assume that your partner is a decent person who shares your desire to work things out.

- Do use a soft and direct tone of voice.

- Do report your own feelings and accept responsibility for them. It helps to express positive supportive feelings before expressing dissatisfactions.

- Don't use a challenging or threatening or demanding mode of expression.

- Don't waste your opportunity to communicate by complaining to partners about things they cannot change, such as the distant past or personal attributes they do not control (intelligence, wealth, family, ethnic background, height, etc.)

In marriage, successful communication is essential, as it often leads to satisfaction and happiness for both parties. The sharing of thoughts and feelings can keep resentments from building up, and some experts recommend that couples be completely open with each other. However, one person's idea of "total honesty" can be another's idea of "destructiveness." Tact is still necessary in any relationship.

Of course, effective communication is no guarantee that a couple will resolve all marital conflicts; some differences may never be resolved. Larger events outside of their lives such as war or the state of the national economy, can make some couples incapable of handling their own conflicts. Sometimes, differences and disagreements are large enough to require the couple to seek pastoral or other professional help.

Accepting Relatives and Friends

You have probably noticed in advice columns in the daily newspapers that many letters come from young married people who are having problems with the family or close friends of their spouses. In the early years of marriage, learning to accept each other's family and friends can be a problem.

Newlyweds seldom think about all of the different interactions that go along with marrying. They sometimes even overlook relationships with parental families. When you marry, you are taking on three or more different roles. You are not only a partner in marriage, relating to your spouse. You are also a married son or daughter, relating to your own parents in new ways. Also, you are an in-law, relating to your mate's parents in a manner that might be similar to, but not the same as, your relationship with your own parents. Added to these primary roles are the new relationships you form with a mate's brothers or sisters, cousins, aunts,

Whether in-laws live nearby or far away, phone calls help to maintain contact and communication.

uncles, grandparents, family friends, professional advisers (doctors, lawyers, clergy), and work and school colleagues.

Often, conflicts arise with relatives because, as in other aspects of marriage, each partner's family differs in attitudes and expectations. In order to achieve a workable relationship with your future mate's family or inner circle of friends, you will need to compromise. If both sets of families want holiday visits, you can alternate visits. If your friend and your spouse do not get along, you can continue your friendship on a separate basis. You might make efforts to become involved with your in-laws or to fit into the activities and interests of your mate's friends. Some points to consider when working towards a successful adjustment follow.

Relatives are people, too. Many parents, for example, have no intention of interfering or meddling with married offspring. However, they must often learn how to "let go" and allow their children to make their own choices. In the same way, young married people must learn to live independently.

Although the jokes about mothers-in-law usually refer to the mother of the wife, studies show that the majority of in-law problems concern the mother and sisters of the husband. Even so, the stereotype of the dominating, troublesome mother-in-law hardly fits the vast majority of in-laws. These new relatives often are very helpful to a young couple and provide a variety of services. If problems do arise, they are probably due to a parent's inability to exchange the long-held role of caretaker and advice giver for the new role of supportive "friend" of the new family.

Contact with both families is important, but you need not overdo visits. Most young couples maintain their own homes or apartments, so it is not necessary to have daily contact with in-laws unless it is by mutual preference. Visits should be diplomatic, of course. It pays to have a good sense of humor and to use tact, as well as to communicate effectively.

In time, as a couple grows and changes, relationships with relatives often change. What once might have been considered meddlesome behavior can come to be regarded as deeply appreciated aid, especially if a couple needs help with basic necessities. Even family disapproval of a marriage tends to modify or gradually change over a period of years, particularly when grandchildren arrive.

For Review

1. What are some reasons for conflict in a marriage?
2. Why do some couples avoid having arguments?
3. What are some of the problems that can arise between a mother-in-law and a daughter-in-law?

6 Chapter Review

Summary

Married couples assume a variety of roles during their lives together. These marital roles change as the partners grow as a couple and as individuals. Their roles also are influenced by their images of themselves, their ideals, parents' marriages, and cultural backgrounds.

Because marital partners bring their varying attitudes toward money into their marriage, financial conflicts can be a frequent source of disagreement. Couples who decide jointly how to manage their finances are better able to resolve these issues.

Although a certain amount of conflict occurs in every marriage, couples can often resolve disagreements through open and honest communication with each other.

Each partner's relatives and friends are another potential source of marital conflict. However, when a couple compromises to achieve workable relationships with each partner's relatives, they can find solutions to the problems that occur.

Vocabulary

Complete each of the following sentences with one of the vocabulary words below.

budget
√ dual-earner family
√ marital role
√ reciprocal
role making

1. Often called the "two-paycheck marriage," both partners in a _____ hold full- or part-time jobs.
2. A husband's or wife's _____ is determined by his or her parents' marriage, ideals, self-image, and cultural background.
3. A family _____ is an effective way for couples to work together to manage all of their finances.
4. Marital partners who have _____ roles believe in giving and receiving in their relationship in a way that is satisfactory to them both.
5. When couples participate in _____, they formulate written contracts that specify the marital roles of each partner.

Chapter Questions

1. How have people's attitudes about marital roles changed?
2. Name three factors that affect the roles a husband and wife accept. Which one do you think is the most influential?
3. Is it important for a couple to discuss roles before marriage? Why?
4. How does cooperation between husband and wife strengthen a marriage?
5. What do you think are the advantages and disadvantages of role making?
6. How can a couple ensure that they both share home responsibilities?
7. What is the purpose of a budget?
8. If you and your spouse were a dual-earner

family, how would you like your incomes to be managed?

9. Why do you think a couple might be reluctant to discuss difficult areas of conflict in their marriage?

10. How can a couple keep resentment from building up in their relationship?

11. How can a person successfully relate to his or her in-laws?

Skill Activities

1. Human Relations Scan one or more newspapers to find syndicated columns that offer advice to readers on marital and family problems. Read and then analyze each letter to identify the conflict in each one. Then, write your own advice responses to five letters. In each letter, outline your detailed recommendations toward the solution of the problem. Use general information given in the text, books, pamphlets, magazine articles, or your own experience and observations to support your advice and opinions. Feel free to agree or disagree with the advice offered in a particular column.

2. Math Utilizing the resources of your school or local library, research different methods of organizing a budget. Once you have studied several approaches to budgeting, select one method that would fit your needs best. Be sure to consider how you might meet long-range financial goals such as education, a major purchase, or getting an apartment. Using your average income over the past three months as a starting figure, draw up a budget that will finance your necessary expenditures, your savings, and your spending money.

3. Decision Making After you have read the text selection about role making on page 99, write your own marriage contract with a partner. Be sure to allow enough time for you and your partner to communicate openly about your attitudes, needs, and feelings as you negotiate the contract. Remember to include the responsibilities of each spouse related to household duties (cooking, child care, yard work, car maintenance, and cleaning), money management, and additional issues you wish to address.

4. Human Relations With four or five other students, discuss your various attitudes about money that one day you may bring to a marriage. To help your group focus its discussion, consider the following questions: Who should manage the money in a marriage? Where did your attitudes about money come from? What should the financial priorities be each month and each year? What percentage of a couple's expenditures should be purchased on credit? How much and what type of debt is acceptable? What priority should be placed on saving and investing money? How should financial disagreements between husband and wife be settled? Is it more important to replace a leaking roof or to have a two-week vacation?

7 Today's Families

As you read, think about:

- how a family socializes its children.
- how family structure and size have changed over the years.
- what different types of family support systems exist.
- what is meant by the family life cycle and financial considerations related to it.

VOCABULARY

socialization	adoption
nuclear family	foster care
extended family	family life cycle

Almost everyone has grown up in some type of family, and most people expect to have families of their own. Everyone has some idea of what a family is, yet it is unlikely that people will agree on what constitutes a family or how to define it. A family might be a couple with no children, a couple with adopted children, a single parent with children, or a group that includes grandparents and other relatives living in one residence.

Families differ in size and makeup, but many family functions, or purposes of the family, are common to all. Some of these functions are discussed in this chapter.

Despite all of the changes that have taken place in society, the family is still one of the most important institutions.

Family Functions

Perhaps the basic function of the family is to provide emotional fulfillment for its members. Children must receive love and affection in order to become healthy, productive individuals. In addition, parents usually expect that their own emotional needs will be met through their marriage and their children.

Another function of the family is to provide security and acceptance. Your family is a place where you belong. Within the family, you can be yourself and feel free from outside pressures. In a crisis, your family can provide necessary loving support.

The family provides a means of identifying individual members. Fairly or unfairly, people often are identified by what is known about their families. You might have heard remarks such as "Oh, the Jacobs's son. He just went to college. He ought to be a good student because his mother and father are both very intelligent." Or "Karen just made the high school swimming team, but that's no surprise. All the members of her family are athletic." Sometimes a negative identification is made. "What can you expect from *those* kids? Their family has always had trouble in this town!"

One important family function is to socialize children. **Socialization** is the process by which children learn behavior that is acceptable to the family and to the rest of society. You learn most of your viewpoints and attitudes in your family. Your family also helps to shape your personality.

Family Structure

Mother, father, and children have always been the basic family structure in every part of the world. There may be a stepmother or a stepfather or a child might be adopted or have foster parents. Nevertheless, at one time or another almost everyone has been part of a **nuclear family,** the term sociologists use to describe the unit including parents and their dependent children.

When most of the people in the United States lived on farms, having a large number of children in a family often meant that the family would prosper. Children did chores, worked in the fields, and helped support the family group. Later on, the grown-up children cared for their elderly parents. Usually, at least three generations lived together or near each other. This type of family is known as an **extended family.**

Over the years, family life has changed dramatically, yet the main function of the family has always been to provide love and security for its members.

What are some of the changes that have taken place in the size and structure of today's families?

Yesterday's Families

In the past, members of farm families grew their own crops, baked their own bread, made their own clothes, and built their own homes. The family provided its members with education, religious instruction, and medical care. The members of the family worked together in and around the home and farm as one economic unit. Team effort was necessary for survival.

At the beginning of the twentieth century, the typical family included four or five children. From the 1900s to the 1950s, two-parent households were common. The mother usually stayed at home to raise the children and manage the homemaking tasks, while the father went off to a job every day. Parents of this time period often believed that their personal happiness depended on the presence of children in the family.

Today's Families

The size and structure of families have been changing dramatically since the 1950s. The number of working mothers has been steadily increasing. Mothers and fathers are sharing more household responsibilities.

There is a large number of single-parent households because of the number of divorces in this country. There are also many *blended families,* or families with stepmothers, stepfathers and stepchildren.

Number of Children During the 1970s, a rapid change in public attitudes about family size took place. Young women between the ages of 18 and 24 surveyed by the Bureau of the Census reported that they expected to have only one or two children. Some married couples said that they no longer believed it necessary to

Adjusting to the arrival of a sibling is often difficult for a big brother or sister.

have children in order to enjoy a satisfactory home life.

A variety of factors determines family size. Economics is a basic factor. Young people expect to provide good housing, clothing, and nutritious food for their families. Most also expect to have an active social life, with rewarding friendships. Many hope to provide educational opportunities that will allow their children to go as far as their abilities can take them. In short, many citizens of the United States desire a quality of life that can be very expensive.

Family size is also affected by the general health and the educational levels of couples. Further, the partners must consider whether they are emotionally ready for children.

Many women wait several years after they marry to have children. Some delay childbearing so that they can establish themselves in a career or achieve educational goals. Still others feel it is important to build a strong marriage before bringing children into the family.

As a result of all these factors, family planning has received much more attention in recent years. Different methods have been developed to prevent pregnancies. Some of these are controversial, and certain religious groups forbid their use. Most American couples today, however, try to plan the size of their families and in what years the children will arrive.

Adopted Children

When couples want children but cannot have their own, adoption offers one way to create a family. However, this is not an easy route to parenthood. **Adoption** is the process of taking another person's child into one's family through

Practical Tip

To take good pictures of small children:

■ Move in close to the subject or use a zoom lens.

■ Have another person keep the child's attention.

■ Aim for an uncluttered background.

■ Aim for spontaneous, natural looking shots.

■ Take pictures outside when possible.

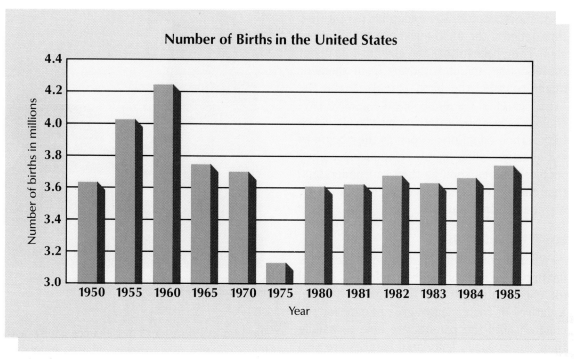

Number of Births in the United States

Number of births in millions

Year	
1950	
1955	
1960	
1965	
1970	
1975	
1980	
1981	
1982	
1983	
1984	
1985	

Year

Source: U.S. Bureau of the Census, 1985.

legal means. The adopted child has the same rights and imposes the same obligations on the family as would any biological child.

Usually, couples who want to adopt a child apply for one through a state or county adoption agency, unless they are adopting a relative's child, friend's child, or stepchild. One of the functions of the adoption agency is to determine whether a particular husband and wife are fit to become adoptive parents. To this end, workers in an adoption agency screen prospective parents, investigating their health, financial status, and educational background, and visiting their home. Obtaining this kind of information helps the agency place a child in a family where people can share their love and encourage a young person to develop in positive ways. The needs of the child, not of the parents, are the primary concern of the adoption agency.

One of the most difficult questions adoptive parents have to face is when to tell a child that

Adoption is an alternative for couples who cannot have their own children.

he or she is adopted. Some adoptive parents feel threatened if the child questions the relationship. They believe that the child, if told about the adoption, might withdraw from them or might consider the birth parents to be the "real" parents. Generally speaking, child psychologists today believe that children should be told of their adoption as soon as they begin to ask questions about family relationships. They should know as soon as they can understand that they have been especially chosen to be members of their family.

Foster Children

When a couple divorces or separates or a death or other crisis occurs in a family, a child (or children) might need a temporary home. Relatives or friends may agree to care for the children until the parents are able to handle their duties again. Unrelated families are also often willing to provide the basic necessities and a loving home for children in crisis. This arrangement is called **foster care.**

Some children are placed in foster homes by doctors or members of the clergy. More often, foster care is a formal agreement between a family and the courts or social agencies that have the responsibility for finding homes for abandoned, orphaned, abused, or disturbed children. In such instances, foster parents receive payment for their services from the state or placement agency. Occasionally these families are able to adopt children they have cared for over a long period of time.

Families with Handicapped Children

Many families must cope with the problems of caring for a child with a physical or mental disability. The presence of a handicapped child affects not only the parents, but their other children as well. The handicapped child may require extra attention or special medical treatment that can put a strain on the entire family.

This mother is helping her son use a computer assisted communication device.

The families who deal most successfully with this difficulty are those whose individual members can work together for the benefit of everyone.

Mentally Handicapped Children Children who are mentally handicapped have difficulty learning. Mental retardation can take many forms, from mild to severe. A child who is educable, that is, mildly retarded, can learn to live and work fairly independently, but may need special educational programs to succeed. A child with more severe limitations may be trainable, or capable of learning certain skills, but must live and work in a sheltered setting. A child who is profoundly retarded usually needs more attention than the average family can provide. He or she may need institutional care.

It is important for parents to treat a mentally retarded child as much like their other children as possible. A mental handicap does not interfere with a child's need for love, discipline, and acceptance. Furthermore, families need not cope with the problems alone. In most communities, help is available through both public and private programs.

Wheeling Free

"Okay, ready? Set. Go!" Paul yells. He and his longtime friend, William, are off, racing down the street in front of their homes. It is not an unusual activity for two lively 16-year-olds, but there is one difference. Paul's legs are paralyzed from an injury to his spinal column. "A dumb accident while horsing around with my younger brother," he explains.

For more than a year, Paul has been in a wheelchair. He is trying out a new lightweight model. His able-bodied friend has borrowed Paul's old, bulky wheelchair for the race.

"No fair!" William calls as Paul expertly wheels past him to the finish line. "You've had practice!"

Indeed Paul has had plenty of learning time with the wheelchair. After the accident, therapists at the rehabilitation center taught him many self-care skills, including how to transfer from the bed to the wheelchair—no easy task at first.

Paul soon became adept at not only getting into the chair, but also at maneuvering in and out of buildings—if he could get his wheelchair through. That could be a big IF sometimes. Some buildings have narrow doorways and no ramps.

At home, Paul's parents got rid of such structural barriers. Doorways were widened, carpeting was replaced with tile flooring, a non-slip ramp was built over the stairs to the kitchen, and a large closet was redesigned to create a bathroom with a special shower seat.

When it comes to daily living, however, Paul's parents have tried to maintain their usual family pattern. They decided that pity and over-protection would only harm Paul more. So they have helped him become as independent as possible, and they expect him to do his share of the household chores, including cooking, cleaning his room, doing laundry, and taking out the garbage.

Fortunately, Paul is also able to attend high school with all his classmates. At school he uses an elevator to get to classes on the second floor. He rides to school on a special van with a lift. When Paul learns to drive, he will get a car equipped with hand controls for gas, brakes, and steering.

"Sometimes," Paul says, "other kids stare at me like I'm some kind of freak." It is hard, too, being on the sidelines, watching rather than playing in team sports. Outside school, however, Paul has joined a basketball team called the Free Wheelers. All the team members are in wheelchairs and play basketball by the regular game rules except that players are allowed two "pumps" on their wheels between dribbles.

Paul gets no special privileges in class. He cannot sit at a desk so he has to roll up beside a desk to have a writing surface. He plans to take electronic classes since the training might lead to a career later on. As he says with a smile, "Electronics is something I can do sitting down."

You can make access to buildings easier for handicapped people by respecting this sign when you are parking a car.

Physically Handicapped Children

Physically handicapped children face limitations because of their bodies. They may be visually or hearing impaired, confined to a wheelchair, or have conditions such as cerebral palsy, asthma, or diabetes. Physical handicaps may be caused by heredity or environment. They may appear at birth, later in life, or as a result of an accident. Some handicaps can be minimized by corrective surgery, physical therapy, or other medical treatments. Others, however, are incurable.

When a child is severely handicapped, parents must make the difficult decision of whether to care for the child at home or to place the child in an institution where he or she will receive the constant attention required. The parents must consider not only the needs of the handicapped child, but also the needs of their other children. If institutional care is needed, parents should investigate their choices and seek medical advice to find the best place. If they keep the child at home, they should take advantage of all the community resources available to them to help the child reach his or her potential.

Myths and Facts About the Physically Handicapped

Federal laws passed in the 1960s and 1970s require that schools provide facilities for educating handicapped young people and that ramps, wider doorways, and toilet facilities in schools and other public buildings be accessible to handicapped people. As a result, millions of handicapped students have been able to attend regular classrooms, and between 250,000 and 300,000 disabled young people graduate from public high schools each year. However, handicapped people still face a primary barrier — the attitude able-bodied people have about handicaps. There is still much ignorance, fear, stereotyping of and discrimination against the handicapped. The myths below represent just a few of the attitudinal barriers that handicapped people face.

Myth	Fact
Handicapped people are odd and do little for themselves.	Handicapped people are people first; their handicaps do not change their interests and personalities. Many handicapped people work and live independently.
Wheelchair use is a tragedy.	People who cannot walk do not lead lives of despair. A wheelchair gives a handicapped person some freedom.
All wheelchair users are ill, and a person can get a disease from the handicapped.	People use wheelchairs because of disabilities caused at birth or by accidents or disease. A disability is not contagious.
Handicapped people do not like to talk about their disabilities.	Many handicapped people can joke about their disabilities. The handicapped want to have normal give-and-take with others.
People with physical disabilities also have mental handicaps.	Being physically handicapped does not mean a person is also mentally disabled. In fact, physically handicapped people resent being treated as children.

What are some of the special challenges facing a single parent?

Single-Parent Families

The Bureau of the Census reported in 1982 that over eleven million families—a little more than one of every seven families in the United States with children in the home—were headed by single parents. Most single-parent families were created as a result of divorce or separation. Sometimes, however, parents were widowed.

Most single-parent families, about 9.4 million, are headed by women without a husband in the household. Single-parent households maintained by the father alone number less than 2 million, but that figure may increase. Recent trends show that more fathers are being granted custody of their children.

Single parents face some of the same problems encountered by parents with mates, but the problems often are much more difficult to solve without a partner. Since a single parent usually is employed, child-care services are often necessary. Such services can be both expensive and inconvenient, especially if child care is not available during working hours.

Most single parents have financial worries. As a group, their incomes are usually lower than those of two-parent families.

Further, single parents frequently suffer from loneliness. Their social life is restricted, especially when they have small children. One parent must earn the living, care for the home, prepare the meals, and perform all the other tasks required to keep a family functioning.

In spite of the problems, evidence exists that some single-parent families manage well. Recent studies show that single parents have more opportunities to express themselves when they are not hampered by another adult who is hostile to them. Also, some children from one-parent families acquire more household skills and are able to accept more responsibilities than children who have grown up within a traditional family structure.

Childless Families

In the past few years, more young people have been expressing their intent to remain childless. According to one study, about five percent of all married couples make deliberate decisions not to have children. These couples have formed family units that consist of two people: a wife and a husband.

Some people may label such a decision "selfish." A childless couple may be subjected to a great deal of pressure to have children. Their critics may express the idea that "a family isn't a family without children."

One reason couples give for choosing not to have children is the desire for a higher standard of living than they could enjoy if they had children. Sometimes, a wife wants to pursue a career without taking time out to have children.

Some couples say they want to remain childless because of population and environmental problems; they fear the future and foresee a decline in world conditions. Others decide not to have children because they want the freedom to travel or to spend their leisure time on activities they believe will bring more self-fulfillment.

For Review

1. How have family roles changed since the turn of the century?
2. What is the basic family unit called?
3. What are some of the factors that determine family size?

Family Support Systems

If the family unit cannot function without help, or if members have problems getting along, the tendency is to regard the family as a failure. Even its own members may agree with this judgment. However, as one sociologist has pointed out, "the American family, as idealized, is an overloaded institution." The goal of perfect functioning is simply not realistic. Some experts are convinced that even a healthy nuclear family, in today's complex society, may need the support of other groups at times.

Extended Families

Isolation can be a problem for nuclear families. Yet, nuclear families are usually part of extended families. An extended family is often loosely defined as all relatives who are direct descendants of an individual. In other words, your grandparents, aunts, uncles, and cousins from either your mother's or father's side can make up your extended family. The group might include three or four generations. Today, these people often do not live near each other. When distance separates the various members,

family ties can weaken. When an individual needs help, no family members are available.

The extended family, with members living close together, is still the conventional way of life for some people. Relatives contribute as much to the welfare of individuals as do the father, mother, and children of the nuclear group. Many ethnic groups have heritages that reflect strong family bonds. Young and old are not set apart from one another. Instead, the goal is mutual support.

An extended family can be a network of caring people of all ages. Suppose, for instance, that an aunt decides she will care for an infant nephew when his mother goes back to work; or Grandma loans money to her grandson when he and his bride need help to make a down payment on a house. Possibly, an older cousin helps a younger cousin get a job, or learn a trade, or enter college. In times of crisis, the members of the extended family can help comfort one another, too.

It is often through the extended family that a particular culture is passed on to individual

Family rituals are important throughout life. Members of this extended family plan a reunion each summer.

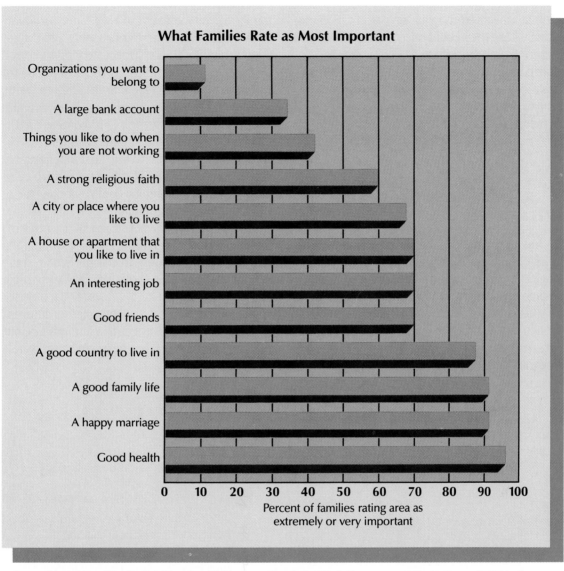

What Families Rate as Most Important

Organizations you want to belong to	
A large bank account	
Things you like to do when you are not working	
A strong religious faith	
A city or place where you like to live	
A house or apartment that you like to live in	
An interesting job	
Good friends	
A good country to live in	
A good family life	
A happy marriage	
Good health	

Percent of families rating area as extremely or very important

Source: Adapted from "The Quality of American Life" by Angus Campbell, Philip E. Converse, and Willard L. Rogers. © 1976 by the Russell Sage Foundation. Reprinted by permission of Basic Books, Inc., Publishers.

members. The members learn from earlier generations what is expected of them in religious, educational, economic, political, and other aspects of life. Family rituals help teach the culture of the group as well as maintain family ties. Holiday celebrations, births, funerals, graduation ceremonies, weddings, and many other life events bring families together, helping to preserve their customs and traditions.

Substitute Families

Some people share living quarters or live in separate housing in a communal arrangement with other people to whom they are not directly related. Such arrangements are not new in the United States. Small communal groups were established for idealistic or religious purposes even before the United States became a nation.

Members wanted utopian, or perfect, communities where they could raise their children and be free from "worldly" or "evil" influences.

Frequently, those who join such communities today give as their reason that they want to be part of a larger family. Often they lack or have lost a family of their own. They refer to the larger group as a substitute extended family.

Family Life Cycle

One factor common to all families is the element of change. Just as individuals go through stages of life from birth to death, so families change in a fairly predictable way. Sociologists call this pattern the **family life cycle.** As children grow up, there can be anywhere from seventeen to twenty or more years of joys, sorrows, and anxieties that cause changes within a family. If you look at your own family or at any family with children, you probably see scenes something like these: Mother trying to coax a fearful kindergartener onto the school bus for the first time, Dad teaching the kids to swim, brother cooking the evening meal for the first time, sister winning the photo contest for the local newspaper, and family vacations at the beach with all the relatives. Most families mark off the special events of these years with ceremonies, such as religious confirmations, bar or bat mitzvahs, and graduations.

Your family might not fit perfectly into each life cycle stage. Yet in any family, members' roles change according to the particular stage of family life. At each stage, the family operates in a different manner.

Various scholars have designated different time periods for the stages in a family's life, but the one used most often begins when a couple marries.

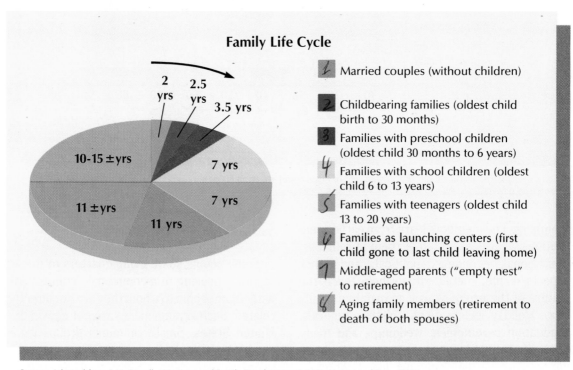

Source: Adapted from E.M. Duvall, "Marriage and Family Development" (N.Y.: Harper and Row, 1985).

Married Couples with No Children

When couples are just starting out, they develop ways to earn, to share, and to spend income. That is the time, too, when couples strengthen their physical and emotional bonds and learn how to get along with each other's relatives.

Setting up a household together and adjusting to each other's personalities, values and goals are other important tasks in this phase of the family life cycle.

Childbearing Families

Stage one continues until the first child is born. Caring for a baby brings big changes into a couple's life. Adding the roles of mother and father to those of husband and wife can put strain on a marriage. First-time parents have to readjust their attitudes toward money, time, space, and careers. Keeping up with a baby's schedule and learning how to make the baby happy, secure, and healthy take up a great deal of time and energy. Couples in this stage of life often find new friends who also have young children. Together they share the problems and triumphs of helping babies grow and develop.

The family life cycle begins when a couple gets married.

The challenges of having and caring for a baby often add a new and joyous dimension to a married couple's life. Couples who have a second child soon after the first have to deal with the fast-paced life of a willful toddler as well as with the demands of an infant.

The arrival of a baby brings many changes to a couple's life. What are some of these changes?

Families with Preschool Children

Even though preschool children can do many things for themselves, they are still very dependent on their parents. Parents must set and enforce rules, answer questions, and provide for all their child's physical, emotional, and social needs. The financial strain of this can be quite great, especially when day care is needed. As young children's interests develop, parents begin to introduce their children to people and places around, as well as outside of, the neighborhood.

Families with School-Age Children

The start of school for a child is the beginning of a new era for the family. School-age children are more independent than pre-schoolers. They are also beginning to develop social lives outside the family. As the children make new friends and acquire new interests, the pace around the home becomes more hectic. Parents frequently find themselves chauffering children to lessons and sports activities. Despite their developing interests, school-age children are still dependent on the family for love and acceptance, as well as for financial support.

Families with Teenage Children

Caring for babies and toddlers is a physically exhausting job, but being the parents of teenagers is mentally exhausting. Families with teens experience a roller coaster ride of emotions as the child and the parents struggle to find a comfortable balance between independence and dependence. This is a time in the life cycle of a family when the child both rejects and shows a great need for his family's love and understanding.

Family Life Cycle
Left Top: Families with Preschool Children
Middle: Families with School-Age Children
Bottom: Families with Teenage Children
Right Top: Families as Launching Centers
Middle: "Empty Nest" Families
Bottom: Families with Aging Members

Families as Launching Centers

As children leave home to start jobs or go on to college, the family enters the launching stage. The intensity of the teenage years begins to ease up and parents try to offer only encouragement and support as their children prepare to start their independent lives. Young adults feel a sense of security when parents respond in this way.

"Empty Nest" Families

When the last child has moved away, the parents begin to focus on each other again. For some couples this can be a difficult period of adjustment, especially if they neglected their relationship during their years of parenting. Eventually the couple can settle into a new routine which allows each individual to pursue interests and relationships. The parents are still interested in their children's happiness, but they no longer have the day-to-day contact with their offspring.

Families with Aging Members

Elderly couples spend their later years enjoying personal interests and utilizing skills. They also enjoy watching their children go through the family life cycle from stage one. Weddings, births, and graduations are sources of pleasure for older couples as they mark the important stages of the life cycle.

For Review

1. How does an extended family help its members preserve traditions?
2. What are some of the strains of families in the child-bearing stage of the family life cycle?
3. Which stage of the family life cycle allows for a married couple to pursue their own interests?

7 Chapter Review

Summary

Although the characteristics of each family vary, their purpose is the same. They provide emotional fulfillment, security, and acceptance for their members, and are responsible for the socialization of the children.

The nuclear family is the basic family unit. Most nuclear families are part of extended families. Years ago, the extended family structure provided caring and support to its related nuclear families.

Today, the rise of single-parent households, blended families, and changes in the size and structure of the nuclear family have created greater variation in family organization than existed in the past. Families with foster, adopted, or handicapped children face many additional challenges.

As society and the family have altered, so individual families change throughout the stages of the family life cycle, from marriage through child rearing to old age.

Vocabulary

Use the following vocabulary words to complete the paragraphs below.

adoption
extended family
family life cycle
foster care
nuclear family
socialization

The family performs many functions for its members. Through the process of ___1___, children learn the behavior, values, and attitudes that are acceptable to the family and society as a whole.

Until the twentieth century, most parents and their children were part of a larger unit called a(n) ___2___. In this type of family organization, a(n) ___3___, consisting of a mother, father, and children, lived with grandparents and other relatives. Children who have been permanently separated from their parents may become members of new families through ___4___. When parents temporarily cannot care for their offspring, state social agencies can arrange for homes, or ___5___ for their children. Regardless of a family's size or structure, all of its members experience different stages of the ___6___ as their roles and lives change.

Chapter Questions

1. Identify four functions of the family.
2. Based on your knowledge of American history, what changes during the 20th century contributed to the declining importance of the extended family?
3. How does the family socialize children?
4. What is the difference between adoption and foster care?
5. Describe two of the problems single-parent families confront.
6. What are some of the reasons couples give for choosing to remain childless?

7. Name two benefits provided by the extended family. In your opinion, what are some of the disadvantages of living close to the extended family?
8. What are substitute families?
9. Discuss the three different categories of mental handicaps.
10. Describe the stage in the family life cycle that your family is now experiencing.
11. From your own family experiences and your observations of your relatives' and friends' families, which stage of the family life cycle puts the greatest strain on a couple? Give several examples to support your answer.

Skill Activities

1. **Reading** Research and write a brief report on early family-like societies in the United States, such as the Shakers, New Harmony in Indiana, North American Phalanx in New Jersey, and Brook Farm and Fruitlands (Bronson Alcott) in Massachusetts.

Describe one communal society, or compare and contrast two or three societies. Consider the following questions: What benefits did these societies offer to an individual? What roles did men, women, and children play? How do these groups compare with substitute families described in this chapter? What were the disadvantages of belonging to communal societies? After completing your report, discuss your findings with your class.

2. **Communication** Investigate your family's history by talking with your parents, grandparents, or other relatives. Record the names of your grandparents, great-grandparents, and other ancestors on a chart or a family tree. Information about how to organize a family tree can be found in books on genealogy in your school or local library.

Once you have a family tree, interview family members to determine what one of your ancestor's families was like. Consider the following questions to help you prepare for these interviews: Where did the family live? How did they make a living? What was their daily life like? What role did religion, education, and entertainment play in their lives? How did the extended family influence them?

As you compile your information, write a description of the family you researched. Use the preceding questions to help you organize your family history.

3. **Social Studies** Study the figure on page 119 "What Families Rate as Most Important." With your classmates, rank each of the items listed in order of their importance. Start with the number 1 for your highest priority item and end with 12 for your least important rating. Tabulate the class results and compute the percentage of students rating each area as most important. For instance, what percentage of students rate "Good Friends" as most important? Transfer the data onto graph paper, using the figure on page 119 as a model.

8 Having a Baby

As you read, think about:

- how raising a child affects a couple's relationship, roles and economic decisions.
- how much it costs to raise a child.
- what a woman can do to keep herself and her baby healthy during pregnancy.
- what factors contribute to birth defects.

This chapter discusses how parenthood affects a couple's life. It will also describe the stages of prenatal development and what a mother can do to keep herself and her baby healthy during pregnancy. Finally, the chapter describes the birth process and what happens during the mother's stay in the hospital.

VOCABULARY

prenatal	umbilical cord
zygote	placenta
uterus	fetus
amniotic sac	rubella
embryo	toxemia

Becoming a Parent

Society traditionally has considered parenthood to be a basic part of marriage. If couples were biologically capable, they had children. Today, however, some couples are choosing not to have children.

Many social and emotional pressures affect a couple's decision. Following are some of the influences that might encourage a couple to have children:

- Their close friends are having babies.

- Their parents want grandchildren.

- They fear others will question their biological capacities to reproduce.

- They fear others will accuse them of selfishness if they do not have children.

- They are concerned about who will care for them in their old age.

- They feel that children symbolize their marriage union.

Influences that could discourage a couple from having children include the following:

- Their education is incomplete.

- They feel that they are financially unprepared for parenthood.

- They are both career-oriented.

- They doubt if child raising is essential to their fulfillment as adults.

- They doubt they can do a good job of parenting.

Effect on a Couple's Relationship

Being a parent is one of life's greatest challenges. Parenthood gives life a new dimension for the individual parents and for the couple, as well. Adjusting to parenthood, however, can be

Waiting for the arrival of a first baby is a time of excitement and anticipation.

a difficult task. Personal stress increases for both parents during the transition to parenthood. Among the changes they experience are having less time for themselves, having less time with friends, and feeling physically fatigued.

Most couples, however, believe that having children brings spouses together. In one nationwide study, parents' most common reasons for believing that children were good for a marriage included the following:

- Child raising is a task that both parents can share and it has an important common goal.

- The experience of helping children and watching them grow makes a couple feel closer.

- Children, a product of love and unity, symbolize marriage.

There is no doubt that with the birth of the first child, family life must be reorganized in a number of ways. Roles shift, habits change, and attitudes are modified.

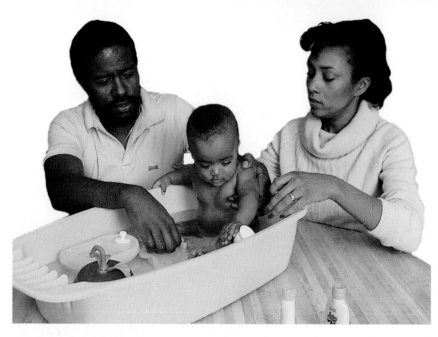

Bath time is one child care routine that can be shared by both parents.

Changing Roles

When husband and wife become father and mother, they must find time and discover ways to learn their new roles. Some couples rise to the occasion and become more efficient and organized, while others become overwhelmed and frustrated. Whatever happens, shifts are likely to occur in other life roles and activities. For example, couples may now find that going out anywhere is not as easy as it was before. Errands now may have to be run by one parent instead of by both. Activities such as visiting one's friends or going to the movies may require much more advance planning.

While many women give up outside employment after their baby is born, for some this is only a temporary measure. After a brief maternity leave, they go back to work. According to the United States Department of Labor, 55 percent of all mothers with children under 18 years are in the labor force; of this number, 45 percent have preschool-age youngsters.

If both parents work, child-care can become a problem. If there are no relatives or friends who can help, parents might hire a child-care provider, find a good child-care center, or work different shifts so that one parent can be home with the children. These are not easy solutions.

Couples need to define clearly what responsibilities they expect from each other.

Economic Factors

Children are considered economic assets in Third World nations. The more children in a family, the better off the parents are likely to be. This is because children work together with their parents to support the family, much as in the pioneer days of the United States. Children also provide security for their parents' old age. In industrialized countries, however, raising a child is a major life expense, and the rewards are more often psychological than financial.

The dual-earner family, in which both parents have paying jobs, is very much a fact of life today. In the United States, 45 percent of all mothers with preschool-age children are in the labor force. Over one-half of mothers with school-age children are working outside the home. The financial costs of raising children often help parents determine whether both go out to work.

Direct Costs How much money is needed to raise a child? The initial costs of having an infant — doctor and hospital bills, food, diapers, clothing, furniture — are only the beginning of a large outlay. Much more money is needed as the child grows.

Housing costs may be the largest child-raising expense. The birth of a child often means that a couple needs more living space. Many young couples live in apartments until their first child is born. They may then start to consider the need for more space and a yard, or for a better neighborhood and schools. For most new parents, purchasing a home of their own would be ideal, but when real estate prices are high, this option becomes increasingly difficult to realize. High rents may put even larger apartments out of reach. However, most people are willing to spend whatever they can in order to get the living space they need for their families.

Indirect Costs Indirect costs refer to the potential income lost if a parent leaves his or her job to raise children. Indirect costs equal about half the amount of direct costs. This brings the total expense of raising one child to a very high figure indeed. Most people who consider becoming parents are not prepared for the high costs involved in bringing up a child.

Child raising costs go beyond the initial costs of diapers, clothes and baby equipment.

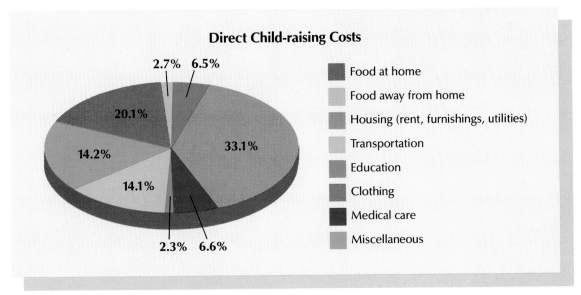

Direct Child-raising Costs

2.7%   6.5%
20.1%
14.2%
14.1%
33.1%
2.3%   6.6%

- Food at home
- Food away from home
- Housing (rent, furnishings, utilities)
- Transportation
- Education
- Clothing
- Medical care
- Miscellaneous

Source: U.S.D.A. Agricultural Research Service, 1989.

Preparation for Parenthood

A sociologist has identified three unique aspects of parenting.

- Parenthood is permanent. Once you become a parent, you will always be a parent. You can give up employment, but you cannot give up parenthood.

- Becoming a parent is not always voluntary. An unplanned pregnancy can occur. People can become parents before they are ready. Other adult decisions such as those concerning marriage or career are seldom involuntary.

- Preparation and training for parenthood is often inadequate. Many people still think that parenting skills come naturally.

Parenting education can ease the transition into parenthood. One study reports that even when only one partner has had a preparation-for-parenthood course, the adjustment to parenthood for both is less severe. Many couples choose to attend classes together.

Today, childbirth classes are offered at many hospitals. Classes are also available through adult education programs, YWCAs/YMCAs, and County Cooperative Extension Services. A major advantage of such classes is that they include expectant fathers as well as expectant mothers. Lessons often provide information on emotional and physical reactions to pregnancy, diet and exercise during pregnancy. These classes also teach the couple important facts about labor, delivery and postpartum care in the hospital.

Attending childbirth classes together is an excellent way for husband and wife to share the first stage of parenthood, the birth of their baby. The couple learns breathing patterns and

How do childbirth classes help parents-to-be prepare for the birth of their baby?

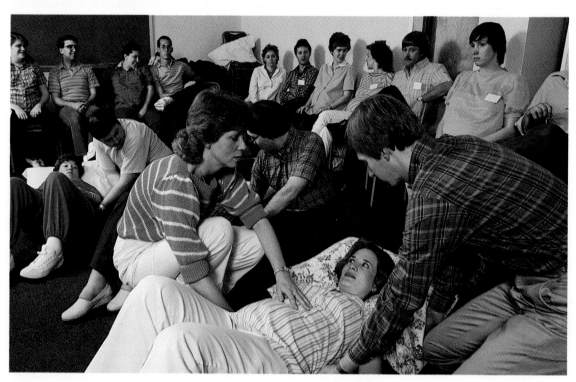

Baby showers are not always just for the mother-to-be.

relaxation exercises together so that the expectant father can help his partner practice throughout the pregnancy. He also can assist during the birth of their child by encouraging his wife to relax and breathe properly.

Many good books and pamphlets contain valuable information about pregnancy, development of the baby, and infant care. Public libraries, family-planning clinics, or cooperative extension services generally have information or literature on such topics as pregnancy and nutrition. When partners can read together, openly and honestly discussing topics related to present and future stages of parenthood, understanding and agreement are likely to result.

At present, few future parents participate in formal parenthood education, even during pregnancy. Thus, the birth of a child can seem like a very abrupt change. People do not have time to adjust slowly to becoming parents; there is no transition period. Suddenly, new parents are confronted with a total, 24-hour-a-day responsibility, with few clear-cut guidelines for successful child raising. They usually learn on the job.

Pregnancy

The unknown can sometimes be frightening, and for some couples pregnancy is very much "the unknown." The prospective parents may not understand what is happening inside the mother's womb. They may not know what precautions are necessary to protect this new life. Parents can better protect a baby if they understand its **prenatal** development, or the growth and changes that occur before birth.

Prenatal Development

A mother normally carries the developing baby in her womb for nine months. Yet it may not be until the fifth month that she can feel the child move inside her or hear its heartbeat. From conception to this time, most of the important prenatal development takes place.

Early Stages A woman becomes pregnant when the egg, or ovum, from a woman, is joined with a man's sperm cell. The joining of these cells creates a new cell called a **zygote** (ZY-gote). The zygote divides from one cell into two

Fetal Development

1 month

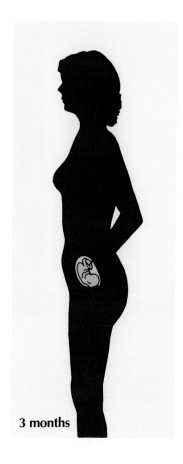

3 months

It is not until a woman is in her last few months of pregnancy that she finds moving around a bit awkward.

cells and continues to divide until it becomes about 90 cells. Near the end of this stage, the fertilized egg travels through the fallopian tube down to the **uterus,** a hollow, muscular organ where the new life develops. About two weeks after fertilization, the egg implants itself into the uterine wall. This step marks the end of the first stage of pregnancy.

The second stage of prenatal development, known as the embryonic period, lasts from the end of the second week until the end of the eighth week. The **amniotic sac** (am-nee-OT-ik SAK), a protective membrane, develops and encloses the **embryo,** or unborn child. This sac contains amniotic fluid, which protects the em-

bryo from shocks and jars, allows it to move around freely, and maintains it at a regulated temperature. The amniotic fluid also keeps pressure off the growing **umbilical cord,** which carries both nourishment and wastes between the embryo and the **placenta.** The placenta is an exchange organ that takes nutrients and oxygen from the mother's body and removes waste products from the unborn child. At the time of birth, the umbilical cord is about 20 to 22 inches in length.

The embryonic period is a very sensitive stage of prenatal development. During this time, essential body systems and organs such as the central nervous system, the digestive

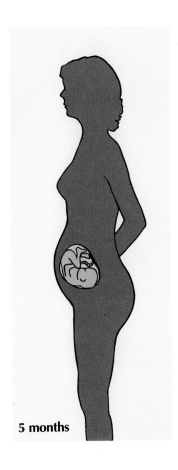

5 months

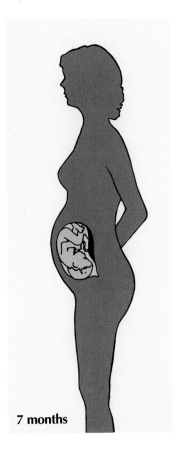

7 months

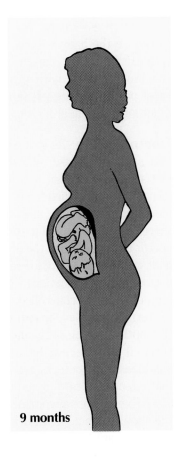

9 months

system, the heart, and the lungs develop. The embryo can easily be hurt by viruses, radiation, drugs, or chemicals in the mother's body.

Fetal Period The fetal period begins at the end of the second month and lasts until birth. The unborn child, now called a **fetus,** is a recognizable human being with a head, arms, body, legs, and feet. Between the fourth and fifth months, the mother begins to feel the fetus move. Further growth and development of body parts and systems continue as the fetus gains size and weight. During these seven months, the fetus grows in weight from about one ounce to about seven pounds.

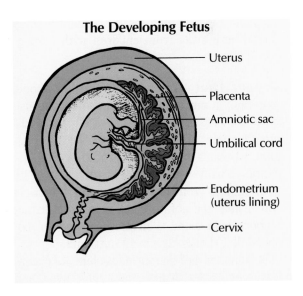

The Developing Fetus

- Uterus
- Placenta
- Amniotic sac
- Umbilical cord
- Endometrium (uterus lining)
- Cervix

Prenatal Care

Before the baby is born, expectant parents have an important parenting role: to provide the mother-to-be with proper care. For the most part, adequate prenatal care is just good common-sense health care.

Doctor's Care As soon as a woman suspects that she is pregnant, she should confirm this fact at a clinic or visit her doctor. Most physicians have a standard fee covering all prenatal medical examinations and the delivery; thus there is no economy in putting off a visit to the doctor until later on in the pregnancy. If a pregnant woman sees a doctor regularly during this period, any complications that arise can be detected early and controlled.

German measles, or **rubella,** contracted by the mother during pregnancy, is frequently associated with severe birth defects, including blindness. The defects are caused by a virus that affects the rate of cell division in the embryo. Even before a woman becomes pregnant, she should take a laboratory test to determine if she has antibodies against German measles. If she does not have these antibodies, she can obtain a vaccine, unless she is already pregnant. To avoid German measles, a pregnant woman should stay away from children with undiagnosed illnesses.

Proper Diet An expectant mother should maintain a nutritionally sound diet because what she eats is what her baby gets. Nourishment travels to the unborn baby from the pregnant woman's bloodstream through the placenta. A baby who gets some or most of its nourishment from low-nutrient foods such as soft drinks and potato chips is being cheated. Unborn babies and their mothers need a balanced diet that is high in all nutrients.

A balanced diet that includes plenty of green, leafy vegetables, fruits, milk, eggs, liver, and whole grain cereals is very important during

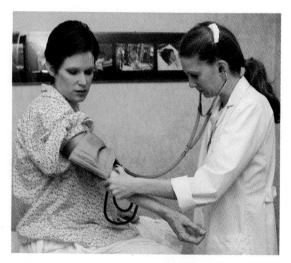

Prenatal care involves regular visits to the doctor. These check-ups are vital to the health of the mother and baby.

Practical Tip

A pregnant woman should meet the following minimum food requirements:

- **Milk** One quart daily of whole, low-fat, or skim milk, or buttermilk; or equivalent values of cheese or yogurt.

- **Meat, Fish, or Poultry** At least eight ounces daily. Nuts or legumes may be substituted.

- **Fruits** At least one citrus and one other fruit daily.

- **Vegetables** One potato and two to four servings of other vegetables daily. One green, leafy vegetable daily. One yellow vegetable four times a week.

- **Butter or Fortified Margarine** One to two tablespoons daily.

- **Bread and Cereals** Two to four servings daily, preferably whole-grain or enriched, including enriched pasta.

pregnancy. Doctors often advise a supplement containing iron and folic acid, which an unborn baby needs in large quantities. Calcium, found in milk and milk products, is also needed in large quantities for babies' bones and teeth.

Most pregnant women are advised to eat about 300 extra calories a day. They usually gain an average of 24 pounds during the nine-month period. An expectant mother should stay clear of crash and fad diets, as they seldom include all the necessary nutrients.

Researchers have linked prenatal nutrition not only with the growth of the fetus, but with the development of its brain and the central nervous system as well. There is evidence that malnutrition (especially an inadequate supply of protein) during the fetal period may result in learning difficulties throughout a child's life.

A proper diet will also help reduce the chances of the mother developing **toxemia.** Toxemia results from kidney malfunction and a subsequent buildup of fluid in the body. High blood pressure and the swelling of hands, feet, and legs are the usual symptoms of toxemia in the pregnant woman.

Proper diet is important during pregnancy. The developing fetus depends on the expectant mother for nutrients.

Weight Gain During Pregnancy

	Pounds	Kilograms
Fetus	7.5	3.37
Placenta	1	.45
Amniotic fluid	2	.90
Uterus (increase)	2.5	1.12
Breast tissue (increase)	3	1.35
Blood (increase)	4	1.70
Maternal nutrient reserves	4 to 8	1.70 to 3.60
	24 to 28	10.59 to 12.49

Source: S.R. Williams, Essentials of Nutrition and Diet Therapy, 3rd ed. (St. Louis: C. V. Mosby, 1982).

There are special exercises for pregnant women. Keeping in shape is an important aspect of a healthy pregnancy.

Rest and Exercise Even if an expectant mother follows a good diet, she may still experience fatigue, particularly during the early months of her pregnancy. A pregnant woman should maintain a balance between rest and exercise.

Although physicians usually recommend that a woman continue her normal activities and exercise throughout pregnancy, an expectant mother should avoid strenuous activity. Pregnant women should not lift heavy objects or take up activities such as skating, which involves the risk of falling. Most sports require a keen sense of balance; during pregnancy, a woman's center of balance shifts. She may find that she loses her balance more easily, particularly during the latter months.

Potential Hazards

During pregnancy, a woman must be careful to avoid exposure to hazards that may harm the unborn child. This warning is especially important during the embryonic period. If a mother is careful to stay away from radiation, alcohol, and drugs, she will increase her chances of having a normal, healthy infant.

X-rays An expectant mother should avoid having X-rays taken, because radiation may damage the embryo or fetus. If a dental X-ray is necessary during pregnancy, the dentist should provide protective covering for the mother's body. A pregnant woman should always alert the X-ray technician and doctor or dentist to her condition.

Alcohol All drugs, including alcohol, are transmitted from the mother's bloodstream to the fetal circulatory system. Expectant mothers should avoid drinks containing alcohol, as excess alcohol can cause low birth weight and mental retardation in infants. Experts who have studied birth defects for the March of Dimes state that babies of teenagers who drink excessive amounts of alcohol suffer on two accounts. The children may be born too small or too soon because their mother's bodies are not mature enough to meet the demands of pregnancy. In addition, the babies may suffer *fetal alcohol syndrome,* which includes abnormally small heads and brains, mental retardation, heart defects, and possibly behavior problems.

Smoking The drug nicotine also threatens the unborn child. Research indicates that cigarette smoking may increase the chances that a woman will have a low-birth-weight baby. Smoking inhibits the flow of blood through the placenta, which decreases the supply of oxygen and other nutrients to the fetus. As a result, the amount of poisonous carbon monoxide reaching the fetus increases, and fetal growth slows.

Other Drugs Caffeine, a drug found in colas, chocolate, and tea, as well as in coffee, has recently been tested by the Food and Drug Administration. Laboratory animals that were subjected to large doses of caffeine produced

Mama Hale's Babies

In the heart of Harlem in New York City is an old brownstone house, one room wide and five stories high. This is Hale House, one of the most effective centers for the treatment of drug-addicted babies in the United States. The success of this small institution is based on the simple philosophy of its resourceful founder, Clara Hale. The babies who are brought to her, dreadfully ill with the painful addiction they have inherited from their drug-addicted mothers, are cured by the simple prescription of good care, security, and most important of all, patient affection.

Clara Hale — known to everyone as Mama Hale — has spent half a century caring for children. When she was a young woman, her husband died, leaving her with three infants and very little money. In order to be with her own children, she quit her jobs cleaning houses and working at a movie theater and began taking care of her neighbors' children.

Soon she had a dozen children who spent the week in her five-room apartment in Harlem. The children's mothers paid Mama Hale what they could, but sometimes they could not pay at all. "I never had a problem," Mama Hale recalls. "The only real trouble was being poor, and I could always manage that." Her daughter remembers how much attention Mama Hale gave to each child and the fun they all had with games and music and happy mealtimes.

Over a decade ago, Clara Hale considered retiring. However, the growing need for care centers to rehabilitate babies with inherited drug addiction convinced her that she still had important work to do. Clara Hale knew very little about addiction, but she knew a lot about caring for babies. She decided to provide care for drug-addicted infants.

For this project, she needed larger quarters. Her daughter Lorraine, who has a doctorate in child development, found financial help from both public and private funds, and the present Hale House was opened. Lorraine now administers Hale House, and Mama has trained ten child-care workers in her method of child care. Hale House also works closely with doctors, psychologists, and social workers.

Mothers visit Hale House as often as possible, and, seeing how secure and happy their babies are, encourages them in their own struggle to return to a healthy, fulfilling life. Mothers are helped by other agencies to overcome their own addiction and eventually accept the responsibility of caring for their children. When a young mother admires the gleaming furniture in the Hale House living room, Mama Hale tells her, "Some of this furniture is new, and some is older than you are. I bought every piece myself. You can do that too. You can make a nice place for your child. You can make it through the drug program. You can go back and get your education. And then you can get anything you want."

From the over six hundred babies that have come to Hale House, only a dozen have had to be placed for adoption.

Clara Hale, founder of Hale House, has made an outstanding contribution to the treatment of drug-addicted babies.

many offspring with birth defects. Apparently, animal fetuses could not metabolize, or break down and process, the caffeine. Of course, the question remains as to how much of any substance may be consumed before it will cause harm. Research still has not shown how much caffeine humans can safely ingest. Common sense would seem to indicate caution, since doses from several different sources may add up to an overload.

A pregnant woman should avoid medication, unless prescribed by the doctor. Many people routinely take aspirin, decongestants, or laxatives when necessary. During pregnancy, absolutely no drugs should be taken without the doctor's knowledge. Scientists have not determined all the effects of drugs on the unborn child. More and more evidence suggests that pregnant women should stay clear of all drugs unless they are prescribed by a doctor.

The Thalidomide babies born in the late 1950s and 1960s serve as a grim reminder that drugs affect unborn children. Thalidomide, a tranquilizer taken by many pregnant women, caused children to be born with gross deformities such as malformed or missing limbs.

The effect of drugs on the unborn child is evident when a pregnant woman is addicted to illegal drugs. Babies born to drug addicts experience withdrawal symptoms, which include high-pitched crying, body tremors, and vomiting. The sucking reflex may be severely weakened for up to four days. If untreated, these infants may suffer convulsions and die.

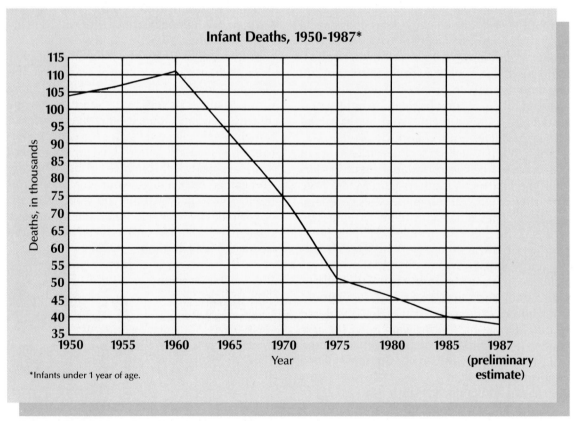

Infant Deaths, 1950-1987*

*Infants under 1 year of age.

(preliminary estimate)

Source: U.S. National Center for Health Statistics, Statistical Abstract, 1989.

Potential Complications

The longer a fetus remains in the uterus, the greater its chances of survival. A premature birth, or one that occurs before the end of the full nine-month period, can create problems. Babies born early may well survive, but such infants often require skilled medical care.

High-risk Infants Babies born too early and/or too small (weighing less than 5½ pounds) are considered to be high-risk infants. Many low-birth-weight babies are just too immature to take over from the mother all life functions, and so they are susceptible to a number of problems.

Respiratory Distress Syndrome (RDS) results from immature lungs. The baby cannot get enough oxygen, and survival is threatened without special respiratory assistance.

Hypoglycemia is a condition of low blood sugar resulting from the infant's inability to store glucose in the liver in a form usable to the body. Symptoms include body tremors, irritability, and lack of interest in eating.

Premature infants often have anemia, or insufficient iron in their blood. They may require blood transfusions or at least iron supplements in their diet.

In a condition known as hypothermia, body temperature decreases. Premature infants often have not developed enough fat to maintain body temperature. For premature babies to survive, they must stay in a sterile, warmed compartment called an incubator.

The problems of the low-birth-weight infant can be serious enough to result in neonatal death (death during the first month of life). According to a report of the Center for Health Statistics, in 1985 more than 30 percent of infant deaths occurred during the first seven days of life. While many factors, including congenital abnormalities, account for these deaths, at least eight percent of all infant deaths in 1985 were related to short gestation and low birthweight.

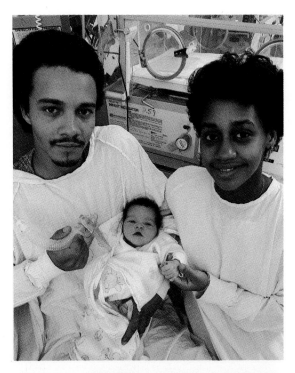

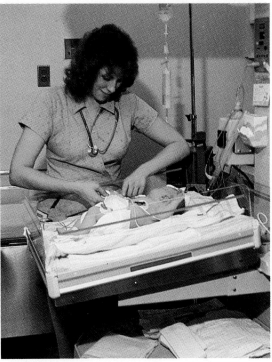

Specialized medical care must be given to babies that are born too early and/or too small.

Major Birth Defects

Defect	Description	Medical Care
Caused by inherited factors		
Cystic fibrosis	Malfunctioning of pancreas; frequent respiratory infection	Detected by sweat and blood tests; treatment of respiratory and digestive problems
Down's syndrome (mongolism)	Mental retardation with some physical defects (chromosomal abnormality)	Detected by amniocentesis; treatment by corrective surgery, special training
Hemophilia	Blood clotting malfunction (even minor cuts result in extensive bleeding)	Detected by blood tests; treatment by injection of clotting factor
Huntington's chorea	Mental and physical deterioration, death	Appears in middle age; treated by special medication
Phenylketonuria (PKU)	Body cannot use food to create essential amino acid; can cause mental retardation	Detected by blood test at birth; treatment by diet with missing amino acid
Sickle-cell anemia	Malformed red blood cells deprived of oxygen; affects persons of African background	Detected by blood tests; treated by blood transfusions
Tay-Sachs disease	Enzyme deficiency resulting in mental retardation; affects Jewish persons of Eastern European background	Detected by blood and tear tests, amniocentesis; no treatment
Caused by environmental factors		
Congenital rubella syndrome	Infection of mother by German measles causes heart defect, deafness, brain damage in child	Prevented by rubella vaccine. Detected by antibody tests; treatment by corrective surgery, physical therapy
Congenital syphilis	Infection of mother by syphilis results in multiple abnormalities in and infection of child	Detected by blood test, examination at birth; treatment by special medication
Caused by inherited and/or environmental factors		
Diabetes mellitus	Insulin deficiency; excess sugar in blood; weight loss	Detected by blood and urine tests; treatment by special diet, insulin
Low birthweight/prematurity	Birthweight under 5½ pounds (2.5 kilograms); immature body structures make survival difficult	Prevented by proper prenatal care. Detected by examination at birth; treatment by intensive care
Rh disease	Antibodies in blood of Rh negative mother destroy blood of Rh positive baby; loss of oxygen causes mental retardation, death	Prevented by Rh vaccine. Detected by blood test; treated by blood transfusion

Mothers of all races, ages, and income levels may give birth to low-birth-weight infants. However, studies indicate that low-birth-weight babies may occur more frequently among mothers who are fifteen and under, mothers who are poorly nourished or have health problems, and mothers who smoke, drink, or take drugs. Teenage mothers are more likely to have high-risk infants. Mothers in this age group are often undernourished and cannot provide proper nutrition for their unborn children. At the same time a mother must provide nourishment for the growing fetus, she must meet the nutritional needs of her own growing body. The notion that a baby will take what it needs from its mother is true only if the nutrients are there to be taken.

Infants with Birth Defects The National Foundation of the March of Dimes defines birth defects as mistakes in body formation or function that occur as an unborn child develops. They may be caused by heredity, by disease, or by something unknown that happens to an infant while it is growing inside the mother's womb. Sometimes, heredity and environment may work together to produce the defect. All defects are not necessarily apparent at birth; some defects cause problems later on in a child's life. The March of Dimes estimates that some 60,000 children die yearly as a result of birth defects.

For Review

1. How do the roles of husband and wife change when the couple has a baby?
2. What are the three stages of prenatal development?
3. Why should a pregnant woman avoid drugs unless a doctor prescribes them?

What is the role of the father during labor and delivery?

Childbirth

An average pregnancy lasts about 280 days. At this point, the infant usually is ready to take over its own life functions from the mother. Labor refers to the work the woman performs in giving birth to a child. As a result of uterine contractions, the infant separates from the mother's body to begin functioning independently.

Normal Delivery

There are three stages involved in labor. The first stage, sometimes called the cervical stage or the dilation stage, is usually the longest. During this preparatory period, the uterine contractions completely open, or dilate, the *cervix,* which is the opening in the uterus through which the baby will pass. The cervix must dilate to nearly 4 inches (10 cm) before it is large enough for the baby to go through. The uterine contractions are totally involuntary; the mother cannot control them. However, she can ease the discomfort by relaxing and concentrating on different breathing patterns.

During the later part of cervical dilation, the physician may give the mother a mild pain-controlling drug. It is given sparingly and close to the time of birth because the drug can also affect the baby. Drugs given in large doses or administered too soon may cause the baby to be born sluggish; the child would then have difficulty in beginning to breathe. Pain-controlling drugs also reduce the mother's ability to help during delivery. For these reasons, some mothers prefer to have no drugs at all during childbirth.

Birth is the second stage of labor. It extends from the time the cervix is completely dilated until the moment when the baby is independent of the mother's body. First, *crowning* occurs: the baby's scalp appears. Babies usually are born headfirst. Doctors must offer greater assistance when a child is delivered buttocks first, or in the *breech* position.

During the third and final stage of labor, the *afterbirth* separates and is expelled. The afterbirth is the placenta and the amniotic sac with its surrounding membrane. This stage of labor usually occurs within twenty minutes of the baby's birth.

Caesarean Delivery

In approximately five percent of births, a normal delivery may not be safe for the mother or for the child. A mother may have an adverse health condition, such as diabetes or toxemia, which can affect the birth. The cervix may not dilate at all, or it may not open up enough for the baby to pass through.

During labor, a common hospital procedure is to attach a device to the mother's abdomen that measures both the infant's heart rate and the intensity of the uterine contractions. This *fetal monitoring* may detect problems as the labor and delivery progress.

Physicians perform a *Caesarean section* when normal delivery is considered dangerous or impossible. They deliver the baby through a surgical incision in the mother's abdominal wall and uterus. The mother's recovery usually takes longer after a Caesarean section than after a normal birth.

To determine whether a Caesarean section is needed, physicians use a "picture" of what is going on inside the womb. Instead of using X-rays, which can harm the fetus, doctors in some hospitals can now use a recently developed technique called *ultrasound*. High-frequency sound waves, reflecting off the body, form pictures of the body's interior on a monitor, similar to the way that sonar detects depths or objects in the ocean. When doctors have an idea of how the cervix is dilating and are aware of the position and size of the fetus, they can decide what action to take. Ultrasound also aids in pregnancy diagnosis. It shows whether a pregnancy is progressing normally and if there will be multiple births.

The Hospital Stay After Delivery

Hospital-care arrangements for mothers and newborns may differ from one hospital to the next. Care usually takes one of two forms, traditional care or rooming-in.

Traditional Care Under traditional arrangements, the pediatric nurses in the infant nursery of the maternity ward usually care for the newborn. If the mother had a particularly difficult delivery or is in poor health, this option might be the most desirable. Generally, babies are brought to their mothers' rooms at feeding time. If a mother feels strong enough, she can usually have her baby brought in at other times as well.

Rooming-in In this arrangement, mother and baby are cared for in the same room. Many hospitals now make this option available. According to some experts, rooming-in has the following advantages:

- The mother can observe her baby constantly, thus providing greater security for the newborn.

- Babies seem more content and cry less.

- Parents can become acquainted with their infant while having medical personnel to reassure and guide them.

- Parents develop confidence in caring for their infant.

- Fathers have the opportunity to play a significant role in child care right from the beginning.

- The bond between infant and parents begins to develop immediately.

Postpartum Care

Depending on the individual institution, women generally stay in the hospital for 2 to 3 days with a normal delivery and 5 to 7 days with a Ceasarean Section. During their stay, women

This new mother is giving her baby a careful inspection.

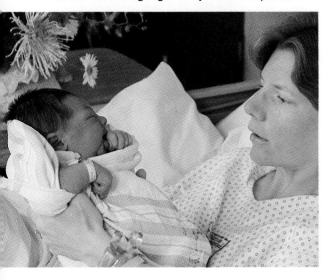

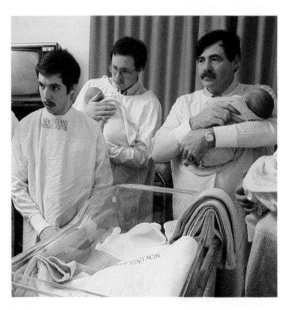

Many hospitals have classes for new fathers. Here they learn how to feed, bathe, and diaper infants.

rest and recover from the delivery of the baby. They learn self-care routines as well as many routines for caring for their new baby. Classes in bathing and feeding the baby are given in most hospitals. If a woman chooses to breast-feed, often the doctor or nurse will let the woman put the baby to breast immediately after birth. This action stimulates the woman's body to secrete the hormones that signal the release, or let-down, of milk. *Lactation* is the term used to describe the woman's production of milk. Many doctors encourage breast feeding because of the advantages it gives both the baby and the mother.

For Review

1. Why do some mothers prefer not to have drugs during childbirth?
2. What can doctors learn from the process of fetal monitoring?
3. What is the difference between traditional care and rooming-in for new mothers in the hospital?

8 Chapter Review

Summary

Parenthood greatly alters the relationship of a couple. Their roles and responsibilities change as they struggle to meet the demands of a newborn. Prenatal classes provide parents-to-be with essential information about pregnancy, prenatal development, childbirth, and infant care. An understanding of prenatal development is important so that parents may protect their unborn child. Since the embryo is especially vulnerable to viruses, radiation, and chemicals, a mother must avoid all harmful substances whenever possible. Proper nutrition and prenatal care also help to ensure the health of both mother and child.

During normal childbirth, a mother proceeds through three stages of labor. If a normal delivery becomes dangerous or impossible, a baby can be delivered by Caesarean section. Hospital care for newborns includes either traditional care or rooming-in arrangements. Many couples prefer rooming-in so that they may care for their newborn shortly after birth.

Vocabulary

Match each of the vocabulary words with one of the definitions that follow.

amniotic sac
embryo
fetus
placenta
prenatal
rubella
toxemia
umbilical cord
uterus
zygote

1. _____ cell formed from the joining of the female egg cell and the male sperm cell
2. _____ disease that is associated with birth defects if contracted during pregnancy
3. _____ occurring before birth
4. _____ carries nourishment to the unborn child and wastes to the placenta
5. _____ disease characterized by kidney malfunction and a subsequent buildup of fluid in the body
6. _____ the fertilized egg implants itself onto the wall of this organ
7. _____ unborn child during the second stage of prenatal development in which essential body systems and organs are formed
8. _____ organ that takes oxygen and nutrients from the mother's blood and removes wastes from the unborn child
9. _____ protective membrane surrounding the unborn child
10. _____ unborn child during the final stage of prenatal development, characterized by the growth and development of all body parts.

Chapter Questions

1. Name four of the pressures that may influence a couple to have a child before they are ready.
2. In what ways might having a child bring a couple together? How might parenthood drive some couples apart?
3. What are the costs that are involved in raising a child?
4. What benefits arise from a husband sharing prenatal classes with his wife?
5. What can new parents do to prepare for their new 24-hour-a-day responsibility?
6. Why should a woman visit her doctor as soon as she thinks she is pregnant?
7. How does eating a balanced diet benefit a mother during pregnancy?
8. Why is alcohol consumption particularly risky for a pregnant woman?
9. High-risk infants are born more frequently to which groups of mothers?
10. What is a Caesarean section and why would it be used?
11. What takes place during the postpartum period in the hospital?

Skill Activities

1. Reading Research the modern methods of childbirth (labor and delivery) in recent magazines and journals. Locate the titles of related articles in *Reader's Guide* to periodicals. After reading three or four magazine articles, prepare a brief written report in which you describe some of the childbearing options that are available to today's parents.

2. Math With a partner, determine the average cost of having a child. Begin by forming a list of all the services and items a newborn will need in the following categories: medical care (doctor and hospital expenses), food, health care products, clothing and bedding, and furniture and baby equipment (stroller, backpack, carseat). To find these costs, talk to new parents, consult store catalogs, and/or visit stores. Your public library has resources that list the average costs of prenatal, childbirth, and infant medical care.

Once you have gathered your data, figure the total dollar amounts in each category. Then compute the overall total. With your partner, decide which costs are absolutely necessary and which could be eliminated. What steps could a couple take to keep these costs down? When you have prepared your findings, present an oral report to your class.

3. Critical Thinking With four or five other students, participate in a group discussion that focuses on how the media portray men as role models and fathers. Think of television shows in which men (fathers, neighbors, coaches, teachers) interact with children. List all of the qualities that the characters exhibit. Then discuss how these qualities might negatively or positively affect a child's development.

9 Growing and Learning

As you read, think about:

- how parental nurturing affects infant development.
- how infant behavior brings responses from parents.
- why young children are self-centered.
- how parents can help young children understand and deal with feelings.

Children learn more in the first five years of life than they will in the rest of their lifetimes. They learn how to walk and talk and how to use language. This chapter describes the physical, emotional, intellectual, and social development of children during the first few years of life.

VOCABULARY

nurturing
bonding
reflex
fontanel
motor abilities
sensory abilities
toddlers
peer interactions

Development of the Parent-Infant Bond

"You can't pay anyone to do what a mother will do for free." This Russian proverb refers to the care and sacrifices most parents willingly provide to meet their children's needs. Yet what, exactly, are these needs? Food, clothing, and shelter have long been considered the basic human needs, but providing just these is not enough. History and research indicate that love and **nurturing,** or the physical expression of loving care, are equally vital to a child's development and growth. A strong parent-infant bond, or close emotional attachment, is high on the list of a child's essential needs.

In the thirteenth century, a German emperor decided to find out what language would be spoken by children who grew up never hearing speech. The emperor arranged for foster mothers to care for orphaned infants. Although the foster mothers fed and bathed the children, they did not speak to them or coo over them. The project was a failure; not only did the children never talk, but they all died at an early age.

Recently, researchers conducted a study of premature infants who had to be taken from their mothers and placed in incubators at birth. A higher than normal number "failed to thrive" once they were taken home. They did not grow, gain weight, or develop patterns of behavior at a normal rate during their first few months.

Studies seem to confirm the idea that parents who are not allowed to care for their babies from the start are more likely to experience feelings of inadequacy or guilt once they bring their babies home. Perhaps this is one reason why some of these parents are unable to be as nurturing as their babies require.

Parental Attachment

Research reveals that the first few hours after birth are important to the development of **bonding,** a mother's attachment to her infant.

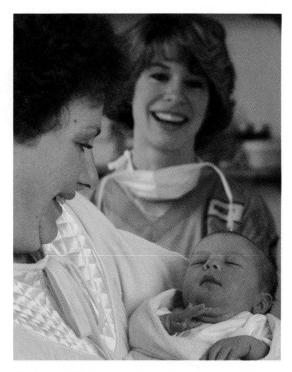

The parent-infant bond has been shown to be a crucial factor in a baby's physical and mental growth.

(Little research has been done on bonding between fathers and infants, but psychologists believe that the same pattern probably exists.) Immediately after birth, the infant tends to be quiet and alert. This calm, wakeful state makes the first few hours an ideal time for parents and infants to get acquainted with each other. When held close, newborns will look at their parents' faces. This behavior seems to attract parents and keep them attentive.

Although newborns do not really smile, their smile-like expressions are also intriguing to parents. The "smiling" suggests that the infant is happy and content. The **reflex** of grasping, a response that occurs automatically when parents insert a finger into the palm of the baby's hand, tends to interest and involve parents.

When parents sense that their babies are responding to them, they derive more pleasure from caring for them. This pattern works to the advantage of both parent and child: the more

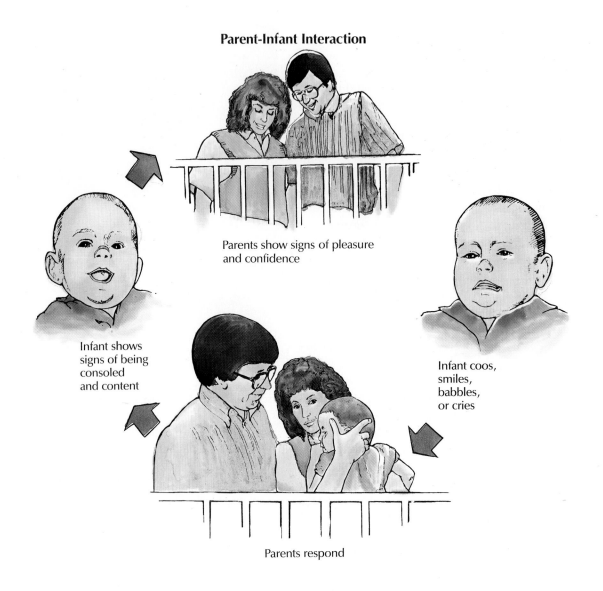

Parent-Infant Interaction

Parents show signs of pleasure and confidence

Infant shows signs of being consoled and content

Infant coos, smiles, babbles, or cries

Parents respond

parents do for a baby, the more he or she responds to the parents. The more the baby responds, the more the parents want to do.

All of an infant's positive responses to parents' actions and reactions affect the parents' growing love. Since babies often coo and babble when they are happy, parents are likely to imitate their baby's sounds. This starts an interchange of mimicry that delights parents and baby alike.

Picking up and holding a crying infant usually makes the infant quiet and content. This response in turn makes parents feel successful. Since many infant cries result from hunger, holding and feeding satisfy both baby and parents. Close contact strengthens the bond between them. The parents become more confident each time they successfully console their child. This confidence and strength is needed at times when a child is extremely upset or ill.

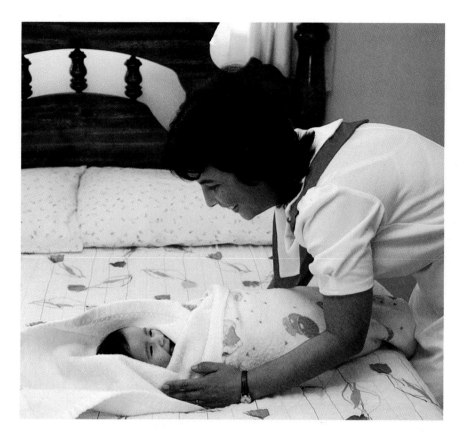

An infant's need for love is as strong as his need for food, warmth and protection.

Infant Attachment

Parents' attachment to their infants becomes the basis for infants' attachment to their parents through the process of interaction. In the early months of life, when the infant cries, smiles, or moves, the parents react by cuddling, talking, smiling, changing, or feeding the child. In turn, the infant responds with contentment and satisfaction.

An important source of babies' attachment to their parents is recognition. Infants gradually learn to distinguish their parents from others and recognize their parents as the people who supply pleasure, love, and care.

By the time an infant is four or five months old, he or she has usually developed a strong attachment to one or both parents. For this reason, parents may find their infant will put up a major fuss if they try to leave the infant with a babysitter. Researchers have identified the following characteristics of infant love:

- The infant is more likely to go willingly to a parent than to anyone else.

- A parent can soothe and calm the infant more easily than can anyone else.

- The infant shows less anxiety in new or different situations when a parent is present.

A parent can provide a constant source of support and security for an infant. This sense of security gives babies the courage to explore their surroundings and master new skills. Studies show that parental comforting does not make babies more dependent and helpless, but actually serves to increase their growth toward independence. Most children with supportive, encouraging parents develop confidence as they grow through infancy and childhood.

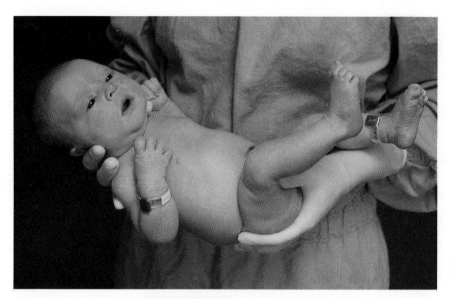

The physical appearance of a newborn baby may surprise or even alarm first-time parents.

Infant Characteristics

An infant, or newborn baby, may seem like a package of mysteries to first-time parents. Once parents begin to care for their new baby, they become familiar with infant characteristics and routines.

Physical Characteristics

Newborn babies are not as cute as many parents expect them to be. Small and wrinkled, they seem oddly shaped. The skin may be red and blotchy. The head may be cone shaped for a day or two from the pressure of delivery. The abdomen looks rounded, even distended. Arms and legs appear stick-like in contrast to the head, which is one-fourth the size of the total length. The average birth weight is about 7½ pounds, and the length is about 20–21 inches.

The **fontanel** is a soft spot on top of the newborn's head. It is the space that allows for movement of the bones during birth. It closes as the bones grow together by the time a child is two years old.

Babies are born with blue eyes. It takes several weeks for the true color to develop. Puffiness of the eyes results from natural pressure during birth. Swelling usually goes down in a day or two, giving the baby a more normal appearance.

Newborns have varying amounts of hair on their bodies. Some have soft down on their heads, others have coarse hair over their shoulders and down their spines. Both patterns are normal and usually rub off soon after birth.

What Infants Can Do

Newborns have many basic abilities. They breathe, cry, swallow and digest food. They spit up, cough, and eliminate waste products. Their senses enable them to smell, taste, hear, see, and feel. They begin interacting with the environment immediately upon birth.

Reflexes All newborns have reflexes that function to protect them. These last until voluntary movements are learned, at about 3 months of age. If you gently stroke a baby's cheek, he will turn his head in the direction of your finger and open his mouth. This *rooting reflex* occurs because he is searching for the mother's breast to begin feeding. Also, every baby is born with the reflex to suck. Whenever something is put in their mouths, babies begin to suck.

Hold a newborn upright underneath the arms, let his feet touch a firm surface, and he will move his legs in a walking or stepping motion. This *walking reflex* functions as encouragement to stand upright and walk.

A newborn baby automatically tightens his fingers around anything that is pressed into the palm of his hand. This *grasping reflex* is so strong that immediately after birth he can support his whole weight by grasping on to your fingers.

Infants react to stimuli with their entire bodies. Hearing a loud noise, or being handled roughly causes newborns to throw out their arms and legs. The fingers are outstretched like an attempt to catch something. As the limbs slowly fall back toward the body, knees bend and fists are clenched. This entire set of movements is the *startle reflex.*

Caring for your Infant

Babies are totally dependent. At first, a baby's needs can seem overwhelming. Parents must provide food, clothing, comfort, and love. As parents get to know their babies, they adjust to the demands of infant care.

Feeding

One of the decisions a mother must make is whether or not to breastfeed her baby. Many women choose breastfeeding because breast milk helps babies build immunities against allergies and many diseases. This method is also popular because it is very convenient. Some mothers prefer to bottle feed their babies. Commercial formulas supply the recommended nutrients and come in a variety of forms requiring differing amounts of preparation.

Whether a mother gives a baby her own milk (Left) or formula (Right), feeding time is satisfying for both a mother and child.

Daily Schedule

An infant's schedule for the first six weeks of life includes periods for feeding, sleeping, bathing, and playing.

Since each baby is unique, there is no such thing as an ideal schedule for a baby. Some pediatricians suggest that parents steer their baby toward scheduled feeding and nap times. Others say it is more important for parents to be flexible. For example, some babies cry to be fed every two hours. Other babies take four hour naps. By the time a baby is three months old, she will be on a more predictable schedule.

Different Kinds of Cries It is normal for babies to cry. Crying is the way an infant communicates her needs. Babies cry when they are hungry, wet, tired, too hot, too cold, or overstimulated. Many babies have a fussy period at the end of the day just because they need to let off steam. The immediate reaction to a baby's cry should be to respond to it. This reassures the infant that someone is paying attention to him. Failure to respond may cause both short- and long-term distress. A baby may swallow air

What is your reaction when you hear an infant crying? Since crying expresses a need, the best reaction is to respond to it.

when he cries, which causes discomfort and makes feeding difficult. Prolonged crying may exhaust a baby, causing irritability and difficulty in soothing him. Over time, if parents do not respond to a baby's cries, the infant may learn that his needs are not important. This parental apathy can make it difficult for the child to form deep, loving relationships. Once parents know what different cries mean, they can cope with this part of infant behavior. Each baby has his own crying "language." One infant, for example, may have a whiny, halfhearted cry when bored. Another baby might have a frantic, high-pitched cry if in pain. Most parents quickly become familiar with their baby's different kinds of cries, especially the hunger cry since it is heard so often.

Adjusting to Infant Care

Before parents take a baby home from the hospital, they usually meet with their physician, who answers any questions they may have. As soon as parents take over complete responsibility for the care of their infant, they rapidly learn to interpret their baby's needs. Getting to know their baby so that they may respond confidently to his or her needs is probably the most difficult part of infant care for most parents.

Time and Energy Requirements

Bringing a baby home usually is a joyful occasion. It is also a time when parents are apt to be tired. Hospital maternity wards are seldom restful, quiet places, and the excitement surrounding the birth is exhausting in itself. Nevertheless, bringing a newborn home is not a restful experience, either. The newborn rarely sleeps through the night during the first few weeks, and regardless of how tired parents are, they must meet the baby's needs, sometimes at the expense of their own.

In order to make things easier for themselves, some parents adjust their schedules so they can rest when the baby sleeps. Sharing the responsibility for the care of the newborn can help, too. In addition, having someone to help out at home for a few days after the baby comes home may ease the adjustment.

Social and Emotional Factors

Research indicates that the first stage of parenthood can involve a high amount of stress. Some researchers have even described the transition into parenthood as a crisis because of the intensity and number of changes that occur when a child joins a family. The mother is very focused on the daily needs of the infant. When she is not caring for the baby, she must care for herself. It is important for a new mother to rest and eat well, especially if she is breastfeeding the baby. Unfortunately, a husband often feels neglected because his wife is so busy caring for herself and the baby. To promote good feelings between the new parents, the father should take over some of the baby's care. The couple will feel closer because they share an involvement with their baby.

Shared Parenting

Throughout history, fathers have not been very involved in child care. This tendency has given rise to the notion that they should not or cannot handle the responsibility. Today, the view that fathers are unable or reluctant to care for their children is beginning to change. Studies show that fathers, if given the opportunity, become as emotionally involved as mothers and are just as capable. Fathers today are often present at the birth of their child and develop an attachment to the baby right from the start. Babies also become attached to their fathers.

Sharing child-raising responsibilities helps fathers learn more about the development of their children. They and their children become

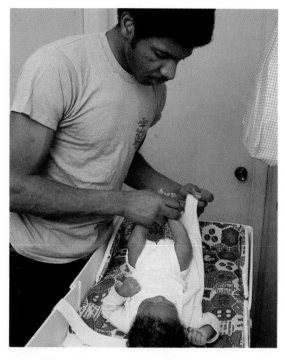

Today fathers are more involved in child care than in the past. How does this affect the family?

better acquainted. Fathers who actively participate in child care have the potential to develop strong and satisfying parent-child relationships. One study reported that in play situations with both parents present, eight-month-old infants sought out their fathers.

Shared parenting also can provide each parent with a chance to relax, away from children. Some parents have found it helpful to plan a regular time each week when one parent takes charge of the children so that the other is able to enjoy some free time.

Perhaps the most comforting aspect of shared parenting is the mutual help, understanding, and support that each partner can give the other. Parents who support one another can provide more consistent and effective child guidance. When parents are able to talk over child-raising difficulties, problems can seem a lot easier to solve.

Development in the First Year

As children proceed through childhood, their development follows predictable patterns. For example, babies usually creep before they stand, and stand before they walk. If parents understand the common developmental trends or patterns, they know what to expect when their own children reach certain ages and stages. Parents who expect too much may put undue pressure on their children to succeed. Parents who expect too little may be overprotective. Parents should always remember that there is a wide range of ages at which children "normally" do certain things.

Physical Development

A child's rate of development can be affected by the type of care he or she receives. Proper food and rest are essential to supply the energy a child needs for continued growth. Plenty of exercise is also vital for growth.

Growth During the first twelve months of life, healthy infants grow very rapidly. Infants often triple their birth weight by the time they are one year old. At birth the brain contains all the nerve cells it will ever have — about 100 billion. However, the central nervous system continues to develop until about age two. Cells that supply and support the brain cells continue to grow, and the brain becomes larger. Development of an insulating sheath, or covering, for some nerve fibers also occurs in the first two years. Insulation of nerve fibers permits them to conduct activity more rapidly. As a result, other abilities develop. Because of this rapid growth, adequate nutrition is highly important to a baby's health.

Motor Abilities In addition to weight gain and brain development, a rapid increase in **motor abilities,** or the coordination needed to

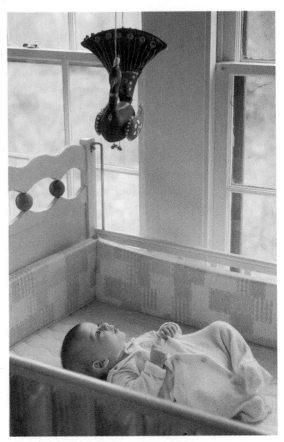

A four-month-old infant enjoys looking at a brightly colored mobile above her crib.

perform various skills, occurs during an infant's first year. At birth, infants cannot lift their heads or roll over. By six months, however, many can sit up. At one year, most children can manage to get around on their own. Some still crawl on their hands and knees. Others walk along holding on to furniture, or with someone holding their hand. Still others can walk by themselves. No two babies develop at exactly the same rate.

Learning Through Sensory Abilities

In most cases, infants are born with all their **sensory abilities** working; they can see, taste, feel, hear, and smell. It is through their five

When placed on his tummy, a three-month-old infant can lift his chest and head.

What sensory abilities are stimulated when an infant crawls through the grass?

Learning how to walk is part of a toddler's move toward independence.

A child who wants to be independent is determined to feed himself, even if that means making a mess.

Motor Development

 **1 month**
Chin up

 2 months
Chest up

 **3 months**
Reach and miss

 **4 months**
Sit with support

 **5 months**
Sit on lap, grasp object

 **6 months**
Sit in high chair, grasp dangling objects with palms

 **7 months**
Sit alone

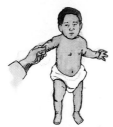 **8 months**
Stand with help

 **9 months**
Stand holding furniture

 **10 months**
Creep

 **11 months**
Walk when led

 **12 months**
Pull up on furniture to stand

 **13 months**
Climb stair steps

 **14 months**
Stand alone

 **15 months**
Walk alone

senses that children learn about the world starting in their first year of life.

Sight Babies can see at birth, and from the first day of life they show interest in their world. Some objects appear to interest them more than others. According to some studies, newborns, when they are held, spend most of their time looking at an adult's face. Babies even enjoy looking at photographs or drawings of human faces. Naturally, they enjoy their parents' faces most of all. Besides being highly responsive, the human face has contrasting colors, which babies find fascinating. A checkerboard design of black and white will also keep an infant visually interested for a long time. A baby between three and seven weeks of age most likely will focus on your eyes when cradled in your arms. However, if you hold the baby away from you, the baby's eyes may stray. This reaction probably results from the fact that infants under two months seem to have a fixed focus about eight inches from their eyes.

As babies get a little older, they enjoy looking at brightly colored or moving objects. For example, a four month old might enjoy staring at the animal mobile hung over the crib. Babies who spend most of their waking hours in a crib looking at the ceiling are limited in their learning opportunities. Parents can give their baby more interesting things to see and learn about by moving the infant to different rooms, or by placing the baby near a window, preferably in a sturdy infant seat away from drafts and strong sun. Infants enjoy watching the movements of patterned curtains or swaying tree branches.

Taste From the first day of life, a baby begins to learn that sucking results in a satisfying feeling. Babies use their mouths and their sense of taste to explore the world. Throughout the first year and into the second, babies will put everything that comes within their grasp into their mouths. Therefore, playthings should have rounded edges. They should also be washable, and too big to swallow. Parents should keep tiny objects out of a baby's reach, and check all toys for small parts that might come off.

Feeling Newborn infants react to the prick of a needle when given a blood test after birth. This indicates that at birth they are sensitive to the sensation of pain. As babies grow, they become sensitive to temperature and textures.

The sense of touch may be important in helping babies develop feelings of security. Parents know that a baby usually stops crying when picked up and held. Studies also show that picking up and holding an infant upright against the parent's shoulder serves to make the infant content and alert. While many parents fear they will "spoil" their infant by picking him or her up each time the infant cries, researchers have observed that the contrary can often be true. The babies of parents who were most responsive to their

Safety Tip

To keep a baby safe from household accidents:

- Never leave a baby alone on a high place such as a bed; keep crib sides up so the baby cannot roll out.

- Keep stairs and walkways well-lit and clutter-free to remove danger of tripping while carrying a baby.

- When a baby begins crawling, put up safety gates or lock doors leading to dangerous areas or stairs.

- Never leave a baby alone in the bathtub. The baby could be scalded by hot tap water, slip and fall, or even drown.

- Keep sharp objects such as scissors, razor blades, and pins out of reach.

cries in the first year cried less and less during that year. The babies of parents who did not pick them up each time they cried tended to cry more often and for longer periods.

Hearing Researchers have noted that parents of newborns tend to talk to their babies in high-pitched voices. Interestingly, newborns seem to respond most often to high sounds. Sounds can soothe babies, too. An infant might go to sleep or be quieted by the sound of a music box or the singing of a lullaby.

Babies make their own sounds during the first year, too. In the first few months of life, they seem to take pleasure in hearing their own voices. When they are older, they may enjoy playing sound games with their parents. When parents mimic a baby's babbling, the baby may repeat the same sounds again.

Sounds play an important part in a baby's learning process. Infants soon learn to recognize the sound of approaching footsteps, and they react to the reassuring sound of a familiar voice. Talking to an infant is one of the best ways to keep him or her alert. It also lays the groundwork for speech development, as the baby attempts to repeat parents' words. Many experts recommend that parents talk to their children during all contact with them, such as during bath time and diaper changing. It makes little difference what they say, but the tone of voice and facial expressions are important. It is from these sounds that a baby senses feelings. During the first year of life, babies need to learn that they can trust their parents to provide care, love, and attention.

Smell There has been little research on the infant's sense of smell. Yet, researchers have observed that newborn babies react to unpleasant and strong odors by turning their heads away and altering their breathing rhythms. Research has also shown that babies react positively to certain smells, such as the smell of their mothers' breast milk.

Toddlers are very curious about their environment. Removing everything from a drawer is simply their way of exploring.

Development in the Second Year

During the second year, children's personalities continue to develop. Children often express their wants more forcefully. Language skills develop in young children as they try to understand and control their world.

Physical Development

By twelve months, many children can toddle, or walk along in short, uncertain steps. **Toddlers** develop in other ways as well that make them better able to explore the world around them.

Growth and Appetite During the second year, children's growth rates slow down. A child who ate most foods during infancy may

Toddlers usually play beside each other rather than with each other. This is called parallel play.

These children are excited by the colors and textures of poster paints.

A sand box is one place a toddler can entertain himself for a long period of time.

During the "Terrible Twos" parents begin to set limits. Often these limits are for the child's safety.

now show less interest in eating. As growth rates slow, children develop smaller appetites. With such small appetites, toddlers can easily fill up on sweets and snack foods and not be hungry at mealtime. It is therefore important that everything they eat be nutritious. A variety of foods, served in small portions, will help ensure an adequate diet.

Motor Abilities Motor coordination improves greatly during the second year. An awkward walk becomes smoother and sometimes turns into an awkward run. Climbing becomes a new skill for young children.

Toddlers use both hands to carry, push, and pull, and they enjoy activities that require the use of their whole bodies. For example, a two year old might feel proud and competent about being able to carry a giant stuffed animal around the house.

Because motor abilities increase at a rapid rate, a toddler's enthusiasm for trying out new skills, such as climbing, may sometimes prove

Safety Tip

To prevent burns:

- Never leave a young child alone in the house.

- Check materials used in clothing and blankets for flammability.

- Keep matches away from children.

- When cooking, turn pot handles toward the back of the stove.

- Keep hot liquids and foods and hot electrical equipment such as irons or coffee pots out of reach.

- To protect a young child from hot grease or food spills, do not let the child wander in the kitchen during meal preparation.

dangerous. Parents need to be aware of the potential hazards in the environment as toddlers develop new motor abilities. At the same time, parents should encourage their children and express interest and pride in their progress. These attitudes promote toddlers' efforts and give needed reassurance.

Learning

A child's second year of life is very different from the first, since the child is now able to move around and use some language. Suddenly, the toddler finds all kinds of new and interesting objects within reach. People begin to understand his or her words.

Exploration Toddlers seem to have boundless energy; fatigue, when it sets in, is about the only thing that can stop their activity. At this age, children are constantly on the go, busy learning about their world, or as some people say, "always into something." Toddlers are full of curiosity. With few things off limits to them because of their growing abilities, they reach for more and more objects. As they explore, they find great joy in taking things out, off, or apart. Finding out how to do things is a constant source of entertainment.

Parents sometimes regard toddlers' curiosity and exploratory activities as deliberate mischief and may severely restrict them for this reason. Nevertheless, these activities are a necessary part of a child's learning process. It is an adult's job to provide safe opportunities for the toddlers to explore. For safety reasons, areas such as medicine cabinets definitely should be off limits, and sharp or breakable objects should be out of a child's reach. On the other hand, areas such as cabinets full of pots and pans can provide worthwhile places for investigation. Young children need freedom in which to explore and learn.

Toddlers are willing to try almost anything they see other family members do. Their efforts often exceed their abilities. Cries of

The King of Playgrounds

It is a Sunday evening in April, 1985, in the small town of Mount Vernon, Iowa. A swarm of kids whoop and holler as they bounce on a rubber bridge, skid down a twisting slide, and scamper up some castle turrets. Their parents and several hundred other adults, all wearing big grins, look on. These people have just completed building a playground. The children had a share in designing it. The whole neighborhood helped: raising money, lending tools and equipment, and collecting lumber, old tires, and other materials to use in its construction.

This is no amateurish job, however. The multi-leveled wooden structure is both sturdy and handsome. It was designed and supervised by one of America's most talented architects—Robert Leathers, also known as the "King of Playgrounds."

Leathers has been designing playgrounds for over fifteen years. At first, he planned playgrounds as a nonprofit hobby, separate from his other architectural work. Now that he is commissioned to do over 60 playgrounds each year, in all sections of the country, their designs are part of his architectural practice.

All Leathers' playgrounds are built by community volunteers. Each is a unique structure, designed to fit its particular site, and each includes ideas suggested by the children who will use it. They are not only designed for active play, they also excite the children's imagination with special features like a huge, playful dragon whose tail forms a corkscrew slide.

Robert Leathers has always been interested in group projects. He suggests this may be true because he was an only child, who spent seventh grade alone at home, temporarily paralyzed from polio. His interest in architecture also began in his childhood when he built a series of tree houses in the woods that surrounded his home in Bangor, Maine. He has designed and supervised the building of over 350 playgrounds all over the country. He has also designed a play area for the two giant pandas given to the Washington National Zoo by the people of China. This wooden structure, also built by volunteers, was planned to resemble the cliffs and ledges of the mountains the pandas come from.

A community playground's construction begins with a twelve-hour day of planning. First Leathers meets with his "playground experts." Children of all ages discuss what they want in their playground. Mazes, forts, ships, or strange animals take shape in the architect's drawings. That evening he meets with parents and other members of the community for their approval of the drawings. Then fund-raising and organizing begin. All sorts of fund-raising events are planned: auctions, performances, raffles, and community dinners. Next, all the construction supplies are collected and volunteer workers are organized. The actual construction takes only four days. They are long, hectic, exhausting days. However, the entire neighborhood agrees it was all worth it when they see the kids race into the playground they all built together.

"Playground experts" give Robert Leathers some of the best ideas for his playground designs.

outrage and wild scattering of toys and papers usually indicate frustration. Parents need to provide toddlers with activities the children can handle successfully. The feeling that "I can do it" is a necessary element in building self-confidence.

Experimentation   Like infants, toddlers also learn a great deal through sensory experiences. They like to play with materials they can taste, feel, and take apart—things that make interesting items for experimentation. However, toys requiring delicate finger movements can be frustrating. Toddlers enjoy action toys as well as objects that move or make sounds because of something the toddler does. Mechanical toys are less satisfying to young children than those requiring efforts at manipulation, such as pull toys.

Social Interaction

In the second year, although children like playing with and near adults, especially parents, they also enjoy playing alone. A toddler's interest in other children is mainly one of curiosity, rather than social interaction. The ability to play with other children and to share comes later, as the child matures.

Toddlers need help in learning that others have feelings. Since they are highly possessive, "Mine!" is a characteristic shout. As they develop language, they also assert their will with others. "No-no" may be used as often by toddlers as parents.

Children enjoy costumes and dramatic play. This is one way they learn how to interact with others.

Development in the Preschool Years

Children's behavior changes rapidly during the preschool years, or between ages three and five. Just when parents think they understand their children, new and sometimes unexpected patterns of behavior appear.

Physical Development

Growth continues at a relatively slow rate throughout the preschool years. Children get taller and usually appear to be thinner than they were during their infant and toddler days. You may hear parents say that their children have lost their baby faces.

Learning

Young children depend almost totally on their past experiences to understand the present. They try to interpret new events by relating them to what they already know. As the quantity and variety of their experiences increase, their interpretations are likely to become more accurate.

> ### For Review
> 1. Describe the motor abilities of a healthy one-year-old child.
> 2. How can parents help their toddlers build confidence and independence?
> 3. Describe some ways to child-proof a house for a toddler.

Learning how to cooperate with other children is a skill preschoolers need to acquire.

As a child's coordination develops, he is able to enjoy activities such as cutting, drawing and pasting.

Picture books can stimulate a child's interest in learning how to read.

Why is outdoor play so important for children?

As children learn to use words to express their feelings they feel more confident.

Language Perception

Preschool children learn to understand their world through language. Their vocabularies increase rapidly as they grow. Simple sentences become more complex as children learn and practice basic grammar.

Long before children know enough words to explain their needs and wants, they communicate their desires through actions. Actions continue to be tools of communication during the preschool years. However, by imitating adults, children learn to use their voices instead of pushing or hitting when they are angry or upset. Language slowly becomes a new and useful way to express feelings, desires, and thoughts.

Children often misunderstand the meanings of familiar words when they hear them used in new situations. For instance, a four-year-old might think a dental record is something to play

"record" to the only meaning he or she knows

for that word. Meanings depend upon the ideas or images the words bring to mind. Parents can explain new meanings to a child as words occur. Interested adults who clarify experiences and word meanings can help their children develop new ideas, understandings, and language skills throughout the preschool years.

Preschool children cannot understand the differences between relationship terms. For example, they may identify most men as "daddies" to other children, and not understand that the same person can have many roles, for example, daddy, husband, brother, or uncle. Also, children interpret what you say literally. For instance, a young child who overhears her parents speaking of a neighbor with a "big mouth" would be confused to see that the neighbor's mouth was no larger than anyone else's. A three year old might look upwards in surprise when his mother exclaims, "Your father just hit the ceiling!"

Asking Questions

Preschoolers ask countless questions. "Why?" seems to be the response to nearly every adult statement. Answering their questions honestly in words and definitions they can understand helps young children learn about their world. When children are old enough to read, parents can help them discover that books can also answer their questions.

Sometimes, the best answer to a young child's question may be another question. "What do you think?" "What would happen if you did that?" These types of questions make children think for themselves. Questioning also helps children think through problems and develop their own solutions and ideas. Turning questions back to children has still another potential value. It can give a clue to a child's ability to think, plan, understand, and decide.

Object Perception Preschoolers need experience to be able to identify whether an object is big, little, light, or dark. Placing objects in order from big to little or from light to dark is an even more complex task. Preschoolers need opportunities to work with materials that are similar as well as with those that differ in color, size, shape, texture, and so forth. With the help of adults and with time and experience, preschoolers grow to understand relationships among different objects.

Social Interaction

During the preschool years, children's interest in other children grows. Instead of just playing beside or near other children, preschoolers want to have playmates. **Peer interactions,** or associations with persons of the same age, are important in the development of social skills. Under the guidance of interested adults, preschool children learn how to get along with children of their own age, as well as with other people.

Through interacting with their peers, young children learn that others also have rights and needs. This learning experience may take some time because young children tend to be "me" centered. This observation does not mean that children are selfish. Rather, they simply do not understand any viewpoint other than their own. Parents can help children see how their words and actions affect other people's feelings with comments such as "When you do that, I feel proud," or "When you behave like this, I feel sad." Children learn to show consideration when they understand how others feel.

To a very young child, sharing a toy probably means losing it. Only through experience and adult assistance do children learn that sharing can have positive results. They find that when they are considerate of other people's feelings and wants, the other people like and accept them. They also learn that sharing means "I get a turn, too." In time and through experiences with others, children learn consideration for others and develop the ability to delay their own immediate wants.

Emotions

Infants and toddlers cannot control their impulses. They show their feelings without considering either the feelings of others or the consequences of their actions. As children grow older, they must learn socially acceptable ways of expressing feelings. When parents show that they dislike the way children show their feelings, children may learn to deny those feelings. Parental messages such as "You don't hate me!" "Boys don't cry!" "Don't be afraid!" tell children that they should not feel angry, hurt, or fearful. As a result, children may feel guilty or rejected. Such messages do *not* make feelings disappear, nor do they help children learn to handle their feelings in more acceptable ways.

Recognizing emotions is the first step in dealing with them. Parents can help children find acceptable and comfortable methods to handle what they feel by saying something like "I know that you are angry with me, but I can't allow you to hit me," or by sharing their own happy and unhappy feelings with the children. Children need the chance to reflect on their feelings and to realize that all feelings — positive and negative — are "natural" and manageable.

When parents closely follow their children's rapid growth and changing abilities, parent-child interactions become more rewarding. Parents are better able to comprehend, accept, and direct a child's behavior in positive, growth-producing ways when they understand the child's changing abilities and emotions.

For Review

1. What is a good way to answer a pre-schooler's questions?
2. Why is it so hard for a toddler to share his or her toys with other children?
3. What is the first step in dealing with children's emotions?

9 Chapter Review

Summary

Bonding between parents and a newborn begins to develop soon after birth. The infant's positive responses to the parents' actions, reactions, and contact strengthen this bond.

A newborn's reflexes, sensory abilities, and other characteristics form the framework upon which all growth and development build. Infants become able to sit, crawl, and stand as their motor abilities develop. As toddlers become more active during their second year, they explore and learn from their environment. Preschoolers gain valuable new skills through their life experiences, questions, parent and peer interactions, and their progress in learning to express their emotions.

Parents who share the responsibilities of caring for their growing child can provide support and understanding to each other as well as more effective parenting to their child.

Vocabulary

Complete each of the following sentences with one of the vocabulary words below.

bonding
fontanel
motor abilities
nurturing
peer interaction
reflex
sensory abilities
toddler

1. The space on top of a newborn's head that allows the bones of the skull to move is called the _____.
2. Important to the development of social skills, _____ helps children learn how to get along with children their own age.
3. In newborns, the function of the _____ response is to protect them.
4. Although newborns do not see, hear, smell, taste, or feel as acutely as adults do, their _____ are functioning at birth.
5. A mother's developing attachment to her newborn is known as _____.
6. The active, inquisitive child in his or her second year is called a _____.
7. A rapid increase in _____ occurs during an infant's first year as muscle control and coordination develop.
8. The loving attention known as _____ is as important to a child's healthy development as the basic needs of food, clothing, or shelter.

Chapter Questions

1. In your opinion, what should hospitals do to promote the development of bonding between parents and their children?
2. Identify three characteristics of infant love.
3. Describe how the motor abilities of a newborn differ from those of a one-year-old.
4. What is the purpose of reflexes?
5. Why do many women choose to breastfeed their babies?

6. Why is it important for a parent to respond to a crying infant?

7. What strategies would you recommend to new parents who are struggling to meet the needs of an infant?

8. What are some of the advantages of shared parenting?

9. Which sensory ability seems to be most highly developed at birth? How do you know this?

10. Describe three specific activities and/or toys that are appropriate to a toddler's level of development.

11. Describe a situation in which a child misunderstands the meaning of familiar words used in a new way.

12. How do you think preschool children can be helped most to develop successful peer interactions?

Skill Activities

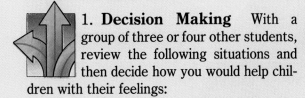

1. **Decision Making** With a group of three or four other students, review the following situations and then decide how you would help children with their feelings:

- A three-year-old is screaming outside of a toy store because he was not allowed to have a toy he wanted.

- Two four-year-olds are striking each other and pulling a toy back and forth between them.

- A toddler is jealous and angry over the arrival of a new baby.

Discuss how you would handle these situations. In what ways do you agree and/or disagree about the most effective way to help a child with these emotions? How do your solutions compare with those offered on page 167?

2. **Human Relations** Learn more about personality differences and the social development of toddlers through observation. To find children to observe, consider your own family, your friends' and neighbors' families, preschools and playgroups. Take notes as you watch children at play. Are there children who seem to be shy or withdrawn? Are there others who seem to be more outgoing? What are their interactions like? Can you see examples of parallel play? What happens when a conflict arises? Compile your notes into a brief written report.

3. **Communication** Create an illustrated poster designed to teach others how to react to a specific child-related emergency such as poisoning, burns, cuts and bites, choking, drowning, or electric shock. Refer to first-aid manuals, articles, and child care books for information. If possible, talk with a nurse, paramedic, or other health care professional for additional information. Present the facts you have gathered as clearly as possible. Use illustrations, photographs, drawings, and other visuals to attractively convey this knowledge.

10 Parenting

As you read, think about:

- how parents can meet the needs of children.
- how different parenting styles affect child behavior.
- why consistency in discipline is so important.
- what choices parents have when selecting child care settings for their children.

Being a parent means being responsible for the growth and development of the next generation—one of life's most important assignments. The responsibility for parenting begins as soon as a baby is born. It is an immediate and total commitment that sometimes produces a great deal of anxiety for new parents.

This chapter discusses children's needs and the ways in which parents can best meet those needs. As you read, you may wish to assess your own talents and capabilities to meet the demands of parenting. The chapter also deals with parents' needs and discusses styles of parenting and support systems for parents.

VOCABULARY

temperament
continuums
restrictiveness
family day care

Meeting Children's Needs

What are children's needs? The most obvious needs are physical. However, children have emotional needs, too. The needs for security, for being accepted, and for self-esteem are equally important in a child's development.

Physical Needs

The most basic needs of human beings are food, warmth, bodily comfort, and rest. Infants respond to a lack of these needs by crying. No amount of cuddling or rocking will quiet a hungry infant. On the other hand, if a three-month-old baby cries because of *colic* or digestive pain, a bottle alone will not stop the crying for long. The infant will stop crying only when the physical discomfort eases. Through trial and error, most parents learn to identify and meet their baby's needs most of the time.

Even as children get older, they continue to react intensely to hunger, cold, pain, and lack of sleep. They often start to "act up" around mealtime, naptime, and bedtime, showing their discomfort in a particular way. To meet their children's physical needs, parents can try to serve meals on time, dress children warmly, and see that their children get plenty of rest. At the same time, children learn that they can count on their parents to keep them feeling healthy and secure.

Emotional Needs

Children's emotional needs are less apparent than physical needs. How well they are met, however, will help to determine the quality of children's relationships and adjustments with other people throughout life.

Security Keeping a child physically well and comfortable builds the foundation for the child's security. Young children feel safe when they know that their parents or other protective adults are always there to help. When a parent

How can a parent provide for the emotional needs of a child?

leaves and a stranger approaches, very young children may feel abandoned and quite insecure and may cry in anger or fear.

As growing children meet new situations, parents can help maintain their children's sense of security in the following ways:

- Establish predictable daily routines.
- Prepare children for change by telling them what to expect.
- Introduce change slowly.
- Do what they say they will do (be consistent).
- Be there when children need them.

Most toddlers have a blanket or stuffed animal that adds to feelings of security, especially in unfamiliar territory.

Acceptance

Children need to be accepted for themselves. They need to know that others think they are fine just the way they are. When parents try to make a child act like someone else, they are telling the child, "You are not good enough."

Sometimes, parents say that a misbehaving child is bad. This term can make the child feel rejected. Children need to know they are loved all the time, regardless of their behavior. In reprimanding a child, parents need to say that it is not the child but the child's *behavior* they do not like. Parents can explain, "I love you, but I don't like the way you are acting."

Parents also should show when their children's efforts please them. When children try to help, parents should thank them. They can accept their children's best efforts even when they hoped the efforts would be better. Praise, hugs, or pats on the back let children know their parents enjoy them for who they are, not for what they may become.

Self-esteem

As soon as toddlers can move around on their own, they try very hard to accomplish many things, often wanting to do everything for themselves. Despite the difficulty of a task, they believe that they can succeed. "Me do it" becomes their motto. When these efforts meet with encouragement and pride, a child's self-confidence grows.

As children develop a sense of worth and capability, they welcome new challenges. They set and reach new goals. As a result, children

A toddler gets a big boost to his self-esteem the first time he dresses himself.

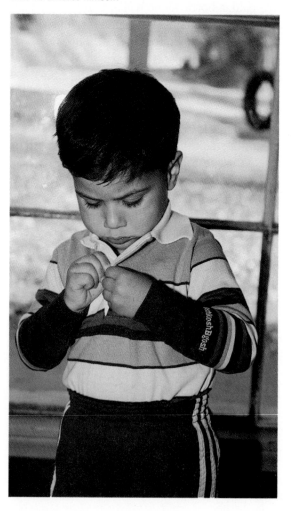

gain new skills, which foster independence. Parents can support children's initiative, or self-starting ability, by giving them opportunities for different kinds of activities. They may provide play materials such as clay, paints, or old clothes, and then encourage children to "experiment" with these materials, or use them creatively in their "make-believe." By recognizing and supporting children's interests, parents can help children further develop their self-confidence.

Children's sense of self-esteem—the opinions they have of their own worth—is based on a personal sense of adequacy and self-respect, and their knowledge that others respect them and recognize their abilities. Making fun of children or laughing at them destroys their self-esteem and their willingness to try again.

Understanding Children's Behavior

All behavior, or action, can be linked to specific causes. To analyze behavior, you must consider the child's basic **temperament,** or inborn characteristics, the situation or experience itself, and the emotions the child may be expressing through the behavior.

Sometimes, parents attempt to deal only with a child's actions, especially when the child is misbehaving. However, it is shortsighted for parents to try to modify actions without considering motives. In order to understand a child's behavior, parents must consider all aspects of his or her personality.

Temperament and Behavior

A child's behavior, in part, is a product of his or her temperament, or personality. Parental behavior and child-raising practices influence children's behavior, but even if parents treat children uniformly, individual children can behave quite differently.

How does this time with his father help to develop this child's self-esteem?

Infants' personalities show marked differences from birth. Researchers have identified a number of areas in which infants may differ. If you are aware of these differences in temperament, you can understand why children may behave differently when faced with similar situations. The following paragraphs describe some basic characteristics in which children can differ. Of course, most children fall between the two extremes of behavior mentioned in each category, and in any child, several of the basic characteristics probably are combined.

Some children are naturally active and outgoing while others are more quiet and shy.

Activity Children vary in activity level. Some children squirm, wiggle, and are always on the go. They show initiative in trying to master their world. Their active natures require close supervision to keep them safe. More passive children may seem content to sit quietly, showing little initiative. Neither type of child is "better" than the other — just different.

Regularity Children also vary in their degree of regularity. Some babies adjust to a regular eating and sleeping schedule within a short time after the birth. Their predictable nature makes it easy for parents to arrange their own routine around their baby's. Other babies never seem to get onto a schedule. Parents find it difficult to predict how long such babies will sleep, or how much or when they will eat.

Adaptability Children differ in their degree of adaptability. Some children meet new experiences, new foods, and new people with enthusiasm. They react positively and willingly to experiences that differ from ones they are used to. For other children, however, anything new or different is upsetting. These children at first resist new foods, shy away from strangers, and react negatively to new situations.

Adjusting to permanent change is harder than accepting an altered routine every now and then. Some children who initially resist change eventually adapt to it. Others may continue to cry and to be upset. Some children react positively and continue to accept change. Others, though positive at the beginning, may later want to return to the old ways of doing things.

Sensitivity Children's levels of sensitivity to the environment vary greatly. One couple explains that their son had such a low level of sensitivity, he would remain asleep if the house fell down around him. Another couple with a highly sensitive daughter declares that, as an infant, she woke up whenever the bathroom light switch was clicked on. Children's levels of sensitivity also affect their responses to changes in tastes, temperatures, and pain.

Mood Children differ in their moods. Some children are generally pleasant, smiling, and joyful. Others seem to fuss and cry a lot. These temperamental differences would obviously affect parents' feelings and behavior.

Ability to Concentrate Children differ in their ability to concentrate. Some children are easily distracted. They may be involved in an activity but quickly lose interest if something else happens. Children who do not distract easily sometimes tune out all efforts to refocus their attention. An activity may preoccupy them so much that they do not notice what is going on around them.

Persistence Children differ in the amount of time they devote to an activity that is difficult for them. Some children keep trying no matter how difficult the task or how many times they are interrupted. Others, less persistent, give up easily or with the first interruption.

Life Experiences and Behavior

In the long run, children's behaviors are products of both their personalities and their life experiences. As they grow and face new situations, children alter their behavior patterns. They learn new ways to handle feelings and situations. What are some of the ways in which children learn new behaviors?

Modeling Children learn from *modeling*— watching and imitating the behavior of others

Some children have the ability to concentrate on a task or game much longer than others.

very carefully. Observe a group of nursery school children at play to see how modeling operates. Much of their play involves imitating adult behavior. From observing others, young children learn not only the proper behaviors for adult roles, but also who should play the roles.

Trial and Error Children also learn from trial and error. When a child is pleased by the

Modeling means imitating the actions of role models such as teachers, parents or even football heroes.

reaction of others to something the child does or says, he or she is likely to repeat the behavior, even when it does not fit the occasion. When a behavior does not bring about the desired results, a child is less likely to try it again.

Relating to Others Children behave differently with different people. They learn that what works with one person does not necessarily work with another. For example, a child cries for a glass of milk when she is with her mother, but when she is with her aunt, she smiles and says, "Please."

All children want and need their parents' attention. They want it so much, in fact, that they would rather have negative attention than no attention at all. This fact probably explains why some children misbehave when visitors are present, or when a parent is on the telephone. Young children find it difficult to share the attention of those who are important to them. They need to know they are still important even when other people are around. A new baby in the home is an emotional situation that many young children find particularly difficult to handle. They can easily feel that they have lost attention that is rightfully theirs to a "rival" brother or sister.

Physical and Emotional States When children are tired or hungry, they are likely to be cranky. (For that matter, so are adults.) Illness, too, can cause children to be irritable or negative. During these times, parents should try to be patient. With love, enough rest, and food, a child's good nature usually returns.

Children's emotions influence their behavior. Even the positive excitement of happy, special occasions can affect behavior negatively. For example, young children at a birthday party can easily become overexcited by too much happening for too long, by too many toys or people, or by too much noise. It helps to keep parties short and to have a limited number of guests. If a child does become overexcited, it can be a good idea to remove the child from the situation for awhile. A quiet walk away from the party with a caring adult calms the child.

Just as too much excitement creates undesirable behavior in children, so also does too little excitement. Young children are active and need to be occupied with interesting toys and things to do. When there is little to interest them, they may get into mischief. Parents who have a supply of "rainy-day" materials, such as clay, paints, puppets, and dress-up clothes, can offer their children variety and prevent boredom.

Frustration also affects behavior. When desires are blocked or success seems impossible, a child's behavior can become unruly. All children reach the point of frustration at some time in their activities. Parents can help by selecting toys and activities that challenge a child's intelligence without being too difficult.

Safety Tip

To keep play time safe, keep the following dangerous toys away from young children:

- Toys with small parts that could be swallowed.
- Objects with small removable parts.
- Toys with poisonous paint.
- Stuffed toys with glass or button eyes.
- Toys with sharp edges.

Adapted from "Our Children's World" by the National Safety Council

For Review

1. How can parents help their children develop a sense of security?
2. What is meant by self-esteem?
3. Describe how children can differ in temperament.

Fathering

Many American men today are learning that there are profound rewards in being active, caring fathers. Spending time with children no longer means just playing ball with sons. Fathers are also feeding babies, pushing strollers, and conferring with their children's teachers. They are spending far more time with their children—both daughters and sons—than their own fathers spent with them.

"Fathering," says Maureen Green, author of a recent book on the subject, "is a job for which there is no training program." She argues that even today most girls are brought up with the thought that they will probably marry and have children. Only rarely does anyone mention to boys that one of the roles they will play is that of father.

This kind of thinking conforms to the traditional stereotypes of parents. Mother stays home, caring for and guiding the children. Dad goes off to work, providing economic support for the family. From Mom, children receive warmth, love, and emotional support. Dad sets rules and oversees discipline. Otherwise, he has little to do with the children, except for a ballgame or two with his sons. Mom thus is the more important parent. If the kids turn out well, the credit goes to her. If they don't, she gets the blame. In the stereotyped family, then, "parenting" really means "mothering."

Today, such stereotypes do not describe how real families operate. Certainly the stereotypes ignore one-parent families, working mothers, and families with stepchildren. Only twenty-four percent of American families consist of a mother, a father, and children. In half of the two-parent families, both parents hold paying jobs.

In an effort to substitute facts for myths, researchers are studying fathers and their children. How important is it for children to receive attention from their fathers? What makes a good father? The findings of researchers on these questions challenge the idea that fathers are less important to their children than mothers.

One of the leaders in the new field of fathering research is Dr. Henry Biller, professor of psychology at the University of Rhode Island. He says flatly, "The presence and availability of fathers to kids is critical to their knowledge of social reality, their ability to relate to male figures, their self-concepts, their acceptance of their own sexuality, their feeling of security." Dr. Biller believes that fathers are important both in the first years of their children's lives and throughout all the later years of development.

What are some of the positive effects that fathers can have on their children?

Being firm and fair is the best approach to discipline.

Providing Guidance and Discipline

Children learn behavior by observing others; in particular, they imitate and identify most strongly with their parents. Sometimes, when parents think they are not being observed, their children are actually watching them and absorbing a great deal. They quickly pick up attitudes, interests, and prejudices.

Several studies suggest some important principles about how children learn through observation. First, children may learn through observation a certain behavior that they do not use immediately but rather store up to use later, in other circumstances. Second, children are more likely to imitate the behavior of adults who have been kind and nurturing to them than to imitate those who have been unpleasant to them. Third, certain responses, such as aggression, are more likely than others to be imitated.

Parents as Models

The actions and attitudes of parents definitely speak louder than words. If parents have "temper tantrums" when they are frustrated, children take cues from this kind of behavior. Telling children that they should be patient when they are frustrated does not work unless adults behave in the same way.

"Do as I say, not as I do" is *not* effective advice, and it certainly is not consistent. Yet sometimes, parents can be tripped up because they overlook or are unaware of the irony of a situation. For example, parents may spank their

Children learn more from what parents do than what they say.

child for hitting another child. This situation provides an example of the use of physical force at the very moment parents are attempting to teach a child not to be physically aggressive. Parental behavior such as this confuses a child.

Modeling strongly affects the fear response. By watching parents overreact to lightning, animals, or other "dangers," children pick up parental fears. However, parents can also teach reasonable safety precautions through modeling.

"Practice what you preach" seems to be the key in teaching children constructive behavior. Indeed, internal modeling by parents can be a powerful tool in teaching children. Parents should try to be the kind of people they want their children to become. In this way, children will be more likely to learn the behaviors that the parents want them to learn.

Clear and consistent rules about homework time help a child develop good study habits.

Rules

Some people believe that discipline means merely punishing undesirable behavior. However, that definition is too limited. Discipline comes from the word *disciple*—one who learns from, or voluntarily follows, a leader. Therefore, it involves teaching, guiding, and setting good examples for others.

Children want and need discipline. Rules and guidelines provide standards of behavior that children can try to live up to. Meeting these standards leads to others' approval of their behavior. This approval fosters feelings of security. If discipline is effective, it does *not* constantly demand the involvement of adults. The best parental discipline promotes self-control and self-discipline in children.

Rules are essential to effective discipline, for they inform children about the beliefs and attitudes that their family and community members consider important. Following are some guidelines for setting rules.

Rules should be clear. Sometimes, children do not know the rules until they break them. Parents then announce the rule and punish the child. When rules are clear and can be easily understood from the beginning, children can judge what they should or should not do.

Practical Tip

To be an informed, effective babysitter:

- Familiarize yourself with parents' rules and guidelines.

- Know the phone number where parents can be reached.

- Find out when parents will return.

- Have all emergency phone numbers.

- Take a house tour. Know where things are that you may need.

- Know escape routes in case of fire.

- Get special instructions for child about foods, allergies, medications.

- Lock doors; do not admit strangers.

- At night ask to be accompanied to and from home.

- Do not have long phone conversations.

Rules should be fair and appropriate for the individual child. Sometimes, children are expected to do more than they are capable of doing. For instance, an average two-year-old child is not able to remember lengthy instructions. Parents should always bear in mind the child's level of development and make only realistic demands.

Rules should be necessary. Parents sometimes set so many rules that they themselves cannot remember all of them. Following are some useful questions for testing rules:

- Is the rule necessary to protect the health and safety of the child or of others?

- Is the rule necessary to protect the rights or property of others?

- Is there a good reason for the rule?

Children can better accept rules when the reasons for them are clear. If the response to a child's "Why?" is "Because I say so — that's why!" the child may feel powerless and become frustrated and resentful.

Practical Tip

To help young children control their temper tantrums:

- If a child's anger can be expressed only through hitting and screaming, let him go to his room to scream and rage and think about what has happened.

- If the child feels bad or wronged she may want to talk and to be held.

- Welcome the child back to the group when he decides he is ready to behave sociably and wants to be with people again.

Elizabeth L. Schariatt ed. Kids Day In and Day Out (New York: Simon & Schuster, 1979).

Consistency

Consistency is essential to discipline. Not only does consistent enforcement of rules tell children that rules are important, but it also helps them learn the rules.

Consistency in enforcing rules in different situations gives children a sense of security. They do not have to test the rules each time to find out what behavior is expected of them, nor do they have to "second guess" their parents. Further, consistency between parents in what they require makes discipline effective, whereas inconsistency tells children that there are ways to get around rules. For instance, when one parent establishes a bedtime hour, the other should not contradict it. Parents should be sure that the rules they set and the behavior they exhibit are consistent. Children's behavior is affected more by parental example than by what parents say.

Nevertheless, occasions do arise when parents should be flexible, or able to bend the rules a little. Flexibility should not be confused with inconsistency, however. Flexibility means that the rules may change somewhat in special situations or because of unusual circumstances. It also means giving children some degree of choice, even within the framework of the rules. It is important, however, that children understand that the rules are being modified and that they know the reasons why.

Consequences

Experiencing the consequences of their acts gives children an opportunity to learn. Parents can help ensure that understanding consequences will lead to self-discipline.

Consequences should be reasonable and related to the situation. For example, if a parent forbids a child to watch TV for a week because the child has left a bicycle in the driveway, the punishment seems unreasonable. There is no relationship between the situation and the consequence. Instead, the parent could revoke the child's privilege of riding the bicycle for three days. The punishment would then seem reasonable because the consequence relates logically to the situation.

Consequences should relate to present and future behavior. For instance, parents might agree to let a child use a workshop area and equipment on the condition that the tools are put away afterwards and the area left clean. If the child fails to live up to these conditions, parents might prohibit the use of the shop for awhile. In this way, the child connects the consequences with his or her past behavior. The parents might promise that the child will have a second chance, after a certain period of time, to prove that he or she can act responsibly. The promise of a second chance relates to future behavior.

Parents should decide upon consequences when they are calm. An atmosphere of calmness helps the parent focus on the situation, not on the child. Anger often results in an attack—if only verbal—on the child. Focusing on the situation allows parents to evaluate it, establish reasonable consequences, and help children decide how to correct their mistakes.

Identifying Parenting Styles

Parenting styles refer to the actions and attitudes parents show in their behavior toward their children. In other words, it is not only what parents do but how they do it that define their parenting styles. Telling children to put their toys away is an action. The tone of voice and facial expressions parents use in the telling reveal their attitudes.

The attitudes and behaviors parents bring to parenting come in part from what they learned from their own parents, who were their models. Parenting style is an important consideration, since it affects both the emotional health and the behavior of children.

How might this mother's warm parenting style affect her daughter's development?

Types of Parenting Styles

One researcher, W. C. Becker, placed parental attitudes along three **continuums,** or lines. The ends of each line represent extremes, with the attitudes and actions of most parents falling somewhere between.

Warmth/Hostility Warmth is evident in friendly, nurturing, supportive parental behaviors. Affection and kindness toward children are examples of warmth. Hostility is evident in unfriendly, cold, or angry attitudes and actions toward children. Parents who constantly criticize and condemn their children are showing hostility.

Permissiveness/Restrictiveness Permissive parents place few restrictions or demands on their children. They do not require

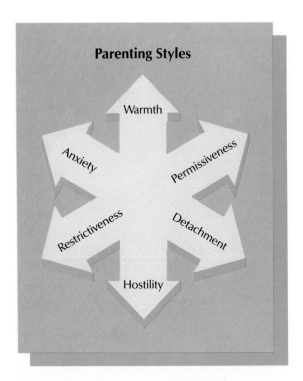

Parenting Styles

Warmth

Anxiety

Permissiveness

Restrictiveness

Detachment

Hostility

when parental warmth is combined with permissiveness, children are more apt to be creative, friendly, assertive, and cooperative with adults. They tend to be fairly persistent in dealing with difficult tasks. One study showed that children reared by parents who are warm but restrictive are apt to be self-controlled, independent, and satisfied with themselves.

When parents are hostile and restrictive, children are more likely to be anxious and to feel guilty. Parental rejection may also lead to self-rejection in children. On the other hand, when parents are hostile and permissive, children tend to be less obedient and are likely to show aggression toward others.

Children who are overprotected but are treated warmly tend to demand their own way and be prone to tantrums. In contrast, children who are strictly controlled and overprotected are apt to be shy and submissive.

Influences on Parenting Styles

Parents are sometimes faced with situations that produce anxiety, tension, and stress. For example, one parent may become unemployed or suffer a long illness. When these conditions combine with a parent's weakened ability to tolerate frustration or to maintain self-control, it is not uncommon for the parent to overreact to children's demands or behavior. As a result, children may become victims of situations they did not create and, perhaps, cannot understand.

Each parent should ask, "Do I like myself?" To care for others, parents must first be able to care for themselves. Parents who did not have their childhood needs met may not have developed a feeling of self-worth. If they grew up with criticism and little encouragement, they may still believe that they are "no good" or "can't do anything right." Parents who are unhappy with themselves and feel unloved may turn to their children for love and care. They lack the ability to nurture their children because they themselves were not nurtured properly.

children to maintain order or to take on responsibilities at home. At the other extreme, parental **restrictiveness,** or rigid control, places many demands and limitations on children's behavior and strictly enforces the demands with punishments. Parents who are extremely restrictive may require children to stay neat and clean and to keep their rooms orderly at all times. At this extreme, they may expect complete obedience even of very young children.

Anxiety/Detachment Some parents may be anxious and overconcerned about every small detail of their children's lives. At the other extreme are parents who remain calm and detached, and have little emotional involvement in their children's lives.

Results of Parenting Styles

Studies have shown that the results of these different types of parental attitudes and actions vary according to how parents combine the three styles. Some researchers have found that

While some parents are overprotective, others are detached and seem to be distant.

If children are treated with warmth and care, they will probably adopt a similar style when they become parents.

Parenting Tasks

	Both Parents (%)	Mother (%)	Father (%)
Discipline the children	83	7	9
Go to Open School Week	76	22	1
Help the children with homework	72	20	5
Speak to teachers if children are in trouble	71	20	8
Decide on children's allowances	67	9	20
Teach the children sports and how to ride bikes	57	4	36
Take children for checkups	35	63	1
Clean the house	33	65	1
Shop for children's clothes	32	66	1
Stay home when children are sick	26	72	1
Prepare the meals	22	77	1

Source: The General Mills American Family Report: Raising Children in a Changing Society (Minneapolis, Minn.: General Mills, Inc.).

Parents' feelings about themselves influence children's developing self-concepts. Children often are able to pick up parents' feelings, even from nonverbal signals. Thus they can sense whether a parent is confident or unsure. Relaxed, secure parents are more likely to raise relaxed, secure children.

Meeting Parents' Needs

Being responsible for meeting the needs of children does not mean that parents' needs must be ignored. Parents need to experience satisfaction, too. In fact, parent care is a vital part of successful parenting. Parents' needs must be met in order for parents to meet children's needs adequately. Parents should find time to pursue their own interests and friendships so that they maintain a healthy self-image.

Needs for Growth

Some parents view their children's achievements or limitations as a reflection on their own ability as parents. In fact, parents themselves are responsible for their own well-being and feelings of adequacy.

Parenthood is a developmental process. As children grow and change, the job of a parent also changes. For instance, the discipline used to correct toddlers' behavior would be inappropriate for and resented by teenagers.

Parents also need opportunities to meet with other parents who have children of similar ages in order to discuss common parenting experiences. When parents hear about other people's children and compare what they hear with their own experiences, they can begin to understand that although children develop in different ways, children of certain ages share some common traits. This fact can be very comforting.

Need for Support Systems

Raising children is a rewarding but very demanding experience. Parents need support and friendship. Having a friend or family member who cares and who will listen without judgment, enables parents to put their own needs and those of their children in perspective. Some parents can turn to their extended families for child care assistance as well as for moral support. When parents live far from relatives, they must look elsewhere for this kind of help. Playgrounds, nursery schools and neighborhood gatherings are just a few places where parents can meet each other and organize playgroups for their children or discussion groups for themselves. In these groups parents can share their experiences of being a mother or a father and give each other valuable support.

One key to being a happy, satisfied parent is taking time to satisfy your own needs.

There are also professional organizations in most communities that provide counseling and other parental support services.

Childhood Immunization Schedule

Recommended age	Diphtheria/ Pertussis/ Tetanus (DPT)	Polio	Measles Mumps Rubella	Hemophilus Influenzae Type B (Hib)
2 months	■	■		
4 months	■	■		
6 months	■	■ (optional)		
15 months[1]	■		■	
18 months	■	■		
2 years				■
4–6 years	■	■		
14–16 years[2]	■			

[1]Single injection for combined vaccines.
[2]Booster injection, and every ten years thereafter.

Source: Healthy People, The Surgeon General's Report on Health Promotion and Disease Prevention, U.S. Department of Health, Education and Welfare, 1979.

Each family must decide which type of child care setting best meets their needs. Many options are available, from family day care to institutional settings.

Working and Parenting

Traditionally, mothers have stayed at home to raise the children. It is estimated that by 1990, 50% of all preschool-age children, and close to 60% of school-age children will have mothers who work. Presently, 75% of all working mothers are working because they have to help support the family. Other women work because it is their choice. In either case, parents find themselves juggling family, home and work responsibilities. It is not easy. Part of the challenge of working and parenting is finding adequate child care, whether it is for 4 hours or 40 hours a week. Because grandparents and other relatives are often miles away, parents must look to organizations for child care options.

Finding Adequate Child Care

Finding and evaluating child care settings are important concerns for parents. It can be intimidating to think about costs and safety. Parents can also feel guilty about not taking care of their children full time.

There are community organizations that can help in providing resources and referrals for quality child care. Friends and co-workers may also offer helpful suggestions. Newspaper advertisements can be effective. They allow parents to structure and then obtain the type of child care arrangement they want.

There are several different types of child care settings. The structure of programs varies, but in every one the most important factor is the quality of the person who cares for the child. Parents need to consider the setting that best fits the needs of the child and themselves. Some child care settings are licensed — regulated by state or governmental agencies. Others are not. It is the responsibility of the parents to assess all of these factors and maintain control over their child's experiences. The following questions can help parents choose the right child care arrangement for their child:

- Is the care provider warm and attentive?

- How and when is discipline used?

- Are there interesting activities?

- What is the background or training of the care-provider?

- Is there first-aid equipment available?
- Is the space clean, attractive and comfortable?
- Is there a plan for sick children?

In-Home Care   A person who provides care in your home for a few hours or on a sporadic basis is a babysitter. A person who is employed in a home on a daily basis, or who lives with the famly, is called a child caregiver or a nanny. These caregivers do what parents do—feed, play with, read to, and supervise the child. The care takes place in a setting that is familiar to the child. Relatives may also provide in-home care.

Family Day Care   In **family day care** arrangements, the people providing the child care take children into their own homes. Although state regulations differ, there are usually from one to seven children receiving care in each family day care home. At least one of the children is often related to the person providing the care. Many parents choose this arrangement because they want their child to be cared for in a home setting.

Child Care Centers   Child care centers provide care to more children than is possible in private homes. These centers can be located in churches, schools, or libraries. Others have been built specifically for this purpose. Many businesses, universities, and industries are creating on-site child care centers. They open early in the morning and close in the early evening to accommodate parents' work schedules. The main purpose of child care centers is to provide for the physical, emotional, and social needs of the children. Child care centers are also involved in the intellectual development of children, but the academic programs vary widely.

For Review

1. What are some of the questions used to judge the fairness of rules?
2. What are some good sources of support for parents?
3. Explain how in-home day care and a day care center are different.

10 Chapter Review

Summary

Parents are responsible for meeting the physical and emotional needs of their children. Effective parenting occurs when there is an attempt to understand children's behavior. Consideration is given to children's temperaments and the life experiences influencing their behavior before decisions are made about how to respond. Providing discipline helps children to develop self-control and self-direction so that they will become more independent. If discipline is to be effective, parents must enforce rules consistently and make sure that their children understand the consequences of their behavior. Couples also need to consider the impact of their parenting styles upon their children's behavior and emotional health.

A responsible parent realizes that his or her individual needs also require attention. Family, friends, neighbors, and community organizations can support parents as they raise their children. They also can help parents find adequate day care through child care centers, family day care, or in-home care.

Vocabulary

Use the following vocabulary words to complete the paragraphs below.

continuum
family day care
restrictiveness
temperament

Parents spend much time responding to a child's needs. They must learn to consider a child's personality, or __1__, to understand and to cope with his or her behavior.

The parental attitudes and behaviors affecting a specific parenting style can be placed upon a __2__, or line connecting two extremes. The extreme of one parenting style includes parents who place little or no limits on their children. At the opposite extreme are parents who maintain rigid control over their children's behavior, which is called __3__.

Because of the rising number of dual-earner families, many parents must find child care for their children. __4__ is an option that many parents prefer because children spend the day in a home setting.

Chapter Questions

1. Describe two specific routines parents can use to help maintain their child's sense of security.
2. Why is self-esteem so important to a child's development?
3. How might parents help children who have difficulty adapting to new situations?
4. From your own childhood experiences, recount a time when you learned from modeling behavior or by trial and error. Remember to explain how the incident you are describing is an example of either modeling or trial and error.
5. Why do you think proper discipline is important to a child's development?

Divorce is a painful experience for all the members of a family.

Divorce

One of the changes that has taken place in many of today's families is divorce, or the legal ending of a marriage. When a couple goes through the process of obtaining a divorce, many people are affected, especially children of the divorcing couple.

Many who experience termination of a marriage feel that they are personal, social, or religious failures. Unfortunately, in this society there are no rituals or customs for helping people who go through the loneliness, grief, and stress associated with divorce.

Factors in Divorce

Over one million divorces take place each year in the United States. Many observers agree that this figure is significant. Yet they also point to the divorce rate, which is usually determined by the number of divorces per 1,000 persons in the total population. In the past few years, the divorce rate has slowed. This fact suggests to some experts that marriages are not breaking up as rapidly in the 1980s as they did in the previous decade.

In analyzing the various characteristics and backgrounds of divorced couples, family experts have identified a number of factors that contribute to the probability of divorce. The rich and the poor have higher divorce rates than couples in the middle-income brackets. Couples who marry in their early teens have a much higher divorce rate than do couples who marry in their mid-twenties. Lack of education is also a factor in divorce.

What problems might cause a marriage to end in divorce?

A couple can rate its own chances for marital success by examining the characteristics of divorced couples. The likelihood for divorce is higher if the following factors exist:

- The backgrounds of the husband and wife are different.

- The families of either or both spouses have a history of divorce.

- The couple was acquainted for only a short time before they were married or had a short engagement period.

- The families or friends of the couple disapprove of their marriage.

- The couple has always had opposing views on the roles of husband and wife.

- The partners have no formal membership in a religious group.

These are only a few of the characteristics that often categorize the so-called "divorce prone." On the other hand, many couples who fit within this category do not divorce. Some couples may remain in less-than-happy marriages throughout their lives. They believe that marriage is sacred and cannot be dissolved. Some parents stay married just for the sake of the children. They may remain in unhappy marriages but become "emotionally divorced".

Compare the marriage rate to the divorce rate during the early 1980s.

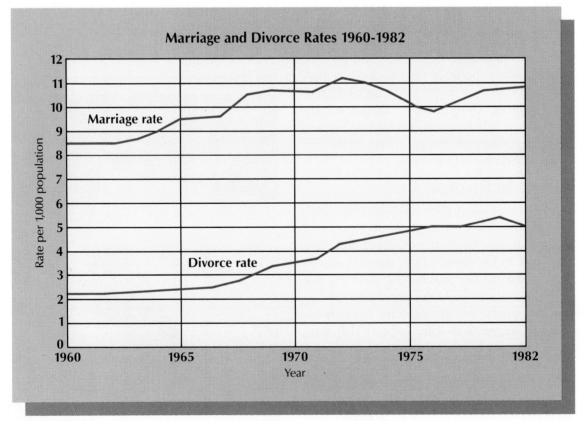

Source: U.S. Bureau of the Census.

Grounds for Divorce

State	Breakdown of marriage/ incompatibility	Cruelty	Desertion	Nonsupport	Alcohol and/or drug addiction	Felony	Impotency	Insanity	Living separate and apart
Alabama	■	■	■	■	■	■	■	■	2 yrs.
Alaska	■	■	■		■	■	■	■	
Arizona	■								
Arkansas		■	■	■	■	■	■	■	3 yrs.
California	■							■	
Colorado	■								
Connecticut	■	■	■	■	■	■		■	18 mos.
Delaware	■								6 mos.
Dist. of Columbia	■								6 mos.-1 yr.
Florida	■							■	
Georgia	■	■	■		■		■	■	
Hawaii	■								2 yrs.
Idaho	■	■	■	■	■	■		■	5 yrs.
Illinois	■	■	■		■	■	■		
Indiana	■					■	■	■	
Iowa	■								
Kansas	■								
Kentucky	■								1 yr.
Louisiana	■					■			1 yr.
Maine	■	■	■	■	■		■	■	
Maryland	■	■	■			■	■	■	1-3 yrs.
Massachusetts	■	■	■	■	■	■	■		6 mos.-1 yr.
Michigan	■								
Minnesota	■								
Mississippi	■	■	■		■			■	
Missouri	■								
Montana	■								
Nebraska	■								
Nevada	■							■	1 yr.
New Hampshire	■	■	■	■	■	■			2 yrs.
New Jersey		■	■		■	■		■	18 mos.
New Mexico	■	■							
New York		■				■			1 yr.
North Carolina								■	1 yr.
North Dakota	■	■	■	■	■	■		■	
Ohio	■	■	■	■	■	■	■	■	2 yrs.
Oklahoma	■	■	■	■	■	■	■	■	
Oregon	■								
Pennsylvania	■	■	■			■		■	3 yrs.
Rhode Island	■	■	■	■	■	■	■		3 yrs.
South Carolina		■	■		■				1 yr.
South Dakota	■	■	■	■	■	■			
Tennessee	■	■	■	■	■	■	■		
Texas	■	■	■	■	■			■	3 yrs.
Utah	■	■	■	■	■		■		
Vermont	■	■	■	■				■	6 mos.
Virginia	■	■	■						6 mos.-1 yr.
Washington	■								
West Virginia	■	■	■		■	■		■	1 yr.
Wisconsin	■								1 yr.
Wyoming	■							■	2 yrs.

Source: The World Almanac and Book of Facts, 1986.

That is, they withdraw physically and emotionally from each other.

Research shows that some couples stay together for economic security, in spite of conflicts. This finding is particularly true when women do not have vocational skills and fear that they cannot survive independently. However, the likelihood of divorce rises when the husband is unemployed.

Changes in Divorce Laws

When most people marry, they assume that their marriage will last "until death," as most traditional vows state. Even if they pledge support for "as long as love lasts," very likely they are hoping for a lifetime commitment.

Laws governing marriage and divorce also have been based on the concept that a marriage contract is permanent. There are many limitations governing divorce. Still, every state has provided for divorce through legislation.

Until recently, most divorce laws were designed to punish the marriage partner who was found "guilty" of wrongdoing and to reward the "innocent" victim. Today, it is possible in several states to divorce without placing blame or proving the fault of one partner in court. Some states have even abolished the term "divorce," calling it "**dissolution** (end) of marriage" instead. Most of these states have provided for grounds that are often labeled "no-fault"— neither party has to be proved to be at fault, or

The results of this study indicate that the highest percentage of divorces among men and women occurs to those who were married in their early twenties. What reasons can you think of to explain why the divorce rate is high at this age level?

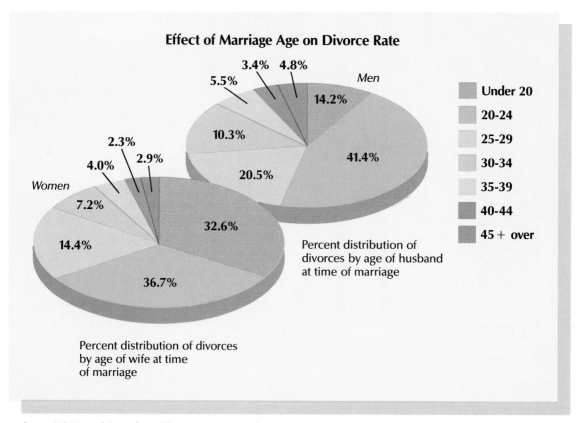

Effect of Marriage Age on Divorce Rate

Men

3.4%   4.8%
5.5%
14.2%
10.3%
41.4%
20.5%

Women

2.3%
4.0%   2.9%
7.2%
32.6%
14.4%
36.7%

Under 20
20-24
25-29
30-34
35-39
40-44
45 + over

Percent distribution of divorces by age of husband at time of marriage

Percent distribution of divorces by age of wife at time of marriage

Source: U.S. National Center for Health Statistics. Statistical Abstract, 1989

Parenting and household management are challenging tasks for a divorced person with children.

both may share the blame for dissolving the marriage. Courts in states with "no-fault" divorce laws recognize that some marriages cannot work and should be dissolved on the grounds of "irretrievable breakdown of the marriage," "irreconcilable differences," or "incompatibility." In effect, these terms mean that there is no chance that the two people involved can continue to live as husband and wife.

Effects on Adults

Most couples who reach the point where "irreconcilable differences" force them apart do not know what to expect from divorce, nor can they foresee the difficulties ahead of them. Despite supposed standards of equality, customs and attitudes in American society do not necessarily allow fair treatment for both partners in a divorce. One mate usually "wins," while the other "loses."

No two divorce cases are exactly alike, but in general, legal decisions favor women when awarding custody of the children, the home, and

Children of divorced parents often have added responsibilities at home.

household property. Men usually must make child-support payments, and sometimes they must also pay alimony to the wife. Fathers may be restricted as to when and where they can see their children. Courts often base their decisions on the traditional view that men are the providers of financial support, and women are responsible for the care of the children. This approach may in fact seem fair when women have not held jobs or have no marketable skills.

In some cases, of course, a man may be better at child care than his wife. In addition, when women have skills or careers, the problem of who will care for and support the children remains, regardless of which parent has custody. In some cases, judges have awarded men alimony as well as child support and custody.

Ex-spouses, whether male or female, often suffer through the crisis of divorce. They may experience anger, bitterness, depression, fear, frustration, grief, guilt, loneliness, panic, and feelings of being rejected and of being a "nonperson." Some communities sponsor chapters of national groups, workshops, or seminars that help divorced persons understand their emotions and "sound off" about their mutual problems. However, most formerly married people must struggle alone to rebuild their lives.

Effects on Children

Early in 1980, there were about 12 million children under 18 whose parents had been divorced. Researchers find that children's reactions to divorce follow a pattern. Few realize that their parents are breaking up, so most are shocked when the divorce comes, even if they have lived in unhappy homes. Many children of divorced parents feel depressed and angry, and they tend to blame themselves for their parents' problems, particularly if they are of elementary school age. Some children may develop poor self-images or become shy and withdrawn. Others may become disruptive, fighting with classmates, destroying property, or acting out their frustrations in some other

way. Preschool children sometimes are afraid that they will be abandoned and that no one will feed or clothe them.

If you or any of your friends or relatives have experienced a family breakup, you may be familiar with other common effects of divorce. For example, visiting the absent parent often becomes somewhat forced or artificial, because it is a "scheduled event," separate from a young person's daily activities. Further, an absent parent might not be familiar with a child's friends or know what he or she is learning in school.

In the 1970s, two child psychology experts studied sixty California families who had recently gone through divorce. After a number of interviews over a five-year period, they found that about one-quarter of the families were doing very well. If an absent parent had been cruel or abusive, children often improved when the other parent showed love and concern. However, according to the researchers, the most crucial factor that determined whether a

Children need to be reassured that they are not responsible for their parents' divorce.

How To Cope with Parents' Divorce

Almost half of all marriages today end in divorce. Being a young person in the middle of a family breakup is a difficult challenge for a teenager to face. Sometimes it is helpful to realize that you are not the only teenager who is coping with stress at home. One young woman expressed it this way: "When Mom and Dad divorced, I was pretty desperate. Then I began to realize that almost everybody at my school had some big problem at home. Some of my friends had a very sick brother or sister. Others had to cope with a drug or alcohol problem in their family. And some were having terrible money troubles. Knowing that I was not the only one with sadness at home was a great comfort to me."

If your parents are separating, it is normal to feel angry and frightened. You may feel rejected by one or both parents. During a divorce, young adults often experience symptoms of depression. They find it difficult to sleep. They may either lose their appetite or find they are overeating. It becomes difficult to concentrate on schoolwork. They feel tired all the time.

There are ways to relieve the stress of parents divorcing. First, it is important to realize that it is not the fault of the children. Even though your parents may get angry at you, they are separating because of problems between them. Do not feel you can solve the differences between them. Try to understand the pain each of them is feeling. It is also necessary to accept the reality of what is happening. Do not get trapped in a fantasy you create that everything will work out. You have to accept the fact that things at home are changing.

Remember that your parents are upset and may say things to you that they do not really mean. Try to talk to each of them about how you feel. You can ask your parents to explain to you what is happening and what their plans are. They do not have to tell you everything. They have a right to privacy. However, it helps to know how changes will affect your own life. You may find it helps to talk with someone outside the family that you trust — an older relative, a close friend, or a counselor.

It is important to focus on other parts of your life. Concentrate on having happy times with your friends. Join some extracurricular activities at school. Work on a special project or hobby you enjoy. Keep in mind that while this is a painful time, it will not go on forever. You may find it is easier to live with one parent or with each parent at a different time than it is to live with parents who can no longer function as a loving couple.

A number of studies of divorce show that children of divorced parents learn how to deal with crisis. This can help them later. They have learned to recognize their own strength in coping with difficult situations. Children of divorced parents can be just as successful in adult life as children from intact families.

Family members can offer each other much needed support during the difficult adjustment period following divorce.

Whether he is with his mother (left), or his father (right), this child of divorced parents feels loved and secure.

child made a good readjustment was the opportunity to maintain "a stable, loving relationship with both parents."

The study revealed that nearly half the families were just getting by, "coping when and as they could." The children in the rest of the families in the study were "bruised: failing to recover from divorce or looking back to the predivorce family with intense longing."

Joint Custody

Some divorced couples try to arrange for **joint custody** in order to reduce some of the negative effects of divorce on children. Joint custody means equal legal responsibility of both parents for their children. Parents who have joint custody may take turns having the children in their homes. Sometimes, parents with young children take turns living in the former family home. For children, joint custody most often means having two homes, and probably two sets of clothes and two sets of toys—one with each parent.

Many experts are divided on the wisdom of joint custody. Most courts are reluctant to grant joint custody in cases where the parents are hostile to one another. The temptation for each parent to "use" the children to punish the

ex-spouse is not healthy. This kind of behavior also can be very harmful to the children. Authorities believe that having two homes may be especially hard on young children. They think that preschoolers need the security and stability of having one home.

Nevertheless, when adults can separate their feelings about former partners from their parental roles, joint custody offers children more contact with both parents than do other forms of custody, and it is closer to the pattern of traditional family life. Many children who have experienced the arrangement say they like it, although they found it uncomfortable at first.

Researchers are closely studying families who have joint custody arrangements. It is hoped that joint custody will offer children more normal lives than what is available under one-parent custody. However, the final verdict is not yet in, and divorcing parents must make up their own minds about the wisdom of joint custody for their families.

Stepfamilies

Although some researchers predict that 45 percent of the children born in the late 1970s will live in single-parent families for part of their

Accepting all the changes brought about by a divorce is easier if a child has this kind of loving relationship with both parents.

childhood, the great majority of children still live with two parents—either their natural parents or, after a remarriage, with a natural parent and a stepparent. The families formed after a remarriage are called **stepfamilies** or *blended* families. This kind of family occurred in the past mainly as a result of death and remarriage. It is now increasingly prevalent as more people divorce and then remarry.

Unfortunately, remarriage does not automatically create a big happy family. This does not mean, however, that the stepfamily will necessarily be unhappy, either. A stepfamily can offer great opportunities for close companionship and personal growth.

When an Illinois couple—each spouse the parent of two children—combined their families, they readily admitted in a *Chicago Sun-Times* newspaper story that it was not easy to blend different family habits, temperaments, and ideas on discipline. Nevertheless, the husband and wife agreed that there was no point in pretending that everything would be perfect or that it would be like the idealized nuclear family. As the wife explained, "We believe that being stepparents is another kind of loving. It's not an attempt to replace the missing parent. It can be an extension of friendship or affection or deep

caring, but it is different. Understanding that helps to make the family work."

Members of a stepfamily may have no clearly defined roles, and there may be quite a bit of confusion over what they expect from each other. Problems may range from what the children should call their stepmother or stepfather (Mother? Dad? proper names?) to whose rules will be followed in the household.

Recent books and articles on the subject describe a number of questions and anxieties with which stepfamilies have to grapple. For example, a new stepmother might wonder whether her stepdaughter will think she has lost her father to "another woman," or whether, through her father's remarriage, she has gained another mom. Some stepparents wonder how to help their own children accept the new mate, who will handle the discipline, and whether their new mates will deal with their own children more severely or give them fewer privileges than the mate's biological children, or vice versa. They wonder what will happen if the two families don't have the same tastes in food or like the same TV shows. What if the new spouse has different views about household responsibilities? What if chores are not divided equally among the children?

Blended families usually face more adjustment problems than intact families of parents and their own biological children. However, no family remains static throughout the family life cycle. Every change may bring on problems or benefits or both for every member of the family.

For Review

1. Discuss some of the characteristics of couples who are likely to get divorced.
2. How can joint custody help or harm children of a divorced couple?
3. Describe some of the common problems in stepfamilies.

The "Empty Nest"

The stage that begins when children leave the home and parents start living as a couple again has received a great deal of attention in recent years. The **"empty nest"** stage, as it has been called, is a time when a husband and wife have to accept new roles. They must begin making plans for retirement and possibly for living alone when a partner dies. Most couples can expect about 16 to 18 years "alone together" in the "empty nest" stage of marriage.

Problems

Some people experience anxiety at the prospect of being without children in the home. Husband and wife may foresee difficulties in adjustment. It can be depressing to realize that half of one's life is over. Health problems may show signs of becoming chronic. After children have moved away, couples may discover that they no longer have much in common, that they do not share similar interests, and that they have little to talk about or to do together.

Parents may miss having young people around to advise, to fix things for, or to kid with, for children often make parents feel resourceful and young. The parents may also find time on their hands and feel less useful with no children in the household. They may need to find new interests in order to maintain a positive self-image.

Discovering new interests together can be fulfilling for a couple during the "empty nest" stage of marriage.

Adjustments

Despite the difficulties of adjustment, the losses and limitations of the "empty nest" stage can be overemphasized. According to recent research, parents who have made successful adjustments to this stage and are happy with their marital life at this point fit the following patterns:

■ The parents had some previous experience with their children leaving home — to go to college, to join the armed forces, or to take jobs in distant communities.

■ The parents occasionally had been away from their children because of job responsibilities, vacation travel, or the obligation of caring for other relatives.

■ The parents had been involved in outside activities, such as membership in civic and religious organizations and various volunteer work assignments. They also had pursued recreational and artistic interests over the years.

■ The couples were involved in activities that both liked and shared.

■ The couples accepted each other's failings and strengths and were not as likely to complain about unfulfilled expectations.

■ The couples usually had experienced less stress in meeting their financial responsibilities and caring for children.

■ The couples had developed satisfactory two-way communication, including good listening skills.

Contrary to popular opinion, near the end of the "empty nest" period, many couples begin to derive a great deal of satisfaction from their new roles and from their new "station" in life. They may develop a sense of mature achievement, with fewer anxieties about personal identity and life choices. The ability to cope with their "empty nest" in a positive way influences a couple's response to aging.

Many older couples enjoy the same recreational activities that they pursued in their youth.

Aging

The term "old age" is not easy to define. Life is a process of maturing from one developmental stage to the next. Growing old is not a fixed, unchanging state. It is simply a phase on the time-line of life.

Aging is a very individual process. People grow old in different ways. The differences depend on factors like income, attitude, health, and family situation. These are the same environmental factors that shape a person's development all through life.

Many people view the final stage of the life cycle as a time with few possibilities for meaningful activity. Nevertheless, the potential for further growth does exist. In fact, increasing numbers of aging persons are visibly active and healthy, and are able to serve others and find self-fulfillment.

Problems

The problems of aging have perhaps been more publicized than have the successful adjustments people make in later life. It is true that some adjustments can be painful for older people if poor health and a low income are built-in factors of their existence. Adjustments also are difficult when a person believes that he or she is no longer needed or useful because of age. Often, an older person must give up a job he or she enjoys. Rarely do young people call upon older people for advice. In a country where youth is emphasized and where goods are manufactured and advertised primarily for the young, it is not easy to maintain a positive self-image as a "senior citizen." However, as the population shifts to a majority of elderly persons, the emphasis in future advertising will change and the image should improve.

There are many elderly people who are able to create and produce until the end of their lives. Some stay active in the creative arts, still others act as consultants for businesses, serve their communities through various nonprofit organizations or religious groups, or spend their time traveling or pursuing hobbies they enjoy.

People in the earlier stages of adult development generally do not realize how many opportunities are available to older people today. Being aware of the positive as well as the negative aspects of aging may help many people find more satisfaction in their later years.

Adjustments

It is important that older couples recognize some of the tasks and adjustments they must make in the aging period. People need to prepare for retirement years in advance.

Most older people receive much less income during retirement than they brought in during the working years. It can be hard to adjust to decreased spending. However, the amount of money required for food and clothing may not

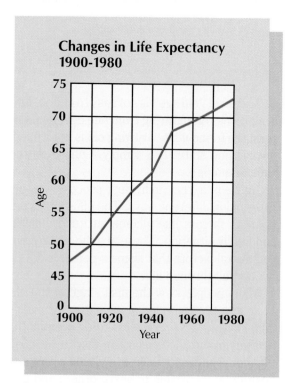

Changes in Life Expectancy 1900-1980

Source: Statistical Abstract of the United States and Historical Statistics of the United States.

Many older persons continue working after they reach retirement age.

be as great at this time. Further, many older people may have finished paying for their homes, thereby reducing housing costs.

Retirement   Occupational level seems to determine when a person retires. Professionals (doctors, lawyers, dentists) gradually reduce their work loads. Executives and managers usually retire according to a schedule. For the majority of the work force in jobs that range from skilled to unskilled, retirement is most likely to be forced. American industry has strongly supported mandatory retirement. Within industry, retirement at age 55 has become more and more common.

For some people, retirement is long awaited. It is a new phase of life offering more time for leisure activities. For many, it is an abrupt change in life style. These people are challenged to find positive ways to make the transition from structured work time to free time. They are faced with the question: What does one do with the knowledge, skills, talents, and wisdom accumulated during a lifetime of work experience?

Some retired people continue to work but they work for themselves, rather than for a business or organization. Others apply their skills through volunteer agencies that provide assistance to institutions such as schools and hospitals. Whatever goal a person chooses for the retirement period, the focus is on internal satisfaction rather than on productivity.

Grandparenting

Being a grandparent can be a great source of pleasure and pride. It has been said that grandparenting allows for all the joys of parenthood with few of the problems. A child sees a grandparent as another adult, besides his parents, who loves him unconditionally. This attitude makes the grandparent feel needed in a very special way. A grandparent fulfills a unique role in a child's life. Not only does the grandparent

With retirement comes time to pursue creative interests. This man receives great satisfaction from working with clay.

provide additional love and support for the child, but he or she is also a source of learning about the past firsthand. Grandparents have wisdom, experience and skills to share with younger generations. Over 90 percent of all children in North America have at least one living grandparent at age 20. Unfortunately, close contact with grandparents is less frequent than it was in the past. This problem is due to the fact that families move so frequently.

Foster Grandparenting   In many communities, programs are designed to match children who do not have grandparents (or who are orphans or foster children) with older adults who want to have contact with children. Adults who participate in such programs are called *foster grandparents.*

For an isolated older person, foster grandparenting provides the experiences of being a grandparent, an experience he or she might not otherwise have on a regular basis. These adults may be living alone, or in institutions. In a foster grandparenting relationship, children benefit from the special attention an older person gives to them. The older person feels needed and loved, so the relationship is beneficial for everyone involved.

Children benefit from the special relationship they have with a grandparent.

Grandparents can teach children about their heritage.

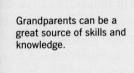

Grandparents can be a great source of skills and knowledge.

Some communities provide services that help older persons live independently in their own homes.

Safety Tip

To avoid falling at home:

- Use rubber mats in bathtub.
- Keep bathroom floor dry.
- Use nonslip rug pads under area rugs.
- Keep wires and cords away from areas where people walk.
- Keep stairways clear.
- Repair loose tiles and tears or holes in rugs or flooring.
- Clean up slippery spills immediately.

Housing Alternatives

Most of the elderly live in houses or apartments where they have lived for many years. In fact, approximately 70 percent of the elderly population own their own homes. Most of the elderly prefer to live independently, in a setting that provides privacy and a familiar environment. However, economic or health reasons may make this impossible. There are other alternatives for those who cannot live alone. Living with relatives, elderly housing units, and supervised care are three possible alternatives.

Living with Relatives There was a time in American society when adults automatically assumed all care and responsibility for their aging parents. Today, although some elderly people do live with their children, it is not a common practice. Living with relatives is a compromise for all involved. When an older person lives with an adult child, the child often makes the decisions. People who are used to making their own decisions often find it difficult to be in this situation. It highlights the loss of independence. However, when poor health, or economic factors require it, this alternative may be the most appropriate one.

Independent Living When health permits, some elderly people live in apartments or housing complexes that are specifically planned for the elderly. The focus is on making independent living safe and convenient. Many of these housing units provide facilities and programs that can satisfy the needs of the elderly who previously lived in independent homes.

Congregate housing provides a semi-independent living arrangement. Each individual or couple has an independent living unit (an apartment or room), usually with private bathroom facilities. They may or may not have their own cooking or laundry facilities. One to three meals may be provided each day. Usually residents eat

Older persons can maintain their independence in housing units especially designed for the elderly.

If a person is not strong enough to return home after a hospitalization, she may choose to go to a nursing home.

at the same time in a common dining area. As is the case with independent elderly housing, there is a wide range of other services that may be available.

Supervised Care Although less than 10 percent of the elderly population may be institutionalized at any one time, it has been estimated that anywhere from 25 to 75 percent are housed in an institutional setting for some part of their later years. A variety of settings is available. This section describes the retirement home and the nursing home.

The retirement home provides for those who have some physical limitations. Nursing or medical care may be available on the site and the institution may or may not have recreational facilities.

Nursing homes may provide nursing or rehabilitative care. For example, if a person breaks a hip and cannot return directly home after a hospitalization, he or she may go to a nursing home for a period of time to get stronger. Long-term severe medical problems make it impossible for others to return to independent living. They may require nursing home care for the rest of their lives.

For Review

1. What are some of the problems couples face in the "empty nest" phase of life?
2. Describe the positive aspects of aging.
3. Describe two types of Elderly Housing arrangements.

Death

In the not-too distant past, a family member who became fatally ill was cared for at home and usually died there. Diseases such as diphtheria and polio took many lives, and people were accustomed to dealing with death as a natural part of the life cycle.

Today, however, with advances in medical science and an average life span of more than seventy years, many people are not exposed to a death in the family until an aged member dies. Even then, the ill person is usually out of sight in a hospital or nursing home. If family members live far away, there may be little or no contact with a dying relative. Only after someone has died do many of the living face the reality of death.

You may already have had an opportunity to gain a better understanding of death and of a person's need to express grief in a healthy way. Possibly you have helped younger children see death as a natural ending to life. Maybe you have been able to discuss the subject with classmates and now have a more comfortable attitude toward the subject.

As you learn about death and its effect on the family, you will probably think about some current issues and problems such as the right of the terminally ill to die with dignity, the importance of having a will, and how to provide for dependents after death. You will discover that the more truthful people are about family losses, the better they are able to "get on" with life in a positive manner.

Awareness

People often avoid the fact of death in American society. Instead of receiving the attention and support they need, the dying must often face death without the emotional support of others.

At some point families have to deal with the loss of a family member.

Families are becoming increasingly aware of the importance of their presence to dying members. Most dying patients would prefer to be in their own beds in their own homes. However, they often require skilled medical care, and families often need relief from the difficulties involved in daily care of a dying loved one. Some terminally ill patients and their families are able to utilize hospice services. **Hospice** is comprised of a team of doctors, nurses, social workers, clergy, and volunteers who provide medical assistance and emotional support to patients in order for them to remain in their homes. The counseling services are also available to the patients' family members.

Psychiatrists and some medical practitioners believe that the dying need to have a say in what they will do in the time they have left. The dying also need help from family and friends to deal with fears and to talk about the many things on their minds. Religious rituals, prayers, and the sharing of thoughts with religious leaders can be comforting to the dying.

Acceptance

According to psychiatrist Elizabeth Kübler-Ross, a dying person can accept his or her own death if that individual is able and allowed to go through stages of denial, anger, and depression. Although not everyone progresses through each stage, the first reaction to the news of a terminal illness is usually "No, not me, it can't be true." Next comes anger or rage and the question "Why me?" Sometimes, a person tries to bargain for more time by making promises to devote one's life to God or to will one's body to science. A dying patient may feel a "sense of great loss" and deep depression, which Kübler-Ross calls **preparatory grief** — a stage that the terminally ill undergo in order to get ready for "the final separation from this world." The acceptance stage often follows.

How do rituals help people deal with their grief?

Grief

After the death of a loved one, family members and friends experience bereavement. No two people face grief in the same way. Some people hold everything inside, while others are more expressive. However one reacts, grief is a healthy emotion.

Researchers once were very critical of the "funeral business" in the United States, since abuses existed that caused survivors to suffer financial hardships. Some recent studies show that conventional funerals with mourning rituals may help survivors accept death and adjust to it in a healthy manner. Other researchers suggest that it makes no difference what procedures are used. The forms of funeral or memorial services, the types of symbols, and the kinds of rites performed vary according to religious beliefs, personal preferences, and the needs of the survivors. Whatever ceremony is chosen, it should have meaning for the bereaved, because it helps them handle their grief.

It is difficult to cope with the loneliness that one feels after a spouse dies.

When counselors offer advice on how to cope with grief, they often encourage frankness: do not try to avoid the truth. It is not easy to face the fact that someone you love has died, but that is the first step in learning to live with grief. One must accept the pain so that time can eventually heal it. Questions, tears, and expressions of grief are all part of one's involvement in this family event.

There is no "right" way to talk to children about death. Explanations depend on such factors as the age of the child, the closeness of the child to the deceased, and the child's other experiences with loss. It is important for parents to teach children about death before there is a family crisis. In addition, parents should allow children to join in expressions of sorrow following a death.

Widows and Widowers

When a woman's husband dies, she becomes a *widow*. A man whose wife dies becomes a *widower*. The onset of widowhood usually takes place suddenly and unexpectedly. Most often it is women who are affected, particularly women over 60. In fact, in North America there are five times as many widows as widowers.

When a spouse dies, the initial process of adjustment is difficult. The newly widowed person must learn to cope with loneliness. Suddenly there is no longer someone to care for; the loss of companionship is a difficult adjustment. After grief begins to ease, the process of creating a new identity and life style must begin.

Some widows must learn to cope with changing their identity from one dependent on the husband's status and occupation to one of single independence. This change is particularly difficult if the widow has been dependent on her husband for decision making.

For Review

1. What is a hospice?
2. Describe some of the stages of grief.
3. How do some of the rituals surrounding death, such as funerals, help people deal with grief?

11 Chapter Review

Summary

Divorce has far-reaching effects on couples and their children. All family members suffer from the pain caused by the separation. New blended and single-parent families must cope with many changes. A joint custody arrangement allows a child to be close to both parents, although at different times.

Couples facing the "empty nest" stage of the life cycle adjust more easily if they have maintained interests and activities apart from their children, and if they are able to communicate well as a couple.

While poor health and low income create problems for some older people, many of the elderly pursue meaningful lives that help them retain their positive self-images.

Awareness, acceptance, and grief are all part of a person's adjustment to the reality of death. Families can help themselves cope with grief if they accept their painful feelings and share the loss openly with each other.

Vocabulary

Match each of the following vocabulary words with one of the definitions that follow.

congregate housing
dissolution
empty nest
hospice
joint custody
preparatory grief
stepfamily

1. _____ legal arrangement in which divorced parents share equal responsibility for their children
2. _____ semi-independent living arrangement for elderly people
3. _____ term used to describe a stage of the life cycle that begins after a couple's children leave home
4. _____ blended family; family formed after a remarriage
5. _____ termination; used in some states to describe the end of a marriage
6. _____ stage experienced by the terminally ill as they face death
7. _____ services provided by a group of professionals to terminally ill patients and their families.

Chapter Questions

1. Why do some couples remain in unhappy relationships rather than seek a divorce?
2. What is the main purpose of "no-fault" divorce laws?
3. How might the courts make their divorce and custody decisions more fair for husbands, wives, and their children?
4. What have science researchers determined to be the most crucial factor in a child's adjustment to his or her parents' divorce?
5. What can parents of blended families do to ease their children's adjustment?
6. How can a couple prepare themselves for the "empty nest" stage while their children are still living at home?

7. How does a person's attitude toward growing older affect his or her adjustment during the aging period?
8. What are some of the changes in life style that people must face upon retirement?
9. Discuss the benefits of a foster grandparents program.
10. How does elderly housing differ from congregate housing?
11. What are the reasons that many people are not exposed to death until an aged family member dies?
12. Describe the three stages that a terminally ill person experiences.
13. What are some of the difficulties that widows and widowers experience after their spouse has died?

Skill Activities

1. **Critical Thinking** Examine the "Grounds for Divorce" chart on page 193. Locate your state and determine what grounds for divorce are applicable. Which of your state's divorce laws are included on this chart? Once you have recorded these answers, investigate your state's divorce requirements and regulations further by talking with attorneys, judges, or other municipal officials. When you have compiled your information, answer the following question: "In your opinion, what laws or procedures can your state's legal system institute or improve to make the process of divorce more fair and/or equitable for both partners?"

Present your information and conclusions in an oral report to your class, or, create a poster that outlines the divorce laws in your state and how they might be improved.

2. **Social Studies** Investigate how people plan for retirement. Begin by researching basic information at your school or local library. What is social security? When and how can it be utilized? What is a pension? How might a self-employed person prepare for retirement?

Make an appointment to meet with a personnel or benefits coordinator at a local factory or corporation. Find out if there is a mandatory retirement age for employees. Is there a pension plan? How does it work? How long must an employee work for the company before benefits can be received? Ask what people of different ages should consider as they plan for retirement. Write a report on what you learned from your research.

3. **Reading** Find out more about Elderly Housing alternatives. Refer to pages 205–206 in your text. Pick one type of Elderly Housing and find out more about it. Consult your local library or local resources that service the elderly population—Councils for the Elderly, Housing Authorities, or actual housing facilities. Find out how the organization and design of the facility suit the needs of the residents. Are the residents of the facility physically independent or do they require many support services? Prepare a brief written report on your findings.

12 Resolving Family Crises

As you read, think about:

- what kind of young people become juvenile delinquents.
- what type of background produces antisocial behavior.
- what organizations offer help to families in crises.

Most families confront and solve many problems over the years. In a crisis, however, a time of severe stress, it is not always possible for a family to find solutions. This chapter discusses types of family crises including juvenile delinquency and family violence. The chapter also deals with ways to handle the problems and resources to help families cope.

VOCABULARY

antisocial behavior
juvenile delinquency
violence
child abuse
hotline

When a person is trying to deal with a crisis, it is difficult to function at school, home or work.

Families in Crisis

There is a big difference between a family problem and a family crisis. Family problems are related to changes that occur in the family life cycle. These problems can be difficult, but solutions can be found. The family crises discussed in this chapter are extremely serious situations that develop when a family member repeatedly commits crimes against individuals and/or society. Families in crisis may need to seek support outside the family.

Antisocial Behavior

Almost half of all major crimes in the United States are committed by people who are not yet legally adults. Some illegal behavior is harmful primarily to the youths themselves, for example, truancy, running away, and illegal drug use. Other actions, such as vandalism, auto theft, robbery, burglary, arson, rape, and homicide, are examples of **antisocial behavior.** It deprives people of life, health, or property and thus poses a threat to society.

Juvenile delinquency is defined as the illegal behavior of children and youths under legal age (in most states, age 18). Many young people engage in an illegal act at some time in their lives; they may steal something, run away from home, or be truant from school. Delinquents, however, repeat their behavior so that it becomes a pattern of living.

Characteristics of Antisocial Behavior

Many people assume that delinquency is the inevitable result of unemployment, slum life, crowded living conditions, or other urban social problems. While these factors do influence behavior, delinquency is also prevalent in middle-class suburbs and rural areas. Why some children become delinquent while others with the same background and living conditions do not, remains an unanswered question.

Study of Delinquents vs. Nondelinquents In a famous study, Eleanor and Sheldon Glueck matched five hundred delinquent adolescent boys from a slum area with five hundred adolescent boys from the same area who were not delinquent. They matched individuals from the two groups according to age, family background, social and economic status, intelligence, and health. The purpose of the study was to discover the differences between delinquents and nondelinquents.

The Glueck study concluded that young people respond to pressures differently. In both groups, crowding, poverty, family problems, and lack of parental love were serious problems. However, it was clear that the delinquents were more aggressive. They showed hostility, defiance, and suspicion and did not submit to authority. They had less self-control and tended to "act out" their anger. They also were more stubborn, less self-critical, less conscientious, less practical, and less realistic.

The study also found that antisocial behavior had been evident in many of the delinquents by the time they were eight years old. Further, while the nondelinquents also faced difficulties in their environment, these youths handled their problems differently. They did not become aggressive or join gangs.

While both groups had the same general intelligence levels, the delinquents had poor verbal abilities and poor problem-solving skills. Delinquents also tended to have failed grades in school; however, their lack of progress seemed to be a result, not a cause, of their problems. On the other hand, the delinquents were more skilled in working with their hands.

Gang Behavior The Glueck study revealed that many delinquents joined gangs. A gang seemed to provide troubled young people with a place where they could win acceptance. Gang members tended to imitate each other and thus to reinforce group behavior. The study did not confirm the commonly held belief that gangs lead innocent young people astray. Rather, the study showed that youths already had become delinquent before joining gangs; they joined the gangs in order to associate with other delinquents. Nondelinquents did not join gangs, but instead sought friends similar to themselves. Gang membership frequently meant engaging in destructive behavior. Conflicts with other gangs over territory, or "turf," were common. Disputes sometimes led to injury or death of gang members.

Vandalism, or the destruction of property, is a common activity of antisocial youths. They often target schools because they are symbols

Vandalism is one type of antisocial behavior.

Antisocial Crimes 1985		
	Ages Under 18	Ages 18 and Over
Violent Crimes		
Robbery	30,154	90,347
Aggravated Assault	36,257	226,863
Forcible Rape	4,830	27,104
Murder	1,311	14,466
Property Crimes		
Burglary	145,254	236,621
Larceny/Theft	386,217	792,849
Motor Vehicle Theft	43,946	71,675
Arson	6,906	9,871
Vandalism	100,353	123,693

Source: Crime in the U.S., 1985 Uniform Crime Reports, Table 33, p. 174, Federal Bureau of Investigation.

Small children have little control over their anger. Scenes like the one above (left) are common. Sometimes adults lose control too, and have child-like temper tantrums.

of authority. Arson is another activity gangs often undertake in revenge for a real or imagined wrong. Lives as well as property may be lost. Gangs also may direct violence against individuals. Sometimes, robbery appears to be the motive in muggings. At other times, inflicting personal injury is an end in itself.

Background to Antisocial Behavior

Although research has not yet explained why patterns of delinquency persist, some areas need further study. These include the ways children learn to express anger, the factors involved in aggression, and the relationship of environmental factors to behavior.

Anger and Aggression Most children express anger. As a child grows, the causes of anger and frustration change. For example, a two-year-old becomes enraged when a toy is taken away. Jealousy and feeling unfairly treated arouse anger in the middle years of childhood. Adolescents often are angered by restrictions on personal freedom and criticism.

Very young children act out their anger by hitting, biting, or kicking. Temper tantrums also express rage, but they are not directed toward a specific object or person. Later, children express anger in words instead of actions, for example, "You make me so mad!" Ideally, as they mature, young people learn to exercise self-control in expressing thoughts and feelings. It is important to learn how to express "I am angry" without displaying verbal aggression toward another person. If a child is afraid to express negative feelings toward the person at whom the anger is directed, the anger is displaced toward a person or object that the child does not fear. Some psychologists believe that people who engage in violent behavior toward strangers actually may be displacing the anger they feel toward persons they know.

Environmental Influences Environment also helps determine how children express their anger and whether their behavior is social or antisocial. Children are subject to many influences other than their parents and families. Neighborhoods, schools, the media, and peers are the most important outside influences. You are probably aware of the powerful influence television has on people.

Students may spend as much as half their time in schools. Children whose friends and teachers accept them can be more relaxed and can turn their attention to schoolwork. Less secure or less popular children may approach learning with fear and discomfort. Each success brings increased confidence, making the child's task easier. On the other hand, failure increases insecurity, bringing further loss of confidence and self-esteem. Whether a child becomes more or less secure, the result affects the child's behavior and choice of friends and associates.

Children commonly want to do what their peers are doing. As children grow, they spend less time at home and more time in the company of friends and schoolmates, whose opinions and preferences become increasingly important. Peer pressure can lead a child to perform illegal acts if the child needs acceptance and approval. This fact is especially true when a child's companions are older, are more experienced, and are looking for adventure. Shoplifting frequently occurs in pairs or in groups. Peer pressure is a factor in drug use, too. The more a person needs to be one of the group, the more difficult it is to resist peer pressure. Students who have gained self-esteem from school successes may be more socially successful and less subject to harmful peer pressure.

Possible Solutions

...ions on the causes of antisocial ...t; however, there is little agree- ...olutions. Some social critics claim ...out unemployment and poverty

would eliminate antisocial behavior. However, the fact remains that delinquents come from all levels of society.

School Programs It has been suggested that schools can help students with behavioral problems. For example, schools could use testing methods to detect weaknesses in student's verbal and problem-solving skills and then act to correct such deficiencies.

Experts agree that the acquisition of reading and mathematical skills is especially important to school success. Although there is some disagreement about methods of teaching, the "helping process" appears to be effective. When older children with reading or math difficulties are specially trained to tutor younger students who have similar problems, both show improved reading and mathematical skills. They also show improvement in other school subjects. In the process of learning how to tutor, the older students themselves are motivated to learn. Tutoring younger children also builds confidence and self-esteem in the older students.

Ten Most Stressful Life Changes

1. Death of a spouse
2. Divorce
3. Marital separation
4. Jail term
5. Death of family member
6. Personal injury or illness
7. Marriage
8. Firing from job
9. Marital reconciliation
10. Retirement

Source: Adapted from Stress: Blueprint for Health *(Blue Cross Association), XXV (1), 1974.*

Family Life

Young people with promising manual skills may prefer a vocational program to an academic one. Vocational education may help some youths set career goals for themselves, while teaching skills that will help the students obtain employment. Student vocational organizations, such as the Vocational Industrial Clubs of America, the Future Homemakers of America, and the Distributive Education Clubs of America, help students develop leadership abilities and interpersonal skills. Although student-managed clubs were not established primarily to assist young people with personal problems, they still can play a part in helping youths who are potentially antisocial to accept authority. Students can also learn how to make job applications, develop job skills, and set career goals.

Community Programs Communities can help troubled adolescents who have left school but who now wish to continue with their education or job training. One community program, Youth Opportunities Unlimited (YOU), is sponsored by a juvenile court in the St. Louis area. Youths 16 years of age and older, who have either asked for help or have been referred by the court, receive job training, placement, and follow-up services. As a result of these services, a large number of young people have completed their high school education and proceeded directly to employment or to college. Follow-up services offer aid in career planning and help with on-the-job advancement.

Trainees need strong motivation to take advantage of the education, training, and employment opportunities that the program offers. Education in the benefits of employment has helped provide this motivation. Community business leaders serve as volunteers to demonstrate what employment is like, what the benefits are, and how to apply for a job. People involved in the program believe they can best change antisocial behavior by providing young people opportunities to develop self-esteem.

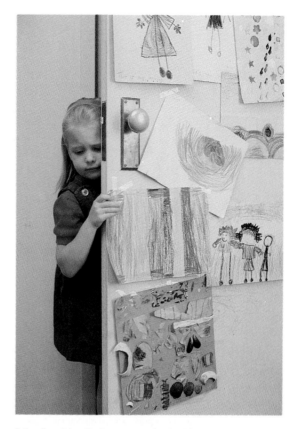

A family crisis affects everyone in the family unit.

Family Violence

Violence is either using physical force against another person, or causing another person to carry out an act by using or threatening to use force. Violence may be used deliberately to cause mental pain, fear, or injury. A person is most likely to become violent under the stress of disagreement, especially when his or her authority is questioned. Many people view violence as an attempt to assert authority and control. Although the idea is hard for many people to accept, violence does occur within families. Newspaper articles and television programs have helped arouse public awareness of this disturbing issue. Perhaps you know of groups in your community that help combat family violence or aid its victims.

How can communication among family members help to prevent violence?

Spouse Abuse

Violence against one's marital partner may range from verbal cruelty to severe physical abuse or even homicide. Statistics show that wife abuse is reported more often than husband abuse, no doubt because social stereotypes of manhood discourage men from reporting such incidents. Although most calls the police receive concern family disputes, much marital violence goes unreported. Society tends to believe that what happens in a marriage is no one else's business. Some people even believe that the abused partner is at fault in some way. (Case studies show that this belief is rarely true.)

Even when marital violence is reported, the abused spouse may remain in the violent situation rather than seek outside help. Reasons for this choice may include the following:

- Seeking help may seem a painful and embarrassing admission that one's family life is not always happy.

- Fear sometimes paralyzes a person's ability to take self-protective action.

- Some people believe that children are better off with two parents, even when one is violent.

- Low self-esteem may keep a person from seeking help. People who feel like failures may come to believe that they deserve or should expect marital failure. Perhaps their situation resembles the one that existed for them at home when they were children.

- Lack of personal or financial resources may cause wives in particular to remain in a marriage. Research has shown that wives who are unemployed, who have no independent financial resources, or who have less than a high school education (resulting in limited job skills) are most inclined to tolerate abuse. They see no way to care for themselves or for their children outside the marriage.

- Lack of community support may leave an abused spouse few alternatives. Public agencies often have no guidelines available for coping with cases of spouse abuse. Laws protecting one spouse from abuse by the other are very recent and many communities have no protective shelters for spouses who wish to escape from a violent marriage.

Child Abuse

Every state has a legal definition of child abuse in order to identify and prosecute reported cases. Generally, **child abuse** refers to mistreatment of a child under 18 years of age by a person responsible for the care and well-being of the child. Mistreatment may involve physical or emotional injury or neglect. Therefore, child abuse is any action or condition that interferes with a child's physical, mental, emotional, or social growth.

Inflicting bodily harm on a child is the most visible form of child abuse. Emotional scars are left as well. Psychological and emotional abuse means failing to provide a child with the love and encouragement necessary for the development of a stable, healthy personality. For example, if a parent repeatedly rejects a child by calling him or her a "dummy" or labeling behavior as "lazy" or "no good," the parent is emotionally abusing the child. This type of abuse destroys a child's self-esteem. However, it is difficult to identify because it leaves no bruises or broken bones. Sometimes, physical symptoms do appear as a result of emotional stress, and they can lead to a failure to thrive.

Another form of child abuse is neglect, which includes failure to provide necessities such as adequate food, clothing, shelter, or health care. Leaving young children at home alone for long periods of time or allowing them to run around in the streets at late hours are examples of parental neglect. Sometimes parents cannot afford to provide the necessary care for their children, or they are so preoccupied with problems of their own that they cannot pay attention to their children. In these cases, neglect may be a difficult condition to cure.

Reasons for Family Violence

If a child learns how to get what he or she wants by violent means, the child will use these methods again and again, perhaps throughout life. Successful violence tends to be repeated. For some, violence may be the only way they know to gain a temporary sense of power over others and to acquire a kind of respect, even if based on fear. Reports of some family violence indicate that the abusive person regards the abused as a possession rather than as a person with feelings. Also, some abusers have been found to be mentally ill.

Social Approval Society appears to approve the use of physical force to some degree. Seeing a child being spanked in a supermarket may distress some observers, while others may thoroughly approve. In general, force is considered acceptable in disciplining children. Parents may believe a child's undesirable behavior means that they have lost control of the situation. Abuse, then, becomes a desperate attempt to regain control.

Stress Violent behavior is closely related to stress. A person who is tense and under pressure is less able to cope with annoyances and is more likely to become angry and to overreact. A burned dinner or tripping over a child's toy may be the last straw. Any number of factors may trigger stress and increase the possibility of the abuse. Loss of a job, for example, can cause much anxiety. Poor health, poor housing,

---

Safety Tip

To spot victims of child abuse, look for these signs that may indicate abuse:

- Extreme shyness, fearfulness, nonresponsiveness or low self-esteem.

- Physical or emotional difficulties (stomach aches, nightmares, bed wetting).

- Violent or highly aggressive behavior.

- Not wanting to be left alone.

- Unexplained bruises or other injuries.

- Change in appetite.

- School problems, inability to concentrate on assignments.

Losing a job is especially stressful for a person who has a family to support.

and overcrowding lead to stress, which may then lead to outbreaks of violence.

Background of Violence According to family researchers, people who were abused as children are most likely to abuse their own children and spouses. If children observe that parents use violence to solve problems, maintain control, or change behavior, the children may turn to force also.

For Review

1. Explain what is meant by delinquent behavior.
2. What did the Gleuck Study reveal about the behavior of gang members?
3. What are some of the reasons for family violence?

Crisis Resolution

Most families in crisis are able to heal themselves without outside aid. In fact, one study shows that most families prefer to work out their own solutions to their problems. Family self-help is most effective in building competence and self-esteem. Still, some events are too complex or too shattering for families to handle by themselves, especially when members of the extended family are not available, or when too many problems occur at the same time. A problem may then become a dangerous crisis.

Coping with a Crisis

Social researchers have noticed a pattern in the responses of families to crisis. When trouble comes—perhaps loss of a job—the first reaction is often shock, and then life goes on for awhile as if nothing had happened. The family needs time to accept the fact that something painful has happened. Recognizing a crisis is the first of many adjustments that must be made.

In the next stage, the family attempts to muster resources to cope with the crisis. If the crisis involves unemployment of the breadwinner, the family may assess its savings, attempt to borrow money, and consider moving in with relatives. The crisis usually is not resolved at this stage, however, and the situation often gets worse; disorganization may set in. Living patterns may be disrupted, children may miss school, and illnesses may occur.

After a period of time, possibly weeks or months, an upturn takes place. Conditions gradually begin to improve. Relatives may help take care of the children, or the breadwinner may find a new job. The family begins to reorganize. In the final stage, reorganization becomes firm. Family members settle into new roles and different patterns of behavior. Gradually, the family begins to accumulate resources to handle future problems.

Calling a hotline is one way a person can get information and support when she is in a crisis.

Community Resources

When a crisis occurs, a family needs information or assistance to supplement its own resources. Relatives are the most likely source of help in an emergency. However, if relatives do not live close by, families can turn to community services.

Hotlines Some communities provide toll-free telephone services called **hotlines.** Hotlines are manned by trained volunteers who provide information, understanding, and reassurance. Hotlines are often advertised on billboards, radio, and television. Frequently, they provide a 24-hour source of information and emergency aid. They handle problems such as parental stress, suicide prevention, child/spouse abuse, rape, advice to runaways, and drug abuse. A list of hotlines appears on page 222.

Professional Services If a family is involved in a long-range problem, its members may need professional help. Psychologists and psychiatrists offer long-range therapy. They can help with problems such as drug addiction, alcoholism, or violence. If the cost of private therapy is a problem, families should look for

Skilled professionals can help individuals and families resolve problems.

institutions in the community that offer clinic services.

Most communities have mental health centers either associated with hospitals or social service agencies or functioning as separate agencies. Though they differ in size and programs, most mental health centers have 24-hour crisis services and consultation services. Private social agencies such as Family Service of America, Catholic Charities, and Jewish Family Services offer casework and counseling services to families.

Self-Help Groups For people who prefer group counseling, self-help or peer-support groups have become popular sources of aid. These groups serve to reduce the social isolation of members, who share problems and give

Hotlines

If you are thinking about running away or have run away,

Call **NATIONAL RUNAWAYS HOTLINE** 800-231-6946 (in Texas, 800-392-3352)
They provide: counseling on resolving home problems, referrals to local social service agencies and to safe shelters. They will send help to your home in an emergency **abuse** situation or refer you to OPERATION HOME FREE for free transportation home.

Call **NATIONAL HOTLINE FOR MISSING CHILDREN** 800-843-5678
They provide: counseling, referrals to local social service organizations, recommendations of local shelters.

Call **NATIONAL RUNAWAY SWITCHBOARD** 800-621-4000
They provide: help and guidance for such problems as **drug abuse, child abuse,** and **sexual abuse,** referral to local social service agencies and shelters, and transmittal of messages to parents without disclosing the runaway's location.

If you are the victim of or have observed child abuse,

Call **NATIONAL CHILD ABUSE HOTLINE** 800-422-4453
They provide: crisis intervention counseling and referrals to local services. All calls are confidential.

If you or someone you know has a drug problem,

Call **COCAINE HELPLINE** 800-662-HELP (800-662-4357) or **800-COCAINE** (800-262-2463)
They provide: counseling on drug problems, referrals to local support groups (such as **NARCOTICS ANONYMOUS** and **COCAINE ANONYMOUS**), to outpatient counseling programs, and to residential treatment centers.

If you have a drinking problem,

Call **AA (ALCOHOLICS ANONYMOUS)** See your local telephone directory.
They provide: referral to their local support groups.

If you have a parent, friend, or relative with a drinking problem,

Call **ALATEEN** See your local telephone directory under **AL-ANON.**
They provide: referral to local support groups of teenagers who have relatives or friends with drinking problems.

If you feel depressed or suicidal

Call a local **suicide prevention hotline.** Most telephone directories list these and other Crisis Numbers in the Community Services section at the front of the White Pages.

A Second Chance

For over a hundred years, a big oak door in Chicago has provided a path from fear and despair to hope and success. It is the door of the Mercy Home for Boys and Girls, a residential community for troubled teens. Those who come knocking on this door come as neglected, abused, or runaway teenagers. They often have been referred there by school counselors, hospitals, drug-treatment centers, or a government service agency.

The staff of professionals and trained volunteers knows that the first priority for these fourteen- to eighteen-year-olds is safety and security. Mercy Home acts as a substitute family—providing an environment of love, discipline, and high expectations for each resident. It also provides two important challenges designed to prepare each teenager to live independently and successfully in the world. The first challenge is to finish school; the second, is to find and keep a job.

Mercy Home is not a school, but it finds the *right* school for each of its residents, paying private-school tuition if necessary. At the same time, the home provides an atmosphere conducive to academic success: regular study hours, special tutoring, encouragement, and shared pride in achievement.

A similar support system helps residents find jobs. Local businesses that previously have employed Mercy Home residents are now becoming the connections that many kids need to get started.

The emotional scars of these troubled teenagers are addressed on a case-by-case basis. Those who need it are given intensive individual therapy. All residents participate in regular group therapy with the staff of psychologists and social workers and with their peers. They learn to respect one another and themselves,

to modify their behavior, and to confront and heal the wounds left by their previous lives.

The cost per resident has skyrocketed since the institution first opened as Mercy Home for Boys in 1887. It then was a struggling orphanage for kids trying to survive on the streets. In 1988, the gift of a nearby mansion allowed Mercy Home to open a separate residence for girls.

The big oak door of Mercy Home allows passage *out* as well as *into* the community. Some kids run away; some are asked to leave because they don't honor the commitment to confronting their problems, remaining drug and alcohol free, participating in therapy, completing school, and holding a job. However, the vast majority of kids successfully complete several years. Mercy Home stays in touch with all its alumni and offers help to any former resident.

Mercy Home is justly proud of its success. Recent alumni include a number of Ivy League college graduates, a judge, a policeman, and a director of the Chicago Board of Trade. At Mercy Home, however, success is defined more broadly. There, it means "getting your act together"; breaking the cycle of neglect, abuse, and despair; and becoming an independent and productive citizen.

Sharing feelings with someone you trust is a great source of support during a crisis.

each other mutual support. Self-help groups, managed by the members, can be helpful to those who take an active part in the organization. One of the oldest self-help groups is Alcoholics Anonymous (AA). Groups have formed to meet diverse needs—for example, self-help groups of parents of mentally or physically handicapped children. Parents Anonymous is a group of parents who are concerned that they have taken out their anger and frustration on their children, or who fear they will do so.

Sharing feelings with others who have the same kinds of problems helps people feel they are not alone. Members of self-help groups provide support for one another in times of stress. They reassure each other that an understanding person will be available quickly in a crisis and will help as long as necessary.

Family Networks Networks of relatives and friends may intervene successfully in a crisis. Some professionals work with both a family and a large group of the family's relatives and friends. The latter group and the family, under professional direction, discuss, interact, and explore the family's problems. For example, a young drug user who becomes mentally ill might improve with counseling sessions, then move to another state to live with relatives in the network in order to find a satisfactory job and new friends.

Pastoral Counseling Many situations that develop slowly can best be handled in a preventive way, before they overwhelm a family or its members. Religious institutions often have specific programs for those who need help. Many members of the clergy are trained in supportive counseling techniques. Talking to a member of the clergy on a one-to-one basis can be a source of practical and spiritual help.

Crisis Prevention

Researchers have studied some families that have weathered crises well and have identified the factors that contributed to the families' success. Several conditions must be met if families are to manage under severe pressures.

Weathering a Crisis One condition observed in families who manage crises well is family unity—a sense of oneness among family members. Mutual affection, loyalty, shared interests, shared religious commitment, and the

Some people find understanding and comfort in discussing a problem with a pastoral counselor.

How can families work together to survive a crisis?

interdependence of members are the ties that bind families together. A second condition is family adaptability, the ability to adjust to change. How smoothly and efficiently members can make shifts and adjustments in family living patterns is a measure of family adaptability. Channels of communication between family members must be open. Also, past experience in meeting difficulties usually indicates that new problems will be handled successfully. A third factor present in families that weather crisis well is adequate family organization. The well-organized family maintains harmony between family goals and the goals of individual members. The physical and emotional needs of each member, as well as the needs of the family as a unit, are met.

Monitoring Change If a family is unified, adaptable, and organized, the members probably will not have much trouble handling personal problems. Nevertheless, all families have faced problems caused by changes in their lives. Some changes may have been painful, some not. Some were planned; others were unexpected. If you are like most people, you realize that certain significant changes are inevitable. You must make appropriate adjustments, even if those adjustments are painful at first.

Major changes take place in the family life cycle—for example, leaving one's parental home, marrying, having children, and facing illness or death in the family. To avoid inner conflicts, you can monitor the number of changes occurring at any one time. For example, if you or your fiancé(e) breaks your engagement, it would not be a good time for either of you to change jobs or to move to another city. One major change at a time is enough to deal with. It is wise to control the amount of pressure in your life, whenever possible.

A problem that can cause emotional trouble at one time may be easier to handle at another time. Some problems can be deferred, or put aside. By sorting out problems, you can gain a sense of control over them. You may even be able to eliminate some of the problems in the process.

Hotlines, professional care, self-help groups, and religious organizations can assist in resolving family crises. Some families weather crises well—their members are unified, adaptable, and well-organized. Families can keep personal problems to a minimum if their members learn to monitor the changes in their lives and to prepare adequately for them.

For Review

1. What are the stages a family goes through in response to a crisis?
2. Name two national hotlines that help teens with alcohol-related problems.
3. What family resources help people weather a crisis?

12 Chapter Review

Summary

Antisocial behavior is harmful to others and disrupts society. Nearly half the crimes committed in the United States are carried out by juveniles. One study indicates that most delinquents are aggressive, hostile, and defiant toward authority. Patterns of delinquency may be traced to the way children learn to express anger and to other environmental influences, such as peer pressure.

Educators can plan programs to help delinquent students succeed in school. Vocational education and community job training programs have helped young people find jobs and develop greater self-esteem.

Family violence disturbs the family organization and causes suffering among family members. People who abuse their spouses or children often were victims of violence themselves as children.

Hotlines, professional services, self-help groups, networks of family and friends, and pastoral counseling can be helpful resources to families in crisis.

Vocabulary

Use the following vocabulary words to complete the paragraphs below.

antisocial behavior
child abuse
juvenile delinquency
hotline
violence

Illegal actions that rob people of their property, health, or lives often are described as __1__. Today, half of all major crimes are committed by young people under the age of 18. As a result, __2__ has become a serious problem for the schools, the legal system, and society as a whole.

__3__, the use of physical force against another person, does not occur only on the streets. __4__, the mistreatment of children by their parents or other caretakers, is a form of violence that may involve physical or emotional injury, or neglect.

Of the community services available to families in crisis, a __5__ is an excellent source to contact first. It provides information, understanding, and referrals to other agencies that can deal with family crises.

Chapter Questions

1. Name five personality characteristics of delinquents, as noted by the Glueck study.
2. What is the difference between antisocial behavior and other delinquent behavior like truancy and illegal drug use?
3. What are the factors that motivate young people to join gangs, according to the Glueck study?
4. Why might a child learn to displace his or her anger?
5. How do you think parents can help their children to express negative feelings?
6. Under what circumstances would peer pressure be most likely to influence a child to engage in delinquent behavior?

7. Which of the programs designed to help troubled adolescents do you consider most effective? Why?
8. How does child abuse affect a child?
9. What is neglect?
10. Describe the pattern in which families respond to a crisis.
11. What are the advantages of participating in a self-help group?
12. How might families further develop a sense of unity amongst themselves?

Skill Activities

1. **Communication** With a classmate, investigate the different community services in your area that provide assistance to families in crisis. To locate these agencies, talk with members of the clergy and school guidance counselors, and consult your telephone book's yellow pages. Obtain pamphlets, flyers, and other printed material from the agencies you have located. After you and your partner have studied this material, create a "Community Services Directory" in which you list and briefly describe the services provided by each agency or organization.

2. **Decision Making** With four or five other students, decide how families can be helped to cope with each of the following crises: unemployment of the primary wage earner, a child's shoplifting, and severe illness and death of a grandparent. For each crisis, discuss and decide together the specific steps that you believe a family should take toward resolving the situation. Refer to the text for ideas and suggestions on what the family can do to help themselves, and what resources might be able to help them.

3. **Critical Thinking** What situations occur during the life cycle of a family that cause stress? With four or five of your classmates, review "The Ten Most Stressful Life Changes" list on page 216. Then, have each person make his or her own list of other changes that are likely to occur during the family life cycle. (For example, high school graduation or moving to another state.) After completing your lists, review and compare them. Are there any sources of stress that all members of the group have listed? Which changes do you think might be relatively easy to handle? Which would be more difficult? Finally, discuss the personal, family, and/or community resources that would be helpful in dealing with each of the changes.

4. **Critical Thinking** Participate in a classroom debate that addresses the question, "Should the courts treat juvenile delinquents as adults?" Once your debating team has been selected, gather evidence from recent magazine and newspaper articles to support your case. As you and your team members study and organize this evidence, prepare for the debate by developing logical arguments based on the evidence you have collected.

Unit **4** Life Management

13 Choosing a Career

As you read, think about:

- how you go about choosing a career that will satisfy your goals and needs.
- what you can do to prepare for a career.
- how you learn about job openings.
- why people change careers.

Finding satisfaction and self-fulfillment in the world of work is a major goal for everyone.

This chapter tells how to identify a suitable career, how to prepare for that career and how to get the job you want. The chapter also discusses how career opportunities are changing, and why some people leave their jobs to enter different professions or vocations.

VOCABULARY

headhunters

It is important to consider your strengths and preferences when choosing a career.

Planning for Your Career

You will spend a large percentage of your waking hours in some kind of employment. If you have a job that takes 40 hours a week for 50 weeks out of a year, you will spend up to 2000 hours per year engaged in work. It is clearly worth your time to figure out which career would suit you best.

Assessing Your Personal Resources

As you start to think about your career future, you have to take a close look at what kind of a person you are, what talents and abilities you have, and what your goals are.

To assess your resources and limitations, "map" yourself on paper by answering questions about the following factors:

- Personal characteristics: How would you describe yourself? Are you a leader or a follower? Can you demonstrate ability to get things done? Are you self-motivated? Do you take direction well? Do you like being with many people or a few? Are you better at persuading or supervising? What are your hobbies? What activities and classes in school do you enjoy? What makes you happy? What is unique about

you? In a recent survey, 471 employers ranked the characteristics of young people they would most like to hire. Contrary to popular belief, academic grades ranked low, while leadership ability ranked high.

- Strengths: What do you do best? What do you find easy to do? What do you enjoy doing? Do you work best with people, information or things? In what areas or for what skills have you received the most rewards or praise? If you plan to have a family one day, will you be able to balance the demands of family life with the demands of a career?

- Health: Are there ways in which your physical or emotional health is impaired or limited? Do you have serious allergies that would affect a job choice? Would working with machines or statistics be challenging, or would it make you feel impatient?

- Goals: What are your long-range goals beyond developing a marketable skill that will make you self-sufficient? Do you want to have a family someday? How will this affect your career? You will need to get education, training, and experience while meeting the responsibilities of both career and family.

- Preferences: Is status — being esteemed by the community — important to you? Is a high

An interest or talent that is expressed in high school could evolve into a career.

salary important? Do you want to live in a certain geographical location? Is creativity important to you? Do you want to set your own hours?

■ Money: Do you have ample money saved or can you get financial backing for the education and training you need? Will you have to work full-time or part-time as a student? Can you get loans from your family, a college or university, or another source? Can you live at home during your training period?

Gathering Career Information

Once you have spent some time analyzing yourself and focusing on your goals, strengths, and personal preferences, you will probably have a better idea of what kind of job would give you the most satisfaction. Next, you should collect information about specific careers and job titles. For example, drawing might be your special talent, and you want a career that taps this ability. The problem is, you do not know what the specific job titles are that would make use of your artistic abilities.

You may already have used your school's career resources. Perhaps you have talked with a guidance counselor and have looked through the materials available in the guidance office or the careers center. Where else can you look for information?

The Public Library Many public libraries place pamphlets, books, and magazines about jobs and careers in a special section. If the library does not have such a section, look in the card file under "Careers." Or, go directly to the 300 section of the book shelves. Start by looking under the numbers 317.425, and 331.128 and 331.7. These categories include books on careers in general, careers in special fields, and job hunting.

For an overview, you might start with the *Occupational Outlook Handbook,* published by the U.S. Department of Labor. Updated every two years, this thick paperback is an authoritative source of career information for jobs in 300 fields. It contains a good introductory section on job hunting and job requirements.

If you already have a specific career in mind, such as accounting or teaching, look under that title. The handbook not only describes the job, but also tells what education is needed, average earnings, and so on. For each field, sources of additional information are listed. A companion volume, the massive *Dictionary of Occupational Titles,* lists and describes 2,000 types of jobs and related information.

The *Encyclopedia of Careers and Vocational Guidance, Vol. II: Careers and Occupations,* edited by William E. Hopke, is just what the title says. Alphabetical listings of jobs include such information as training required, physical requirements of the job, and where to get experience.

One way of learning about career options is to review materials in your school or local library.

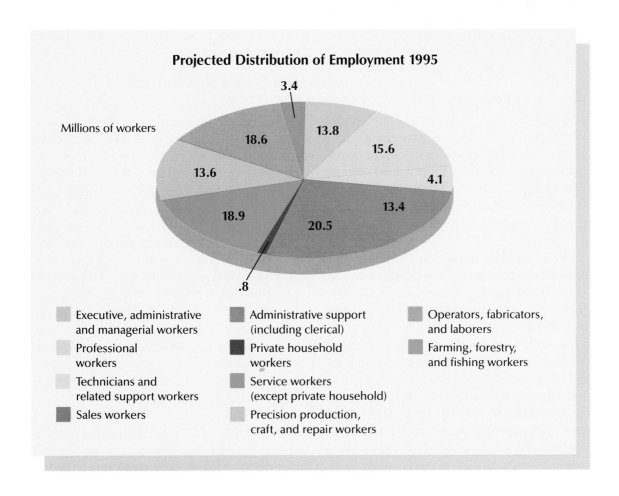

Projected Distribution of Employment 1995

Millions of workers

3.4
13.8
18.6
15.6
13.6
4.1
18.9
13.4
20.5
.8

Executive, administrative and managerial workers

Professional workers

Technicians and related support workers

Sales workers

Administrative support (including clerical)

Private household workers

Service workers (except private household)

Precision production, craft, and repair workers

Operators, fabricators, and laborers

Farming, forestry, and fishing workers

School guidance counselors have practical information about careers that might match your skills and personal goals.

People and Organizations Your school guidance counselors are not the only professionals you can consult for career information. Most states operate Job Service Centers in conjunction with the U.S. Employment Service. The centers are listed in the *Occupational Outlook Handbook.* You may also look in a city telephone book under the listings for the state government.

Do not overlook the informal counseling you can get from individuals who work in your chosen field and who live in your community. The people you or your parents know are good career resources. Most people are willing to talk about their work when you show an interest. Ask them to tell you about its good points and bad points, education needed, and so forth.

Professional organizations, trade organizations, or labor unions exist for a variety of careers. Many publish free career information. For instance, if you were interested in jobs in banking, you could write to the American Bank-

ing Association and ask for career information.

To find the addresses you need, check one of the sources already listed or look in your library for one of the reference guides to professional organizations, associations, and unions. Among these are *Career Guide to Professional Organizations* (Carroll Press), listing 2,000 groups, and *National Trade and Professional Associations of the United States and Canada and Labor Unions* (Columbia Books), listing 6,000 groups.

When you write for information, be brief but direct about what you want to know. Request specific career title information and requirements.

When you look for information on careers, check out as many sources as possible. That way you will know what to expect before you begin a particular job, and you will know how to get the most out of it.

Career Opportunities

In the 1970s, thousands of people planned to become teachers after they finished college or graduate school. Yet, when they applied for teaching positions, there were not enough openings for all. Because school enrollments had dropped, fewer teachers were needed.

By contrast, programmers, analysts, and other people who trained to work with computers found they could pick and choose among job offerings. The reason: the computer field was booming, creating thousands of new jobs.

As you plan a career, you cannot ignore changes in the job market. These changes can directly affect future job openings. Of course, your own interests, abilities, and career goals will be the main factors in choosing a career. However, you must also be realistic about the future of the field you choose.

Fortunately, changes in the job market usually do not occur overnight. Often changes are so gradual that researchers can predict them. Predictions such as these are the task of

According to job projections, will there be many job openings in the careers shown above in the next ten years?

the Division of Occupational Outlook of the Department of Labor.

In the 1988–1989 edition of the *Occupational Outlook Handbook,* the Bureau of Labor Statistics predicted that by the year 2000, nearly four of five jobs will be in service-producing industries. Those expected to grow rapidly include

- Business services
- Health services
- Retail and wholesale trade
- Finance, insurance, and real estate

Occupations expected to grow at a faster-than-average rate include

- Lawyers
- Teachers, librarians, counselors
- Economists
- Psychologists
- Teacher aides
- Health service administrators

Also in this fastest-growing group are dental hygienists, computer service technicians, flight attendants, physical and respiratory therapists, and speech pathologists. All of these statistics must be read carefully, however. Even though an occupation is expected to grow rapidly, it may provide fewer actual openings than an occupation that is large but growing slowly. That is because some areas, like service-producing industries, account for so many of the total number of jobs available.

The following example can help you understand this. Between 1986 and 2000, employment for medical assistants will increase by approximately 90%. That is an astounding increase, which marks this as one of the country's fastest growing fields. In contrast, employment for retail sales workers will increase by about 34%. That's a large increase, too, but nowhere near 90%.

Yet, there will be an increase of 1.2 million jobs for sales workers as opposed to an increase of 100,000 jobs for medical assistants. That's because the existing number of medical assistants is small compared with the existing number of retail sales workers.

Some fields will show no growth between now and the year 2000; others may decline. For example, the number of jobs in manufacturing, mining, fishing, forestry, and agriculture is expected to decrease. This does not mean that many people will not do well in these fields. It does mean, however, that the competition for the best jobs will be stiff.

To find more detailed information about forecasts in the career you are considering, check the up-to-date career materials available from your school guidance counselor or in the public library. Two valuable resources are the *Occupational Outlook Quarterly,* published by the Department of Labor, and *Career World,* a periodical for high school students. Both have articles on finding jobs and on specific careers. Contact with people in the field today will also keep you current on your job prospects for tomorrow.

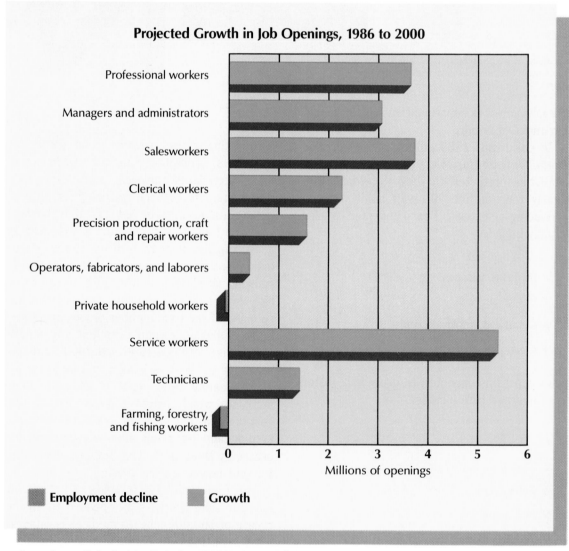

Projected Growth in Job Openings, 1986 to 2000

Millions of openings

■ Employment decline   ■ Growth

Source: Bureau of Labor Statistics, "Projections 2000," March, 1988, Bulletin 2302

Part-time or volunteer work can help you clarify career interests.

Preparing for Your Career

If in your self-assessment you have discovered that you need special training, experience, or education for your career field, you should start now to look into the various educational programs and volunteer or part-time work opportunities available to you. These programs will not only help you prepare for a chosen career, but they could even introduce you to careers you might not have considered.

Part-time or Volunteer Work

While you are still in school, you can start to prepare for a career by getting involved in part-time or volunteer work. Do not underestimate

What skills are being developed in these part-time jobs? How might these skills be put to use in different careers?

the value of this kind of experience and how it affects your career planning. First of all, the more work experience you have, the easier it will be to identify the kind of work you do or do not want to pursue further. All kinds of work experiences — camp counseling, waitressing, babysitting, or pumping gas — help you recognize what kind of work skills you have.

When you start applying for full-time work, employers will look at your background. Many employers feel that work and volunteer experiences help candidates gain insight into the working world and develop leadership ability.

Trade Apprenticeships

Trade apprenticeships available through government programs, labor unions, or employers, enable workers to learn how to do a job while being paid for the work. School guidance counselors usually have information on local trade apprenticeship programs. In some cities, Apprenticeship Information Centers (AIC), affiliated with U.S. Employment Service Centers, are good sources of information. Through trade apprenticeships, you can learn the job skills you need to get the type of position you want.

A high school education is sufficient for most trades. Some trades, however, such as carpentry or electrical work, require more than a high school education. Now that some college graduates are choosing well-paid "blue-collar" careers, job entry into trades has become more competitive. The better your education, the better your chances are for getting a good job in a trade.

College Programs

Students in college today are much more likely to have definite career plans than students in the past. They have become more realistic about their prospects in the complex and swiftly changing job market.

Faced with declining enrollments because of a steady decline in the number of prospective students, many colleges are changing their requirements in an attempt to attract applicants. They are making academic programs more convenient for students with full-time or part-time jobs. Many colleges offer lifelong education programs and night classes.

As you assess your resources and needs for training or further education, write down some jobs that come to mind. Then weigh the costs of your choices. What will you gain from each job? What will you have to give up for its benefits? Try to narrow your selections, even though there is nothing final at this point about your decisions. Making some choices now will give you the confidence you need to begin to chart your own course in the world of work.

Some colleges offer programs that prepare students for specific careers.

For Review

1. List three important questions to ask yourself when planning your career
2. Where can you find information about careers?
3. What job category will have the most job openings through the 1990s?

Besides reading the Help Wanted section of the newspaper, how can you learn about job openings?

College placement services act as liaisons between students and potential employers.

Getting the Job You Want

To get just the right job, you must find a job opening, apply for the job, and have a successful interview. It is important to put as much effort as possible into these processes. Failure to make the right move in any of these steps could affect the outcome of your job search.

The Job Opening

There are several ways to find out what jobs are available. Besides the "Help Wanted" ads in the newspaper, there are private and government career counseling and job placement agencies, college placement firms, and of course, personal contacts. This section will explain three of the methods used to find job openings.

Newspaper Ads "Help Wanted" ads in the classified section of the newspaper are good sources of job openings. It is a good idea to read all the listings in the paper every day, not just the ads under the category that interests you. You might see an ad that gives you a new idea of how to approach your job search. If you see an opening that you qualify for, respond that day, or a more agressive job hunter may get the job.

When you answer a newspaper ad for a job, follow these suggestions so that your response stands out. Give yourself every opportunity to be interviewed:

- Write your letter of response so that you fit the specifications in the ad as closely as possible.

- Keep your letter brief. Include only the most important information.

- If an ad asks you to send your salary requirements, state a wide salary range and add the words "depending on the nature of the duties and responsibilities."

Agencies Private job placement agencies are sometimes called **headhunters.** Companies hire the agency to find suitable applicants for their job openings. Making yourself known to such an agency can be helpful. Once the agency knows you, you might be called for a number of different interviews. Your local state employment office or Job Service Center maintains lists of job openings. Visit the office or center every week to keep up with new jobs listed. The address is in the phone book, under listings for the state.

Personal Contacts One effective method for finding out about jobs and job openings is to set up "information-gathering interviews." In this interview, you are not applying for a job; you are on a "fact-finding mission." First, contact someone who has the kind of job you would like to have. During the interview, ask the person to talk about many different aspects of the job, the positive and negative sides. Find out what kind of background the person has and what other jobs he or she has had. It is also helpful to know what kind of training or education the person completed. This type of interview is helpful in two ways. First, it gives you information about the career that you are interested in. Second, it gives you a chance to establish personal contacts within the organization. You are a familiar face, not just a name on a letter.

You may not get a job as a direct result of this kind of interview, but you have a better chance of being asked in for a real job interview if an opening occurs.

The Interview

Most employers consider the interview the single most important step in getting a job offer. Thus, you should be thoroughly prepared for the kinds of questions an interviewer may ask. Before the interview, find out as much about the company or organization as you can so that you will be able to give informed, interesting answers to key questions such as the following:

- Why do you want to work for us?

- What do you know about our products?

- What are your job goals ten years from now?

- Why should we hire you instead of one of the other applicants?

- Tell me about your last job.

- What special skills do you have?

- What are your weaknesses?

- Tell me about yourself.

First impressions are important. Take time to prepare yourself thoroughly for a job interview.

To have a successful job interview:

- Open the interview with a firm handshake.

- Be prepared. Know about the company.

- Anticipate questions you will be asked. Rehearse the answers.

- Dress conservatively.

- Arrive five minutes early.

- Maintain good posture. Do not chew gum, bite fingernails or talk with hands.

- Maintain eye contact when talking.

Before you have said a word, the interviewer forms an opinion about you from the way you look, walk, and dress. He or she can tell something about your work habits by how you filled out the job application and whether you arrived on time for the interview. (There is *no* excuse for being late.)

For the interview, dress neatly and conservatively. This is no time for jeans or for standing out in the crowd. You should look neat, clean, and businesslike. If possible, scout the business ahead of time. Check out how the employees dress. It will tell you something about what kind of clothes are acceptable there.

Your response to questions such as "Tell me about yourself" gives the interviewer a chance to see how you operate. Your answers should include information that shows why you would be a valuable employee. They should help keep the interview focused on the issue of you and the job. Mention volunteer work and other experience you may have had that might relate to the job. Mention your interest in going to night school to sharpen your skills.

Feel free to ask the interviewer questions about the job and the company after he or she has asked you questions. Ask about opportunities for advancement, company training programs, and company benefits such as health insurance. Your first questions should not be about vacations, sick leave, or holidays, since they would make you sound as if you are more interested in time off than in working.

Follow-up After the interview, if it is appropriate, send a prompt follow-up letter to the interviewer. The letter is another chance to bring your name to the interviewer's attention. You might also want to follow up on your interview by making a phone call to check on the status of the job.

If you walk out of the interview knowing that you failed to get the job, consider it a learning experience and try to analyze what went wrong. You might even want to make notes of things you wish you had said or had not said. Then at the next interview, you will not repeat the same mistakes.

Changing Careers

In November of her junior year, Maggie Signorelli's dad lost his job when the insurance firm where he worked as an office manager went out of business. At the age of 41, Mr. Signorelli had to hunt for a new job.

When Jean Mitchell began applying to colleges, her mother announced that after seven years as a hospital admissions clerk, she, too, planned to go to school. With the encouragement of the hospital administrator, she enrolled in a local college program that trained people for the newly created hospital job of patient representative.

Ed Signorelli and Ruth Mitchell changed careers for different reasons. Yet their experiences are typical of what is happening in the working world. Changing jobs and even switching to entirely new careers is becoming more and more common for many people.

Making a Job Interview Work for You

Everybody finds interviewing for a job nerve-wracking. There is a method you can use to make the interview less stressful. It is borrowed from professional actors who have developed it to overcome stage fright and to help them give a convincing performance.

Think of a job interview as a small play. You are the leading character. By dressing for the part, practicing your lines, and learning how to ad-lib, you can shed most of your nervousness and concentrate on what you have to tell the interviewer.

First, plan your costume. This role demands conservative clothes. A young woman should wear a well-tailored suit or dress. A young man should wear a jacket, a shirt, and a tie. Avoid extreme accessories and bright colors. Even if you have to borrow some of the clothes, dress for the part.

The following incident shows how important the right clothes can be. Several years ago a research team made a study of interviewers' attitudes about job applicants. They set up two interviews with a personnel director. The first applicant was a bearded young man dressed in blue jeans and a brightly-flowered sports shirt. In spite of good qualifications he was turned down. Several days later a clean-shaven young man wearing a dark suit and tie, with a business-style haircut, talked with the personnel director. His skills were good but not quite as good as those of the first young man. He was given the job. When the interviewer was asked her reasons for making her choice, she said the second man was better qualified. She was then told, much to her amazement, that the two applicants were one and the same person. Although she had not been aware that she had made her choice purely on the applicants' appearance, that was the deciding factor.

Once you have chosen what you will wear for the interview, decide what main points you want to present. Think how to answer hard questions such as: "How would you describe yourself? Why should I hire you?" Think of special interests and skills you have that you could apply to the job.

The next step is to hold a rehearsal. Ask a friend or relative to help you role play the interview. Have your friend ask you questions about your background, your skills, and why you have chosen this particular job. If you get tongue-tied when questioned, remember you are playing the part of a self-assured person, eager to learn about the new job. If you begin to ramble on too long or talk too fast, concentrate on giving short, specific answers. After the interview rehearsal, have your friend help you evaluate your performance.

The actual interview will be different from the rehearsals, but you will be experienced in presenting yourself in a positive way. Listen carefully to what the interviewer says. If you stumble over an answer, just stop and begin again. Think of all those other applicants who have not rehearsed. If it should happen that you do not get this job, use this interview as a live rehearsal for the next one.

A neat, well groomed appearance makes a very good impression in a job interview.

Who Changes Careers?

"The average worker under 35 years of age goes about the job hunt once every one-and-a-half years, and the average worker over 35 starts a new job search once every three years." So writes Richard N. Bolles, author of several best-selling books on careers and job hunting.

Of course, there are still people who begin a career in their chosen field and work happily ever after. However, more and more Americans change careers either because they want to or because they must if they want to continue getting paychecks.

Some experts predict that the average worker will change careers three to five times in his or her lifetime. Such averages do not mean that everyone will switch careers. They do indicate that as you begin your working career, you should probably expect to shift careers at least once.

Suppose that you start with a job in one career field. Perhaps you switch jobs once or twice through promotions or by changing employers. As the years go by, however, any one of the following might cause you to change careers:

■ You might realize at age 30 that the career that had sounded just right for you at 18 is no longer stimulating.

■ You might develop a whole new set of interests that leads to a new career. For example, a course in gourmet cooking might lead to a new career in catering.

■ You might find, as Ed Signorelli did, that through no fault of your own, the job market for your chosen field has changed. Either your job has been eliminated or so few openings are available in your field that you have to look for work in another field. (Ed Signorelli, for instance, became a print shop manager.)

■ You might find that some new field that did not even exist when you began working offers exactly the kind of job you want. In the late 1970s, for example, products like video games and hand-held calculators created brand new industries—and new careers.

■ You might find yourself retiring from your first career at an early age, but you want to continue working. Fields such as the military, police work, and fire fighting often permit retirement on partial pensions after 20 or 25 years of work. For someone who started at age 18 or 20, that can mean being "retired" at age 40.

Factors Affecting Career Change

The American economy is like a hand-held kaleidoscope. As you look through the viewer, the slightest shift of your hand changes the pattern. Every shift in the economy changes the pattern of careers open to people. People in the labor force—which includes most adults—simply have to adjust to the shifts.

Another factor that affects job and career change is increased life expectancy. At the turn of the century, life expectancy was about 47 years. Today people live decades longer; in 1980, life expectancy was nearly 74 years.

With longer life expectancy, people also are working longer. At the turn of the century, the average man worked for about 32 of his expected 47 years; the average woman worked about 6 years. Like life expectancy, work-life expectancy has risen sharply. The great influx of women into the labor market that began in the 1970s will influence the figures significantly. Work life for women is expected to rise particularly sharply.

Keeping Up with Career Changes

A fast-changing economy and a longer work life mean that most workers have to learn new skills throughout their working lives. The need for continuous learning is especially strong in high-technology fields such as science and medicine or in manufacturing industries.

This person chose to leave his job as an accountant to start his own video rental business.

Some career counselors say that most workers need more training at least every six years. Often such training is given by the company itself. In workshops and on-the-job training programs, an employee can learn the skills for a new career without changing companies or going back to school.

Literally thousands of career and job courses are available in adult education programs and community workshops, and through correspondence courses and other sources. In one recent year, seven million Americans age 35 or older were enrolled in some form of adult education other than college. Some of them took courses for fun or relaxation. However, most surveys show that about half of the students enrolled to learn new career skills or to improve their existing skills.

College enrollments also reflect the trend toward continuing education. One out of every four college students is 25 years of age or older.

One out of every ten is 35 or older. In the nation's two-year community colleges, half of the students are 28 years of age or older.

Clearly, lifelong learning has become a necessity to most Americans for changing careers or improving old ones. By being ready to reach for new opportunities, Americans can successfully change careers.

For Review

1. Name two ways to answer a "Help Wanted" ad most effectively.
2. What is an "information-gathering" interview?
3. In a job interview, how should you answer the question, "Tell me about yourself"?
4. Name one career in which continuous learning is necessary.

13 Chapter Review

Summary

As teenagers begin planning for their careers, they first should assess their personal characteristics, talents, and abilities, then identify their goals. Gathering information about careers through books, pamphlets, and other resources can help young people make informed career decisions. Professional and trade organizations, labor unions, and individuals working in a young person's chosen field can also provide valuable career information.

A student can prepare for a career by learning about it firsthand through part-time or volunteer work, trade apprenticeships, and various college programs. Job openings found in newspaper advertisements, employment agencies, or through personal contacts can help a person find the right job. The interview is considered to be the most important step toward receiving a job offer. An applicant should be prepared, dress conservatively, and arrive at an interview punctually.

Because of increased life expectancy and a rapidly shifting American economy, many people will change careers one or more times during their working years.

Chapter Questions

1. What are the personal characteristics that make you unique?
2. What special talents or abilities do you have? How might these strengths contribute to the career or job you hope to have?
3. How can you become more informed and experienced in the field that interests you?
4. Why is it important to consult the most recent career resources available?
5. Where should a person look for professional organizations related to career?
6. Do you agree that a person should not pursue a career because there are few projected job openings? Why or why not?
7. How can volunteer or part-time work help you prepare for a career?
8. How have colleges adapted to the changing career needs of today's students?
9. Name four ways to find job openings in a particular field.
10. Compare an "information-gathering" interview with a traditional job interview.
11. What does a prompt follow-up letter convey to a prospective employer?
12. Why is it becoming more common for people to change their careers?
13. What is the term used in referring to private employment agencies?

Skill Activities

1. **Critical Thinking** Collect information about a career that interests you by locating the books discussed in the section "Gathering Career Information" on pages 232–234. After you have consulted four or more resources, write a report in which you discuss the following issues: What are the prerequisites for entry into

this career? What personality traits are best for this type of work? What skills or abilities are needed? What education is necessary and how much will it cost? What roles and responsibilities are part of this career? Finally, based on what you have learned, discuss how you are suited (or not suited) for this career.

2. Social Studies With two or more of your classmates, conduct a survey of the students in your grade to determine the types of volunteer and part-time work that are available to teenagers in your community. Ask all of the students where they work, what type of work they do, and how they believe their job relates (or does not relate) to the job or career they want in the future. When you have finished your survey, tabulate your results. Classify each job by its category. Work categories might include child care, outdoor work, sales, restaurant work, hospital work, and so on. Then develop categories so that you can tabulate students' responses about how they see their current job relating to a future career. Discuss your results with your group before you present your findings to the class.

3. Communication Obtain an "information-gathering" interview from someone working in a career that interests you. First, review "Personal Contacts" on page 241. Next, make a list of the people you, your friends, and your family know who are working in the field you are investigating. Select one person to contact

by letter or by telephone. Once you have an appointment, prepare a list of questions that will give you information you have not found in your reading. For example, what kind of interpersonal contact do you have during an average day? What is the most challenging part of your job? Which aspects of your job do you enjoy the most and the least? What is a typical day like? During the interview, listen carefully to all the information you are receiving. Take simple notes, if necessary. After the interview, write a thank you note to the person you interviewed. Then discuss the new information you have obtained in a brief written report.

4. Reading Compile a bibliography of the career resources available in your school and/or community. After consulting the card catalog and other sources you know, ask the librarian and your guidance counselor for additional references. After you have gathered the necessary information, organize your bibliography according to standard bibliographical rules. Ask your teacher or school librarian for information on how to compile a bibliography.

5. Social Studies With one or more of your classmates, find out what types of trade apprenticeships are available in your community. Your school guidance counselor may have information that will be helpful. Also contact Apprenticeship Information Centers and labor organizations. After compiling all of the information, summarize your findings in a brief written report.

14 Balancing Needs and Resources

As you read, think about:

- what factors affect family management.
- how individual goals, standards and objectives relate to one another.
- how a family's resources affect a family's goals and choices.
- how budgeting can help families manage money effectively.
- what time management practices can be used to improve your use of time.

Management is the development and use of resources to meet personal and family needs and to achieve goals. Home management is the method families use to get what they want out of life. While a family's needs and goals are numerous, its resources usually are limited. The key to good family management is the successful balancing of needs and goals with the resources necessary to achieve them.

This chapter describes the management process, from setting goals and making plans, to managing money and time efficiently.

VOCABULARY

standards	flexible expenses
resources	fixed expenses
feedback	prioritize

Managing Roles

Most people play many different roles in life. People often meet demands on the job, in family life, and in relationships all at the same time. Management practices that help people meet their responsibilities and fulfill their dreams include setting goals, using resources, planning, and getting feedback. Strategies for managing time and money are especially useful for those trying to balance the many demands of pursuing a career and meeting responsibilities to a family. This is especially true when there are dependent children, who require a great deal of care, and whose needs may be difficult to balance with requirements at work.

Setting Goals and Standards

Goals are broad statements of what you want to achieve. Your current goals are the long-range results you have in mind, or the outcomes for which you are willing to work from day to day. You will set other goals as you achieve the ones you are working towards now. You should realize that it takes time and energy to reach a goal. On the way, you will set intermediate objectives for yourself. *Objectives* are the short-range aims that help you reach your goals. You can test them as you go along and change them if they are not helping you.

A family's **standards,** or the quality level of its goals, help determine how much effort family members put forth in trying to reach those goals. Standards are measurable and, in contrast to goals, are readily apparent, or visible. For example, if you swim, what kind of performance do you expect from yourself? Do you usually swim a certain number of laps or a certain distance in a pool? Do you try to increase your skill? The level of skill you expect from yourself is a standard. Your family, likewise, has standards. If an orderly, efficient home is the goal, the standard is the degree of neatness and organization required.

Personal goals may include improving a skill, saving for a car, or planning a trip. What kind of goals do you have?

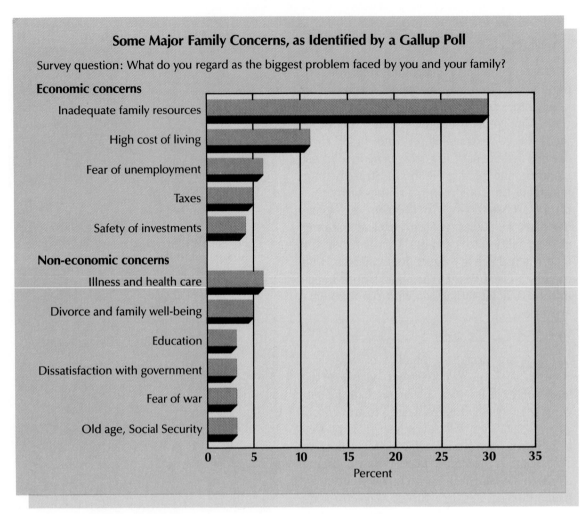

Some Major Family Concerns, as Identified by a Gallup Poll

Survey question: What do you regard as the biggest problem faced by you and your family?

Economic concerns
- Inadequate family resources
- High cost of living
- Fear of unemployment
- Taxes
- Safety of investments

Non-economic concerns
- Illness and health care
- Divorce and family well-being
- Education
- Dissatisfaction with government
- Fear of war
- Old age, Social Security

Percent (0 5 10 15 20 25 30 35)

Source: The Gallup Poll: Public Opinion 1987; George Gallup, Jr., Scholarly Resources, Inc.

Standards should be realistic and possible to achieve. Furthermore, what is appropriate at one time may not be appropriate at another. When family members agree on the same standards of home management, the chances for conflict decrease. Applying standards is an important way to judge the results of your plans and actions.

Family Resources

How you achieve goals and objectives while maintaining your standards depends to a large extent on the **resources**—the elements that are available to your family. Many people think that money is the major, or sole, resource. However, other resources are helpful in achieving goals. Well-managed families use their resources to benefit all members.

Health More than any other resource, good health has a major impact on the well-being of the family. Unlike money, your health cannot be borrowed. Health is a priceless resource that many families take for granted. Access to reliable sources of information and adequate care are important factors in good health.

Information Information resources are numerous and varied. Some of the people you know, for example, relatives, friends, teachers, librarians, and coaches can be valuable sources of information. Other information resources are books, government publications, and the media. The sources that can supply the information you want should be related directly to your goal. For example, the person best qualified to check your homework assignment is the teacher who gave it.

Getting all the information you can about a subject gives you a solid base for making choices. If, for example, you are considering a part-time or volunteer job in your community, you should get the following information:

- Does the work tie in with my interests?

- What kind of people will I meet there?

- Is there anything available to fit my schedule?

- Will it interfere with my other activities?

- Do my parents agree with this idea?

- How can I manage transportation?

- Can I get school credit for it?

Getting this information would require asking questions of your parents, a school counselor, and the prospective employer. Collecting information usually means using a number of different resources. Once you have as much information as you need, you are able to make an intelligent decision.

Energy Energy varies considerably in different individuals, and even in the same person from one time to another. If you examine your habits, you may find that you waste a fair amount of energy every day. The section in this chapter on time-management shows how proper planning can help you save both energy and time. With more energy and more time, you can develop another resource: skills.

Learning how to make efficient use of information is an important skill.

Skills Playing an instrument is a skill. Skills also are used in after-school jobs. Skills may be physical, social, or mental. Physical skills involve muscles, social skills involve insight and poise, and mental skills are as numerous and complex as the branches of human knowledge. Once you master a skill, you perform the activity requiring that skill more quickly and smoothly. You need less effort and concentration. You may become skilled at pitching a ball, typing, knitting, or many other useful activities. The skills you develop rather easily may be related to still another resource: family strengths.

Family Strengths Families often take their own strengths for granted. *Strengths* could be special inherited talents like a good ear for music. They could also be behavioral characteristics such as friendliness or persistence or areas of special knowledge acquired by family members.

The many and varied strengths that families have can be powerful resources for family management.

A person thinking about joining the school band probably would not consider it unless he or she were talented in playing an instrument. All families have some talents that run in the family. One way to discover them is to find out about your ancestors' special abilities. This also will help you establish a practical connection with the past.

Through teaching and example, families set standards of behavior and affect the development of one's character. Courage, perseverance, patience, good humor, and concern for others are just a few strengths many families possess. Special skills and family lore also are worth looking into. For example, perhaps in your family a grandmother's recipes remain favorite dishes. Which of your family's talents, traits, or skills do you hope to keep alive and perhaps pass on to a family of your own?

While family strengths may not always be easy to identify, one obvious resource cannot be overlooked. In fact, it may be the first resource to come to your mind: money.

Money "Money isn't everything" is an expression often greeted with scorn, for apparently some people believe that having more money in hand would solve all their problems. However, it is as important to manage money properly as it is to have it.

Families have to think carefully about how they will spend their money. Most experts would agree that basic needs such as food, shelter, medical care, and transportation to and from school or work should come first. Once these needs are met, how you spend the rest of your money depends on the decisions you make and how you plan to implement those decisions.

For Review

1. Why is it important for a family to set goals and objectives?
2. What is meant by a family's standards?
3. What are some of the important family resources?

The Management Process

The more you understand how families use the processes of good management to achieve their goals, the better you'll be at achieving your own goals, both as an individual and as a family member. Home management, like business management, involves the processes of decision making, planning, getting feedback, and managing money and time efficiently.

Making Decisions

Everyone may feel burdened once in awhile by the vast number of decisions that must be made. Even people with good decision-making skills may find it hard to sort out all the choices that confront them.

Steps In Decision Making Effective decision making usually involves eight steps.

1. Identify the decision to be made.
2. Know your goal.
3. Check available resources; consult authorities if needed.
4. Decide what choices are possible; consider the likely results of each choice.
5. Select the best choice for you; determine the procedures to follow to reach your goal.
6. Act on your plan.
7. Evaluate the results and change your procedures if they don't work.
8. Take responsibility for your decision.

Some families simplify the decision-making process by following these rules: obtain what is cheapest, what is easiest to operate and what is nearby. Such rules can simplify family management, but cause future problems.

The decision-making process, as it was described in Chapter 4, can be used to improve family-management practices.

Cooperation between family members is necessary for effective home management.

Communication Communication contributes to good relationships and good marriages. It is also the key to good decision making. If communication is poor within families, the members are unable to share information or to come up with creative approaches to decision making. Planning becomes more difficult since you cannot take a person's preferences and needs into account when they have not been expressed. Communication within a family presents a challenge because of differences in ages, perceptions, and preferences. If communication among family members is open and satisfying, it will help individuals set worthwhile goals and make realistic plans.

Planning

No family or individual makes plans in a vacuum. The rules and expectations within each society limit what its members can do. Parents, for example, are expected to teach their children certain manners. Your employer expects you to wear clothes appropriate to your job. To sell a certain product or service, you may have to follow regulations that demand getting working papers or a license. Once you recognize society's limits, you can make realistic plans with reasonable confidence of reaching your goals.

Types of Plans Some plans concern events that occur one time only—your high school graduation, for example. Often, such plans require special care because they involve a new experience. At other times, a plan may be used repeatedly to simplify everyday living. For example, clothes shopping, making your bed, and doing homework all are easier if done according to a planned routine. Some plans, once completed, are stored in your mind to be pulled out

What management skills can parents use to deal with the demands of parenthood and household organization?

Getting Your Money's Worth

Your money will stretch a lot further if you follow a few basic shopping rules.

1. Before you set out on a shopping tour, do some planning. Impulse buying is fun, but you may find that after a pleasant day of wandering around buying bargains, you have blown your budget and still do not have the one big item you most wanted. Make a list of the items you want to buy. Estimate how much each will cost. Then check your budget and decide what items you really need. Before you leave home, set a limit of how much you will spend.

2. Compare prices before you buy. Identical products have different price tags at different stores.

3. If you are making an expensive purchase, such as a major appliance or skis, it is worth your time to check product ratings. Consumer magazines are available at the library. They compare the quality and price of major products and list the good and bad points of each one.

4. Choose quality products. A high price, however, does not always mean quality. Always examine the item closely to be sure it is well made. Read the label or the warranty.

5. When purchasing seasonal items such as clothing, sporting goods, or air conditioners, buy off-season when the item is on sale.

6. Decide exactly what you are looking for before making a major purchase. For example, if you are buying a camera, how will you be using it? A lightweight camera that is easy to use may be what you want. If you are seriously interested in photography, you may want a camera that is more difficult to use, but takes sharper pictures in a variety of settings. Is it important to you to have a flash for interior shots, a wide-angle lense for landscapes, or a telephoto lense for shooting from a distance? The sales staff of camera stores can usually answer many of your questions about photography.

7. Beware of the old bait-and-switch practice. This often begins with an ad for a product at a remarkably low price. For example, you see an ad for a color TV for $89.99. That sounds too good to be true. It is. When you show up at the store, you are told the advertised TV is sold out. The salesperson then gives you a big sales pitch about another TV at three times the price of the advertised one.

8. Beware of high-pressure sales methods. Do not let the sales person talk you into buying. If you feel pressured, leave the store and then decide if you want to buy the item.

9. Be very careful about answering ads you receive in the mail or over the phone. Often you are told you have just won a prize. This often depends on whether you sign up for some other item. Hundreds of people are trapped into signing up for magazine subscriptions, or book or record clubs. Do not sign any sales agreement until you know exactly what you are going to be paying.

and used again when similar circumstances arise. For example, vacations at the beach involve similar preparations each year. However, before you can devise a workable plan, you need relevant information.

Gathering Information Information can be gathered through trial and error, research, a brainstorming session, or by consulting others. If you have correct information, you will not overlook possible choices or follow harmful procedures. The less experience you have in doing something the more information you should seek from reliable sources within the family and the community.

Putting Plans into Action How will you put your plans into effect? Do you have all the information you need? It is a good safety measure to recheck a plan before beginning to implement it.

Dividing the work plan into manageable sections often gives you confidence to continue and provides you with an opportunity to see if the result will meet your standard. If it will not, you can adjust your approach. For example, if you want to prepare a special dish to serve guests, you first can serve it to your family to see how they like it.

Cooperating with others often makes a plan easier to carry out. Shopping expeditions for two mothers with active toddlers may be chaotic. Both parents and children return from the store tired and irritated. The mothers might wisely decide to take turns watching the children, thus freeing each other for a few hours of shopping and errands.

Getting Feedback

Feedback, or response, alerts you to possible ways to improve your plan or parts of the plan. It may concern the system of steps you devised, the materials you chose, or the standards you are applying. Some feedback is immediate, such as whether or not the stereo you are considering buying shuts off automatically. Other results are harder to determine. Perhaps as you study for finals, you find that the dance classes you are attending after school require more energy and time than you can afford.

Through feedback, you can gauge the effectiveness of the plan you have chosen. If the plan involves a family goal, family members may need to reevaluate their resources and repeat the decision-making or the planning process.

Managing Money

Most people work hard to earn money. It is important to learn how to manage money so that you can make the most of this valuable resource. Preparing a budget and following it every week or month gives a person greater control of his or her earnings.

Making Up a Budget A budget is a plan showing how much money you will earn and how you will spend your money over a certain period of time. In order to make up a realistic budget you should first keep a record of your income and expenses over a two-week period. To make such a record, make a list of all the things you spend money on. Group your expenses into categories like food, clothing, transportation, medical expenses and entertainment. Once you have kept a spending record, compare this to your income. Now you are ready to write a budget. Divide your expenses into two parts, **fixed** and **flexible** expenses. Fixed expenses are things that must be paid for on a regular basis. Housing costs, electric bills and insurance payments are examples of fixed expenses. Flexible expenses are costs that change from week to week. Clothing, health care, and entertainment are examples of flexible expenses. Using the figures from your spending record, pick a spending limit for each of the expense categories. Try to stay within your budget for a few months. You will probably need to make adjustments in your budget after a few weeks or months have passed. A budget has to be changed frequently to match the needs and circumstances of an individual or family.

When a family uses a budget to manage money, it is possible to achieve recreational goals.

Sample Form for a Yearly Budget

ITEM	JAN.	DEC.	TOTAL
TOTAL MONEY INCOME			
Expenses (fixed)			
Taxes: Federal			
State			
Property			
Auto			
Rent or mortgage payment			
Savings			
Insurance: Health			
Life			
Property			
Auto			
Debt payments: Auto			
Credit card			
Expenses (flexible)			
Operating: Household			
Auto			
Food			
Clothing			
Personal care			
Fares, tolls, other fees			
Medical care			
Recreation and education			
Gifts and contributions			
TOTAL EXPENDITURES			

Managing Time

Do you feel as if you never have enough time? Are you often late meeting friends or keeping appointments? If so, then you are like many people who have trouble managing time. Managing time means using your time efficiently so that you can achieve your goals in life. The following steps will help you make better use of your time:

1. Make a list of personal goals.

2. Look at your current use of time.

3. Reduce the number of "time wasters" in your daily schedule.

Goal Setting   The first step in learning how to manage your time is to make a list of short-term as well as long-term goals. Short-term goals are those things you want to do today, tomorrow, or next week. For example:

- Return books to the library.

- Mow the lawn.

- Go to the dentist.

Writing long-term goals involves careful thought. Try to think about what you would like to accomplish in the next year or in the next five years. A list of long-term goals could include the following:

- Learn to speak Italian.

- Go to college.

- Travel to Europe.

- Lose weight.

Once you have your list of goals, **prioritize** them, or put them in order of importance.

As you accomplish things on your first list, try to think about how your daily activities are helping you accomplish your long-term goals.

Practical Tip

To improve your use of time:

- Keep a log. See where you waste time.

- Set long- and short-term goals.

- Prioritize your goals.

- Focus on one thing at a time.

- Share responsibility when you can.

- Learn to set limits.

Your Daily Schedule   Once you have made up your list of goals, you should look at how you currently use time. Keep an informal diary of your daily schedule for one or two days. Record how much time you spend on each activity. Once you have compared your daily schedule to your list of goals, you will probably want to improve your use of time. One way to do that is to cut down on activities that waste time.

Effective time management can help a person keep up with a busy schedule.

How can the telephone help you manage your time more efficiently?

Time Wasters In order to make more time in your day for the activities that are important to you, you should reduce the number of activities that eat up, or waste your time. The following factors can detract from efficient time use:

- *Television.* Watching television can be a waste of time. Try to watch only the programs that you are really interested in. Limit the amount of time you watch television.

- *Clutter.* People waste a lot of time trying to locate things. If you take time to organize your possessions, your mail, your important papers, you will save time. The use of storage containers, files, and labels will help you sort out the clutter in your life.

- *Telephone.* Be aware of the time you spend on the phone. Try not to visit on the phone with someone you will see in person the next day. Instead of wasting time on the telephone, use it as a time-saving tool. You can use the telephone to do shopping, for example. Instead of driving to a store 20 miles away to buy a certain record, you can save time by calling the store first to see if they have it in stock.

- *Waiting.* Waiting in line, sitting on a bus or in a dentist's office can be frustrating. If you are prepared for waiting, then you will actually enjoy this time by yourself. Always bring a book or newspaper to read when you think you might have to wait somewhere.

Since time is a valuable resource, you will probably want to use time-management practices such as the ones mentioned in this section. Once you have learned how to take control of your use of time, you will be able to accomplish many of your personal and family goals.

For Review
1. Why is effective communication within a family such a special challenge?
2. What are the factors involved in making plans?
3. What is the first step in setting up a family budget?
4. Give two examples of time wasters.

14 Chapter Review

Summary

The management process is an organized way for families to decide on and reach their goals. A family's background helps to shape the goals, objectives, and standards that it chooses to live by. The family's ability to achieve its goals depends on the extent of the resources that are available. These include: health, information, energy, skills, family strengths, and money.

Effective home management involves decision making, planning, interpreting feedback, and managing money and time efficiently. Once family members have made their decisions and set their goals, their plans determine how the goals will be attained. Gathering and evaluating information before executing a plan, putting the plan into action, and analyzing feedback are all important parts of the planning process. Wise management of money, time, and other resources also can help a family achieve more of its goals.

Vocabulary

Complete each of the following sentences with one of the vocabulary words below.

feedback
fixed expenses
flexible expenses
prioritize
resources
standards

1. A person can analyze a plan's effectiveness by evaluating _____.
2. It is important to _____ your short- and long-term goals so that you will know which goals to act on first.
3. The _____ which you set for yourself probably result from the goals and the objectives you hope to achieve.
4. Because the costs of entertainment, clothing, and school supplies fluctuate from week to week, they are considered to be _____.
5. A family's _____ such as money, health, energy, skills, family strengths, and information contribute to a family's ability to attain its goals.
6. A budget accounts for a family's or an individual's _____ which must be paid on a regular basis.

Chapter Questions

1. What is management?
2. What are the factors which combine to make a person's background?
3. How can the setting of goals and objectives assist in helping a person to achieve what he or she wants?
4. Describe two of your family's goals. What are the standards which relate to the potential achievement of these goals?
5. What problems can occur when a family sets unrealistic standards?
6. Why is effective communication important to a family's decision-making process?

7. What are three of your family's strengths? How have they helped your family to achieve its goals?

8. How is managing a home similar to managing a business? How is it different?

9. How has gathering information helped you to formulate a plan during the past several months?

10. How can feedback help a person to improve a plan?

11. Give examples of the fixed and flexible expenses in your monthly budget.

12. Why is it important to prioritize a list of your goals?

13. What do you think are the most prevalent time wasters in the average high school student's day? How do you think this time could be used more effectively?

Skill Activities

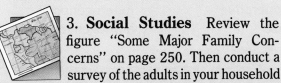

1. **Resource Management** Try to manage your time more efficiently for one week. On Sunday, make a list of your goals for the coming week. Next, create a daily schedule of how you plan to spend your time each day. Be aware of "time wasters" in your schedule. At the end of the week, evaluate your list of goals and your schedule. Which of your goals were you able to achieve? Which were you able to work toward? What time wasters were you able to reduce or eliminate? What role will time management play in your future? Finally, write an essay and discuss your answers to these questions as well as

your other reflections or observations about this activity.

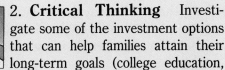

2. **Critical Thinking** Investigate some of the investment options that can help families attain their long-term goals (college education, vacation, home remodeling). Begin by studying how a family can invest $2000. Research in financial magazines, newspapers, and books to gain an overview of the investment opportunities available. Analyze the advantages and disadvantages of savings accounts, certificates of deposit, treasury bills, mutual funds, money market funds, and stocks and bonds. When you have completed your research, draw up an investment plan for such a family. Explain why the investments you have chosen are best for them. Also include advice on how they should invest additional money as funds become available.

3. **Social Studies** Review the figure "Some Major Family Concerns" on page 250. Then conduct a survey of the adults in your household about their family concerns. Write the eleven issues listed in the figure on a piece of paper and ask each family member to rank the items in order of their importance. How do your family's results compare with those presented in the figure? What do you think the factors are that account for the differences you have found? What impact does the date of the Gallup poll have on the results? Participate in a class discussion with other students who have conducted the same family survey.

15 Managing Your Environments

As you read, think about:

- how the term ecosystem relates to families and family environments.
- what is involved in planning a wardrobe.
- how housing meets the physical, psychological and social needs of individuals and families.
- what factors you should consider when you are evaluating a neighborhood.

VOCABULARY

ecosystem	mortgage
manufactured housing	equity
condominium	sweat equity
cooperative	heterogeneous
lease	homogeneous

Families function within several different environments which together make up an ecosystem. This chapter considers some of the environments interacting with you and your family — clothing, housing, and neighborhoods.

Clothing provides an individual with protection and an opportunity for self-expression. Managing a wardrobe involves good management and consumer skills.

Dwellings satisfy many human needs, including shelter, security and privacy. In this chapter, the many housing choices will be described.

Neighborhoods, and the community as a whole are critical parts of a family's environment. This chapter discusses the many factors that determine the quality of a neighborhood and of a community.

Ecosystems

An environment is something that surrounds you. Clothing, housing, and neighborhoods are environments that have a direct effect on members of a family. All the human environments together make up an **ecosystem,** or combination of interacting environments. The term was originally used in the biological sciences to describe the interrelationship of parts in the natural world. This term also applies to families and their environments. Moreover, humans shape their environments, while in turn the environments shape them. Individuals are at the center of a series of ever-widening environmental circles. The circles can be referred to as "near" or "far" environments in terms of their distance from the individual or from the family.

The environments nearest the family are clothing and the home, which in turn are surrounded by the neighborhood and the community. Each environment requires careful management.

A community is part of the family's ecosystem.

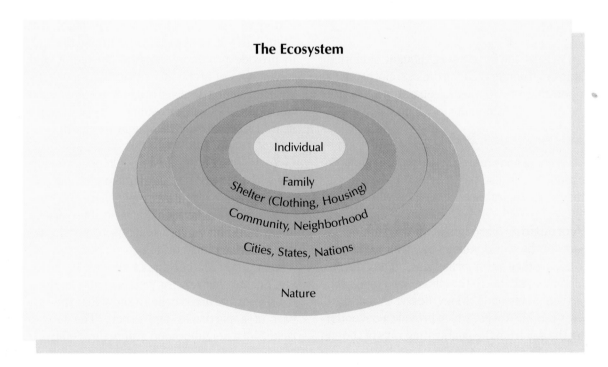

The Ecosystem

Individual

Family

Shelter (Clothing, Housing)

Community, Neighborhood

Cities, States, Nations

Nature

Snowsuits and hardhats are examples of clothing designed to protect the wearer.

Clothing

Perhaps you have never thought of clothing as an environment. Nevertheless, clothes act as a portable environment, separating you from the other environments in which you live.

Functions of Clothing

Clothing does more than form a personal environment. It also serves some basic physical and psychological needs.

Protection Throughout the ages and in all parts of the world, human beings have learned to use clothes as "minishelters." They devised costumes suitable to the climate and geography of their homelands. Many desert nomads still wear tentlike robes, which provide a cover during the day from the penetrating rays of the sun and from the blowing sands. At night, the "tent" may be wrapped closely around the body to provide protection against the biting cold. Inhabitants of arctic and subarctic regions discovered hundreds of years ago that animal skins trap body heat, thus providing a barrier against heat loss to the surrounding atmosphere.

Group Identity Most people need to identify with a group. Wearing similar clothing may indicate that a group of people share the same living conditions, outlook, and heritage. Clothing may contribute to feelings of ethnic, regional, and national pride.

Clothing often becomes a symbol of belonging. School children, for instance, may conform to an informal dress code to show that they are part of a particular age group. The leather jackets of a neighborhood group, the T-shirts of

Think about the way you dress. Do you wear clothes that are similar to other members of a certain group?

a special club, or friendship rings can signify that the wearers "belong." Even people whose clothing represents a protest against traditional forms of dress often tend to look enough alike to be considered a group.

Uniforms contribute to group identity, too. A uniform indicates that the wearer is a member of a particular group such as the armed services, a fire department, or a hospital. A uniform also can appear to confer status on the wearer. Police and airline pilots' uniforms suggest authority and competence. The white uniforms of health care personnel connote cleanliness and professionalism.

Personal Identity Conversely, clothing can fulfill the need to express individuality. In earlier times when all fabrics were hand-woven, individual fabric designs were expressions of creativity and personality. Today, a person's choice of colors, fabrics, and accessories serve the same purpose. By combining these elements in a personal way, an individual expresses a mood, revealing unique qualities and projecting a sense of self.

Lack of interest in appearance often is a sign of low self-esteem. Failure to dress well can be interpreted negatively by others. Bobby Fischer, the world-famous chess player, felt that audiences didn't show him respect until he appeared at tournaments well-dressed. Until that time, he felt that careless dress may have branded him "an uncouth kid" who happened to be good at chess. People who are well-groomed and wearing clothes that suit the occasion usually feel good about themselves. Others, pleased by a nice appearance, will respond positively to the well-dressed person.

Managing a Wardrobe

Managing a family's clothing needs — as well as one's own individual needs — involves all the management steps described in Chapter 14. Wardrobe management also demands consumer skills in selecting and caring for clothing.

Planning People who know the colors, design, and fit that suit them best have an advantage when planning wardrobes. Wardrobe planning is something you learn gradually over a period of time. A good way to begin is to think of your favorite item of clothing — the one you feel most comfortable in and wear most often. Analyze what you like about the garment and how it becomes you. Consider a variety of clothing styles before you decide what suits you best. Also, consult books and magazines that give information about color, line, and texture. Use this information to choose clothing that emphasizes your good points.

Wardrobe planning involves working with what you already have. Look carefully at the contents of your closet. Try on each item of clothing and analyze it. Divide all the garments into three groups — those that you wear often and are suitable as they are; those you like but that need repair, alteration, or cleaning; and those you do not wear because they are out-of-date, were never becoming, or do not fit well. If articles cannot be saved by alteration, they can be sold on consignment to a thrift shop or donated to a charitable organization.

People need self-discipline when deciding between clothing items they need and items they would simply like to have. It is helpful to make a chart of your activities, such as school, work, sports, and so on. You can then list the clothing you need for each activity.

Investment Buying Since clothing is a big part of the family budget, it is important to make wise decisions about clothing purchases. Think of buying clothing as making an investment in your appearance. Spending a little extra

Since clothing is an expensive investment, try to buy items that coordinate with the rest of your wardrobe and that fit your life style and activities.

The Fashionable Female Foot

When we think of changing fashions and how people's life styles are reflected in the clothes they wear, shoe styles seem of minor importance. In the past, however, shoes were a status symbol—particularly women's shoes.

In earlier centuries, members of royalty and the very rich were set apart from the rest of the population by the fact that they did not do hard physical work. One way the rich separated themselves from workers was to dress in such a way that they could not perform physical tasks. In the eighteenth century, wealthy men as well as women wore high-heeled slippers. Workers went barefoot or wore practical, sturdy flat-heeled shoes or wooden clogs. They therefore developed strong feet while the nobles, tottering along in their high-heeled, sharp-toed shoes, suffered from a variety of foot problems. It was so hard for them to walk that they were often carried about the streets in sedan chairs.

It even became the fashion for rich women to wear shoes built on stilts. This style developed first in China and Japan. In the fourteenth century, the idea was taken to Italy. Thereafter, for several centuries, stylish European women teetered about on stilts which were as much as twenty inches high. A woman wearing this peculiar footwear could walk only if supported by a servant holding her on either side.

Psychologists suggest that women wore tight, uncomfortable shoes not only to set themselves above poorer people, but because such shoes made women seem fragile and helpless. A small foot was an important sign of beauty in a woman. A good example of this is found in the fairy tale "Cinderella," in which the most desirable woman in the kingdom is the one with the smallest feet. This concept is even more strongly expressed in the early version by the Grimm Brothers. Here the stepmother has her elder daughter cut off her big toe in order to make her foot fit the tiny slipper.

Women in ancient China went almost as far in order to have tiny feet and win a husband. Their feet were tightly bound when they were infants so their feet could not grow. Adult women could scarcely hobble around, for their feet remained only a few inches long.

The human foot must carry the full weight of the body on a very limited surface. To bear this weight, the toes need room to spread. Pointed-toe shoes constrict the toes and force the big toe toward the center. High-heeled shoes force the feet into an even more unnatural position and make it difficult and even dangerous to run. According to a study by the Podiatry Society of New York State, ninety-nine percent of the people studied had perfect feet at birth. By age five, forty percent had developed problems. By the age of twenty, eighty percent had foot problems.

The situation, however, is now improving. Shoes worn for active work and play are now being designed to allow the feet to function properly. Most important, women no longer need to wear crippling shoes to make them appear fragile and helpless in order to gain a mate or to prove their worth.

This uncomfortable looking antique shoe once was a symbol of beauty and status.

time in the selection of clothing will ensure that you are getting the most for your money. Sometimes spending a little more money for clothing means you get a better product, but high price does not always guarantee quality in a garment. Fabric and workmanship, or how well the garment is made, determine how well a garment will fit, and how well it will wear. When you are attracted to a garment's style or color, be sure to check its fabric content and workmanship before taking it to the fitting room. When you try the garment on, check it critically for fit. It is vital that the fit be satisfactory. If a garment does not fit properly it will be uncomfortable to wear and therefore will not be used.

Here are some guidelines for those seeking maximum value and enjoyment from clothes:

■ Plan your clothing purchases around one or two basic color groups so that the same items of clothing may be used to create various outfits for different occasions.

■ Select items that can be worn with other clothing you currently own. Mix-and-match separates can extend your wardrobe by creating new outfits.

■ Choose simple, basic styles — wardrobe expanders — that can be dressed up or down depending on the occasion and that can be easily coordinated with other garments.

■ Look for versatile garments that can be worn most of the year.

■ Buy the best quality you can afford. Look for natural fibers such as cotton for comfort in hot weather and wool for comfort in cold weather. Synthetics, such as nylon and polyester, are easier to care for. To get the benefits of both, try a blend.

■ Choose accessories that will go with several different outfits. For example, select a pair of shoes that will go with several garments or choose a belt that matches several pairs of pants. For versatility, choose simple designs and solid colors.

■ Avoid fashion fads. Fads and trends change often. If you buy clothing to keep in step with a fad, you will soon be stuck with outdated clothing.

Clothing Stores Many different kinds of clothing stores offer new clothing of the latest design. Some advantages and disadvantages of various types of stores follow:

■ Specialty stores often have the widest variety of styles.

■ Department stores offer more individualized help to customers. Some of their clothes are expensive, but their "budget shops" often offer bargains on new merchandise.

■ Discount stores sell items of varying quality. Check clothing carefully before you buy.

■ Factory outlets carry both quality garments and "irregulars," items that have flaws. Check irregulars carefully, as the flaws are often so minor that the items are good buys.

■ Mail-order stores send out catalogs, useful shopping tools for people who cannot get out easily. However, when you order merchandise from catalogs, you cannot check garment quality or fit prior to purchase.

Items on sale are not always bargains. Before you buy, consider the possible results. If you never wear or use a sale item, it was no bargain. Sometimes, a garment bought out of season may not seem as attractive when the time comes to wear it. Some stores will not accept returned sale merchandise for cash or credit. Once you've bought a sale item, it is yours.

Upkeep If the garment passes the tests of quality and fit, check the type of care required for proper upkeep. Manufacturers must attach a care label to each garment. The label indicates whether a garment should be machine or hand washed, or whether it must be dry cleaned. It tells how to dry the garment — whether to

Clothes that are made well and fit right are clothes that look the best on people.

Clothing Quality and Fitting Standards

Clothing Quality

Seams *Seam allowances* should be at least 1.25 cm (1/2 inch). Seams should be *finished* (overstitched or bound with fabric), especially in garments of fabrics that ravel easily. *Stitching* should be straight; stitches should be short, with no broken threads; stitching should be securely fastened at seam ends. *Doublestitching* should be evident at stresspoints such as underarms or waistline. *Plaid or striped patterns* should match at seams.

Hems *Allowance* should be generous in case lengthening is needed. *Edges* should be finished to prevent raveling.

Grainlines Lengthwise and crosswise threads in fabrics should meet at right angles.

Fastenings *Buttons, snaps,* or *hooks and eyes* should be complete and secure. *Buttonholes* should be stitched on straight of grain, sized to fit snugly around buttons, and finished securely. *Zippers* should lie smoothly and open and close easily.

Details *Collars, pockets,* and *padding* should lie smoothly. *Fabric* should have no snags or irregularities.

Clothing Fit

Jackets and Coats Garment should *fit smoothly,* especially when worn over other garments, with no strain across back and shoulders when extending or folding arms. Garment should *fall in a straight line* from shoulders, with no wrinkling. *Collar* should fit closely and lie smooth and flat against back of neck. *Sleeves* should hang straight from shoulders. Full-length sleeves should reach wrist when arms are bent. *Armholes* should be cut deeply enough to prevent binding.

Skirts and Trousers Garment should *fit smoothly,* with no wrinkles or binding. Garment should be *comfortable* when wearer walks, sits, or bends. *Waist* fit should be snug, but not tight. *Back seam allowance* should be wide enough to allow letting out if needed. *Pleats* or *creases* should hang straight and with lengthwise grain of fabric.

To care for your clothing properly, read and follow the care labels on each garment.

hang it, lay it flat, or use an automatic dryer. Reading labels will help you plan for clothing care.

Daily care of clothing involves avoiding snags, dirt, and spills. Check for and take care of stains or rips promptly. Hanging up clothes immediately after changing can eliminate the need to iron to remove wrinkles. Individuals may handle the upkeep requirements for their own clothing. Or, a family may choose to divide clothing care. Washing, ironing, and mending can be divided among family members.

For Review

1. What is an ecosystem?
2. What are three important functions of clothing?
3. Name some different types of clothing stores.

Housing

A house or apartment is the special place where people share their lives with their families. A home in which family members are comfortable contributes to family well-being in many ways.

Functions of Housing

Homes meet physical, psychological, and social needs. They provide shelter against the elements, offer a sense of security, and establish areas where family members can enjoy privacy.

Shelter The basic purpose of a home has always been to provide shelter. The first refuge for human beings was a cave. Later, people built homes with materials available in their particular geographical region—thatch or reeds, blocks of mud or ice, stones, wood, or animal skins—to meet their need for protection from the elements.

A home should suit the needs and life styles of the different family members.

It is important for a family to have one space in the house where they can share group activities and entertain friends. What rooms in a house can be used as group living space?

Security A home provides a person with security; a sense of belonging develops when people have an environment to call their own. Your home is familiar. You know what to expect there, and so it provides you with a feeling of stablity. People become disoriented when they lose their homes because of financial hardship, through urban renewal, or through catastrophes such as fires, floods, tornadoes, or earthquakes. People who lose their homes lose not only a shelter, but also the place that sustained and nurtured their family.

Privacy and Living Space Privacy is considered a primary psychological need. It allows you to "keep a distance" from others, even though they may be fellow family members, in

order to retain your own sense of being unique. Privacy includes the state of solitude, or being alone, which allows you to be reflective. Furthermore, some privacy is essential for relaxation and for unwinding from the stresses of daily life.

Closely related to the need for privacy is the need for adequate living space. Social scientists have analyzed people's feelings about the space around them. According to Edward Hall, an anthropologist, people surround themselves with an "invisible space bubble." This bubble is a personal space, or the area that must be kept free from intrusions by others if people are to achieve psychological comfort. Personal space is necessary at school and places of work, as well as at home.

Brothers or sisters often have to share a bedroom. This room has been arranged and decorated so that each boy knows which part of the room is his.

Safety Tip

To prevent fires at home:

- Keep storage spaces clear of combustibles like paper, cartons, old furniture and rags.

- Store flammable liquids in closed containers away from heat, sparks and young children.

- Replace worn cords or faulty connections immediately.

- Do not overload outlets.

- Do not use the oven to heat your home.

- Do not smoke in bed.

- Above all, install smoke detectors on every floor of your home and near sleeping rooms.

Personal space includes more than the physical area around you. It includes the range of your sensory input, or what your senses bring to you from your surroundings. The sight of a car turning into a neighbor's driveway, the sound of a dog barking down the street, or the smells from the barbecue next door are examples of how sense impressions enter your space. Most researchers agree that a sense of control over one's personal space is important to individual well-being.

Family members need privacy, but they also need opportunities to interact with and relate to one another. Group living space permits family members to be together and to entertain guests. Ideal group space provides comfort and adequate seating space in attractive surroundings away from distracting household traffic. Group sharing, relaxation, conversation, and discussion of problems, for example, occur more readily in an inviting space.

People use their personal living space to express their individual style.

Needs for space in the home depend on a family's stage in the life cycle. A married couple may be comfortable in a one-bedroom home. People need more space when they have children. The ideal in the United States is to have a room for each child. However, many families cannot afford the ideal arrangement. Often, children must double up and share rooms. Most families find that this sharing works better when each child has his or her own space within the room. When children grow up and leave the home, couples often find that caring for a larger home is too costly. The result is that they move to smaller quarters.

Self-expression Some homes are open and inviting. Within them, children feel free to express themselves, teenagers enjoy "hanging out," and adult visitors relax. Other dwellings may convey feelings of discomfort or tension that make people feel uncomfortable.

A home reflects the people who live there—like clothing, it sends out messages about them. It reveals what they think is important. It reflects and reinforces self-esteem. Thus, housing is an extension of oneself and of one's family.

Practical Tip

To conserve energy at home:

- Turn appliances—lights, TV, radio—off when not in use.

- Boil water in a covered pan. Water boils faster with less energy.

- Use electric pans or appliances to cook small meals or snacks.

- Run the dishwasher only when full. Let dishes air-dry insted of machine-dry.

- Choose and use energy-efficient appliances, checking them periodically.

Mobile homes, adobe houses and log cabins reflect the many types of materials used in the building of single – family homes.

Housing Alternatives

Several different types of housing are available. Whether you choose a single family house, an apartment unit, or a condominium, each type of housing has advantages and disadvantages.

Single Dwelling A single family dwelling is a house that has been designed to be used by one person or one family. The design and size of single dwellings vary greatly. Owning a private house, whether old or new, entails ongoing responsibility for maintenance and upkeep. Attention to heating, plumbing, electrical work, carpentry, roofing, painting, and appliance repair takes time, money and energy. You must also consider lawn care, and snow removal in certain climates.

Buying a house, or having one built can be extremely expensive depending on the community or city where the property is located. To

Whether a family chooses a simple farm house, a modern, victorian or colonial style of architecture, owning a home is part of the American dream.

reduce the cost of buying a house some people purchase a pre-fabricated, or manufactured house. **Manufactured housing** consists of house parts constructed in a factory and then shipped to a home site. Instructions are provided with the materials, which are assembled on site. Manufactured housing can be less expensive because mass production methods are employed.

Mobile homes, another type of manufactured housing, are not easily moved, despite their name. They are an enlargement of the travel trailer and they often have as many as three bedrooms, a living room, dining room or eat-in kitchen and are so large they can be moved only by truck. Mobile homes have two major advantages: they allow persons who move frequently to maintain familiar surroundings, and they are less expensive to purchase or rent than other housing.

Multiple dwellings can accommodate two families or many families.

Multiple Dwelling This type of building accommodates two or more families. Each family has its own unit. Many people live in apartment units, either in large developments that consist of big buildings, or in smaller groupings such as garden apartment complexes. People may also rent units in two-family houses.

A **condominium** is an individually owned town house or apartment unit in a multiple dwelling. Condominiums appeal to people who want few maintenance responsibilities but who also want to own a home as an investment. In addition to the purchase price, condominium owners pay a fee for the upkeep and use of the grounds and facilities that serve all the units.

A **cooperative** is a unit within a building or complex that the residents own jointly. Each owner has a percentage of the building's stock based on the size of the unit he or she occupies. As with condominiums, the shareholders divide the costs of maintaining grounds and common areas and facilities.

Renting a Home

Those who rent a house or apartment may have a need for greater mobility than those who buy a home. People who rent have fewer upkeep responsibilities since the landlord is usually responsible for repair and maintenance.

Triple-deckers and townhouse apartment units are two types of multiple dwellings.

The degree of obligation for upkeep depends upon the **lease,** a rental contract for a specific period of time. The lease states the monthly payment, or rent, that is owed, and usually lists the rules regulating the use and care of the premises. The lease also may specify how much the renter can fix up or alter the dwelling. Before signing a lease, read it carefully to determine your obligations, and look over the premises thoroughly, listing any problems you observe. Submit this list to the landlord and keep a copy for yourself. The landlord should make the necessary repairs before you move in.

The management usually requires one or even two months' rent as security against dam-age to the property. The landlord can keep this sum if the tenant leaves the place in poor condition or breaks the lease (leaves before the time period indicated on the lease). In some localities there are very detailed laws outlining the rights and obligations of landlords and tenants. These laws vary from state to state.

Rental apartment complexes vary a great deal. Some complexes are old, and little is done to maintain them. Some welcome children and pets and have recreation areas, while others have many restrictions. It pays to investigate and to compare the "personality" and benefits of various apartment complexes before making a final choice.

Checklist of Home Living Space

Knowing what to look for before you buy or rent a home can help you decide on the best place for your needs — especially after you've moved all your belongings into it. Following are some of the things to consider:

- Convenient floor plan: paths from room to room, rooms conveniently related to one another (entry to living room, dining room to kitchen, for example)

- Convenient and adequately sized areas for work, privacy, and socializing

- Suitable wall spaces and room sizes for furniture

- Adequate storage space

- Easy cleaning and maintenance

- Furnished appliances in good condition

- Clean, effective heating

- Up-to-date wiring and plumbing

- Conveniently placed electrical outlets

- Windows located to provide enough light and ventilation

- Agreeable window size, type, and placement

- Blinds, shades, screens, and/or storm windows for windows

- Well-fitted doors, casings, cabinets, and/or built-ins

- Extras: air conditioning, carpeting, dishwasher, disposal system, fireplace, patio

- Soundproof walls, especially in multiple dwellings—listen for talking, footsteps, plumbing and equipment noise from other rooms, units, or hallways

- Outdoor space convenient to indoor space, especially in single dwellings

Adapted from Money Management Institute, Your Housing Dollar (Prospect Heights, Ill.: Household Finance Corporation, 1979).

Buying a Home

A home is probably the largest purchase the average person makes. Since most people cannot afford to pay cash for the full price, they make a partial payment that varies according to their income and the cost of the home. This is called a down payment. To pay the rest, they obtain a loan, from a bank or savings and loan association, pledging their house as security. This pledge is called a **mortgage.** The loan is paid off in monthly installments, or mortgage payments, spread over a period of time up to 30 years. The monthly payments include payback on the principal (amount of the loan) and payment of interest (the fee for borrowing the money).

People purchasing homes usually are advised to spend no more than two and one-half times their annual income. Shop around for the best mortgage loan. There are many different types, and terms and rates vary. Visit several banks and savings and loan associations for advice on these matters.

When determining how much you can afford to pay for a home, you need to be aware of "hidden costs." Besides the down payment and monthly mortgage payments, you incur other costs when you purchase the house, or shortly thereafter.

- Closing costs (about $1,500 to $5,000). These are fees for legal services, appraisal of the property, the mortgage application, the loan of the money itself, an abstract or title search (which is a check to see that no one has any "claim" on the property), prorated property taxes (taxes for the part of the year that you will own the house), etc.

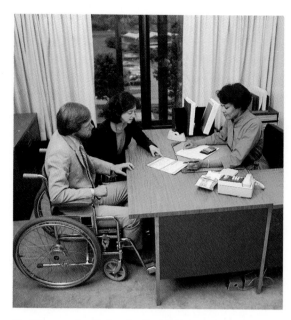
Homebuyers should shop for the best interest rates and fees when applying for a mortgage.

- Mortgage insurance with premiums paid by the homeowner.

- Town assessments, such as for sidewalks, curbs and gutters, public water, and street lights payable to the end of the calendar year. Normally, these are paid by the seller before the house is sold, but, especially in newly built areas, you should check whether any new assessments have been levied and how much they will be.

- Cost of moving to the new location

Other costs must be taken into account when considering home ownership:

- Annual real estate taxes assessed by local governments for community use, such as for schools and parks. These are sometimes included in mortgage payments, sometimes paid separately, annually or semiannually.

- Insurance

- Landscaping desired (mostly applies to new homes)

- Utilities, such as water and sewerage, gas, electric, and telephone. These will probably be billed monthly or quarterly (the seller should inform you of prior years' bills).

- New furnishing needed, including major appliances

- Equipment and tools for repair and maintenance

Buying a home is a long-term investment. As the mortgage loan is repaid, the owner's share of the home increases, while the lender's decreases. Thus, the owner builds **equity,** or property value. Property values go up and down depending on the location of the property and the general economic conditions of the community. An additional benefit to home owners is that they can deduct all interest payments on a mortgage loan from federal income tax. They also can deduct real estate taxes.

One way to cut down the cost of buying a house involves **sweat equity.** This term refers to the work a potential owner does in building a home when a company advances materials and provides a construction loan. A person's time and effort is the down payment, and he or she then pays the company a specific amount each month until the house is completed. The buyer then applies to the bank for a mortgage for the remainder of the purchase price.

Practical Tip

To save heating energy costs:

- Insulate attics, roofs, and ceilings.
- Caulk and weatherstrip doors and windows that allow air leakage.
- Install storm doors.
- Hang insulated curtains or shades.
- Turn down thermostats.

Couples can work together to choose furnishings that reflect their interests and tastes.

Furnishings

No matter what type of housing you choose, you will have to make decisions about how to furnish it. Furnishings need not be expensive to be comfortable and attractive.

Needs A family's stage in the life cycle and family and individual preferences determine furnishing needs. A single person or a young couple furnishing a first apartment have different needs than a family with a new baby or with several children. A couple whose children no longer live at home and who are moving to an apartment or a smaller house have some needs that are similar to and some that are different from those of couples starting out.

Decisions

In management terms, when you make decisions about home furnishings, you define what you need and how much money you can spend. Then you search for information about the different kinds of furniture available and how much they cost. You must also consider how long you want an article to last. If you expect to keep an item for many years, get good quality, using your research as a guide. Several consumer magazines regularly evaluate furnishings and report on the results. Government publications also provide advice. Some furniture stores and shops offer consumer information to customers as a public service.

To meet your budget, you may have to consider discount furniture, used furniture, "knocked down" furniture that you assemble yourself, unpainted furniture, and so on. After weighing the alternatives, decide what is sensible to buy second-hand and what should be new, in the light of what you can afford.

In planning furnishings, think in terms of lighting that will not strain the eyes, colors that will lift the spirits, and furniture that will fit the human body comfortably. You should consider furnishings in terms of their effects on human behavior rather than for fashion or appearance alone. A family's way of life also will influence its choice of furniture. For example, if a family anticipates frequent moves, sturdy furniture that will fit into a number of different settings would be a good choice.

When shopping for furnishings, carefully consider quality vs. price. The goal is to get the best deal for your money.

Goals

A newly married couple will probably have long-term and short-term goals. The short-term goal may be to have just enough furniture to live comfortably. A short-term goal may be to add to the basics over a one- or two-year period as money becomes available. A long-term goal might be to buy desired items in anticipation of moving to a larger home.

Shopping

Once you've made your decisions, you will know just what you want when you arrive at the store. However, there is still more you will need to know. Find out all you can about the article you are considering. Try it out. Sit in chairs to be sure they are comfortable. Check mattresses by lying down on them. Check drawers in tables and chests. Do they slide easily? Do cabinet latches stay closed? Find out all you can about manufacture and finish and the care required to maintain appearance. Read labels and tags for details about construction and upkeep. Consider how you will use the piece of furniture and then make sure it will suit your purpose.

If you are moving to a home where you will need to buy large appliances such as a stove, refrigerator, washer, or dryer, consider buying the existing ones from the previous home owner. Of course, you will need to determine the condition of these items before you buy. If you must purchase new equipment, you can use many of the same decision-making steps that apply to buying furnishings.

For Review

1. Why is privacy an important function of housing?
2. What is the difference between a condominium and a cooperative?
3. Discuss the advantages of renting a house or an apartment unit.

Neighborhoods

The area around a person's home—the neighborhood—determines the quality of family life as much as the house or apartment. A neighborhood is an extension of a person's home base. The people, streets, shops, and landmarks become familiar and make up one's home territory.

Neighborhoods vary in size and shape. A city block and a suburban development are both neighborhoods. Suburban developments usually include open spaces between houses and cover large areas. City neighborhoods are more compact, since more people live on less land. Suburbs depend largely on shopping centers, or malls, for goods and services. Clusters of stores are bounded by large parking areas, since access to shopping centers is mainly by car. City neighborhoods include shops as well as houses or apartments and offer many services—laundries, newsstands, drug stores, groceries, barber shops, and shoe repair shops—usually within walking distance.

Evaluating a Neighborhood

To judge what a neighborhood is like, you need to consider a number of related factors. You should also rely on your impressions of a place after visiting the neighborhood at different times of day.

Community Residents When deciding if you would like to live in a particular neighborhood, you may want to consider community attitudes. Are people concerned about making the neighborhood a better place in which to live? Are they active in community improvement projects?

Is the neighborhood **heterogeneous,** or mixed—that is, are the people living there of different ages, occupations, backgrounds, reli-

gions, and ethnic affiliations? Such diversity adds vitality and excitement to a neighborhood. Diversity allows people with complementary strengths to help one another. On the other hand, living in a neighborhood that is **homogeneous**—most people are similar in background, income level, and ethnic and religious affiliation—makes many people feel secure. They identify with and share certain characteristics of their neighbors. They may develop group consciousness, or a feeling of belonging to a group of like-minded people. This feeling may encourage group efforts as people rally around similar causes or shared goals.

Local Governments Most people underestimate the importance of local government.

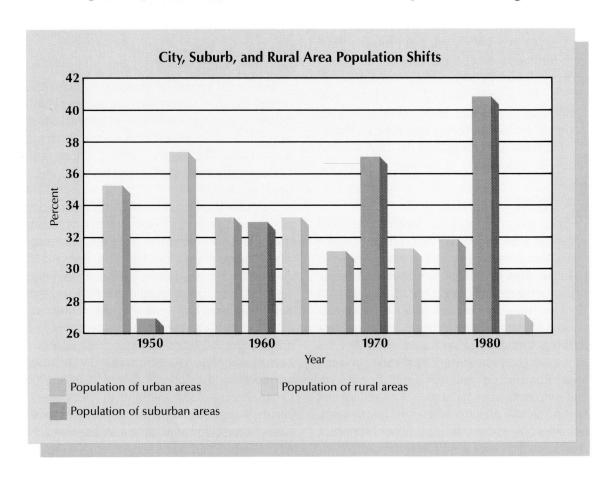

City, Suburb, and Rural Area Population Shifts

Population of urban areas
Population of suburban areas
Population of rural areas

What do you think the positive and negative aspects are for families living in a village? A town? A city?

At least one way to have a voice in local affairs is to be informed and to vote in local elections.

All states are divided into units called counties (except in Louisiana, where they are called "parishes," and in Alaska, where they are called "election districts"). Tax-supported county governments may be the only local governments in some rural areas, providing schools, libraries, and roads. County units are governed by elected officials and a governing body, often called a commission. Sheriffs and their deputies are county law enforcement officers.

In other areas, responsibility for local government is divided between counties and municipalities. The latter include villages, towns, and cities, designated according to population size. Larger municipalities have police depart-

ments of their own, and they may combine with counties to provide some services, such as schools. Counties or municipalities or both may determine safety and health regulations, and may provide hospitals and recreation facilities.

Villages and towns usually are governed by elected boards and executives. Depending on state law, city government may take three forms: (1) mayor and city council, elected by voters; (2) mayor and commissioners, elected by voters; (3) council/manager system. In the latter form, voters elect a council that appoints city department heads.

Zoning Local government officials establish or approve zoning laws that regulate the use of land. The purpose of these laws is to keep industry and commerce separate from residential areas. They specify the types of dwelling that can be put up in a residential area, and the basic changes that can be made in existing buildings. A zoning map is usually available at the city or town hall. There you can get information on the zoning specifics of your neighborhood. Good zoning can allow for people's needs by allocating space for parks, or by placing rental units near public transportation.

Health and Safety Following are some health and safety factors to consider when evaluating a neighborhood:

- source of the water supply
- problems with contamination of air, water, or soil
- reliability of garbage pickup

- nearness to a freeway, airport, or railway where noise may be a problem
- extent of fire and police protection
- access to a hospital emergency room and ambulance service
- sufficient street lighting
- play areas for children away from streets with heavy traffic

Schools For many families with children, a good school is often the most important reason for choosing a neighborhood. Factors that parents can consider in evaluating a school include the following:

- pupil-teacher ratio
- per-pupil cost, or money spent on teachers, books, supplies and so on

One aspect families consider when evaluating a neighborhood is the quality of a school system. Other factors are parks, community organizations, transportation, and libraries.

- library, art, music, physical education facilities
- students' scores in statewide competitions
- opinions of parents with children in the school

Culture and Recreation You also should consider the cultural and recreational facilities in the neighborhood and their importance to your family.

- nearness to parks, libraries, museums, and recreational facilities
- existence of active programs for all age groups at these facilities
- availability of day care center or community recreation center
- access to cultural and recreational facilities
- existence of neighborhood organization working for improvements in the area

Revitalizing Neighborhoods

Many towns and cities and some states have passed laws intended to revitalize older or declining neighborhoods. Neighborhood organizations are provided with information and funds and encouraged to upgrade their local areas. Elected officers are advised to set goals that reflect the needs of the people in their area. Plans made and monitored by neighborhood residents are more likely to succeed than those imposed by outside groups. Many people have found that participating in neighborhood volunteer work is a personally rewarding experience.

Different neighborhoods have different goals for revitalization. A discount food market or a health-care clinic might satisfy a need of a low-income community. A senior citizens' center would serve a neighborhood with older residents. Whether they choose hobby shops, recycling stations, or recreation programs, the people themselves have the opportunity to decide on the community services that best suit their needs.

Many families today are participating in the revitalization of neighborhoods.

In an attempt to upgrade housing and thus to upgrade neighborhoods, a new version of the widespread nineteenth-century practice of *homesteading* has emerged. People who need housing, but who cannot afford the normally high housing costs buy decaying, abandoned houses for modest sums. The condition of purchase is that in five years the purchaser must improve the property to meet building code standards. Those who do so then own title to the home.

For Review

1. What is the purpose of zoning laws?
2. Name three of the health and safety factors to consider when evaluating a neighborhood.
3. What does *homesteading* mean?

15 Chapter Review

Summary

The individual and the family are part of several environments which interact as an ecosystem. Some of these environments include clothing, housing, and neighborhoods.

Clothing provides protection, reinforces group identity, and allows individual expression. Managing an individual's or a family's clothing needs involves careful planning, wise shopping, and clothing maintenance.

Housing satisfies many of a family's physical, psychological, and social needs. A home provides shelter, a sense of security, privacy, living space, and a place for members to express themselves.

In choosing a home, people must decide whether to rent or buy a single or a multiple dwelling unit based on their family's needs, income, and goals. Since neighborhoods affect family life, people need to assess them by analyzing their residents, local government, schools, health and safety facilities, and cultural and recreational programs.

Vocabulary

Match each of the following vocabulary words with one of the definitions that follow.

condominium
cooperative
ecosystem
equity
heterogeneous
homogeneous
lease
manufactured housing
mortgage
sweat equity

1. _____ rental contract
2. _____ a homeowner's investment of labor in building a home with materials and money provided by a construction company's loan
3. _____ having similar characteristics
4. _____ combination of interacting environments
5. _____ individually owned apartment or townhouse in a multiple dwelling or complex
6. _____ homeowner's loan provided by a bank or other lending institution
7. _____ having different characteristics
8. _____ homes built from factory-made parts which are assembled on site
9. _____ monetary value of a home excluding the mortgaged portion
10. _____ independent unit within a building or complex that is jointly owned by residents

Chapter Questions

1. What are "near" and "far" environments?
2. Give an example from your own experience in which people wear clothing to establish group identity.
3. In addition to low self-esteem, how might a person's disinterest in his or her appearance be interpreted?

4. Name three characteristics of a well-planned and well-managed wardrobe.
5. In your opinion, what are the most important factors to consider when buying clothing? Why?
6. How does housing meet a person's psychological needs?
7. What are the advantages and disadvantages of owning a home?
8. If you want to own a single family house and cannot afford one, what other housing options could you consider?
9. How can families benefit from living in a heterogeneous neighborhood? A homogeneous neighborhood?
10. What factors might a young family with children consider to be important in selecting a neighborhood?
11. How does homesteading help to revitalize declining neighborhoods?

Skill Activities

 1. **Math** Research the cost of buying a home, condominium, or apartment building in your neighborhood. Study real estate listings in the newspaper, and talk with realtors, your family, and your friends' families to determine the price range of these homes or buildings in your area. Then meet with a loan officer or other bank employee at one or more local banks to calculate average closing costs. After you have gathered your data, compute the average total cost of buying a home (condominium, apartment building). Prepare and distribute your data to the class as part of a brief oral report in which you discuss your findings.

 2. **Critical Thinking** Plan a redecorating project for a room in your house or apartment that is utilized as a group living space for your family. Redesign this space so that it will encourage more group interaction and relaxation than is now possible. Plan furniture, wall coverings, drapes, rugs, lighting, and other objects with this purpose in mind. Visit furniture and department stores, browse through mail-order catalogs, and consult library references on home decorating to help you "create" a new room. When you have organized all of your ideas, draw a map or floor plan which clearly shows each item you have selected. Mark each item on the floor plan with a letter. On a separate sheet of paper, next to its corresponding letter, describe each item you have included and explain how it contributes to the group living space.

 3. **Social Studies** Research the functions of clothing for people from another country, or ethnic or religious group. Use a variety of library resources to find your information. As you read, look for answers to the following questions: How does the clothing of this group of people serve their physical, psychological, and social needs? What other purposes are fulfilled by their clothing? Write a report in which you discuss the answers to these questions. Include illustrations of some of the types of clothing you describe.

16 Managing Independent Living

As you read, think about:

- why single living is increasing among people in their early twenties.
- what employment and credit problems singles encounter.
- what housing options are available to single people.
- how support systems can be helpful to a single person.

People may be single for numerous reasons. Some young people choose to remain single until they start a career. Others may remain unmarried for a longer period, or permanently, because they enjoy being independent and free of family obligations.

Single people may encounter special problems on the job and in other areas of daily life. Support networks—friends, relatives, and community groups—are as important to single people as they are to married couples. This chapter discusses the satisfactions and challenges of being single.

The Single Life

People may be single temporarily or permanently, through choice or circumstance. Each situation involves its own set of problems as well as advantages. These affect men and women of all ages.

Young Single People

Bureau of the Census figures show that in the past two decades, the number of men and women remaining single during their early twenties has increased considerably. A variety of reasons contribute to this trend. One reason is that as more young adults work and establish separate households, many remain single longer. Other reasons have to do with changes affecting women.

Single people often pursue interests such as music

Postponement of marriage by young adults has increased as shown by the decline in the number of marriages among people in their late teens and early twenties.

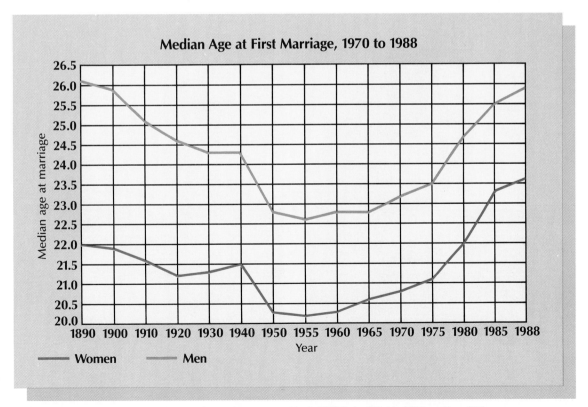

Source: Bureau of Census: "Marital Status and Living Arrangements: March 1988" (Series P-20, No. 433) Issued Jan., 1989.

- More women are in college than ever before. Of the young women who are students, it appears that they have postponed marriage to a later date in order to pursue a college or post-graduate degree.

- Because of the women's movement, society is not as critical of single women. Many women seek jobs in geographical areas away from their neighborhoods or home states.

- More rewarding careers are open to women. The need for financial support from a man has lessened.

- Women may find the prospect of a career more appealing than the idea of home management.

- Postponement of marriage among young women has a corresponding effect on post-ponement of marriage among young men.

Divorced Single People

There are more separated and divorced people in the United States today than ever before. Although approximately four out of five divorced people eventually remarry, the time span between marriages appears to be increasing. There are several million divorced and separated men and women in the United States.

Few people have a realistic picture of the single life of a divorced person. They do not realize that a divorced person goes through painful struggles from the time of the marital breakup until he or she becomes adjusted to it.

In addition to feeling lonely, a divorced person has to cope with many new responsibilities.

Learning new skills and maintaining contact with friends are two challenges for single people. What are other challenges?

The following are some typical comments by singles:

- "Some of my friends think I can do as I please all of the time, but they forget that I also have to do all the chores around my house. That's a lot of responsibility."

- "I don't like being alone during the holidays. I had to put some effort into finding people to share that time with."

- My wife always did the cooking and the cleaning. Now I get a feeling of accomplishment when I do those jobs myself."

- "I like being alone most of the time, but I wonder what it's going to be like when I get old."

Older Single People

The number of older adults living alone is large compared to the number of single people in their twenties living alone. Many older single people are widowed or divorced. Some have never married, choosing to remain single in order to pursue careers or to develop their talents.

One study of older single people, conducted by a sociologist, points out that single people are often depicted as leading half-lives. According to those interviewed, this view is a misconception. Many older single people have led satisfying, productive lives that have been "filled with love and work, friendship and learning."

Single people often have hobbies that occupy their spare time and give them great satisfaction.

Single people must assume all of the responsibilities for household management, including finances.

Special Challenges of Single Life

Whatever their backgrounds and reasons for being single, all single persons must deal with employment, credit, and housing in their daily lives. Being single poses some special problems in these areas.

Employment

Single people are just as serious about their careers as married people. Many have more time and energy to devote to a job than do married persons. Nevertheless, evidence shows that in the past some employers believed that single people are inclined to move more often, to change locations when they marry, and to leave their jobs more impulsively than do married people. However, with more single people in the labor force, employers are having to revise these stereotyped opinions.

Single people can help change stereotypes by speaking up when they observe discrimination against a single person and by attempting, along with their employers, to find constructive solutions to their special problems. They also can try to view the problems they face as a set of challenges to meet, rather than as obstacles to fight.

Credit and Loans

In the past, single people, especially women, were at a disadvantage when they applied for loans and credit. Today it is illegal to deny a person credit or loans on the basis of sex or marital status. In some large cities — New York and San Francisco, for example — women's banks now offer services to meet the special needs of women.

Housing

Many cities have housing and apartment complexes designed especially for single people, particularly young single people. These complexes usually are built with swimming pools, lounges, game rooms, and other recreational features. These planned facilities provide an environment that makes it easier for young single people to meet one another. Older single people may choose apartment units or retirement communities to fulfill their housing needs. Since in American culture being single is still not the most commonly accepted way of living, many single people feel more comfortable among people like themselves.

Living with Parents Although there is a trend in the United States for single people to

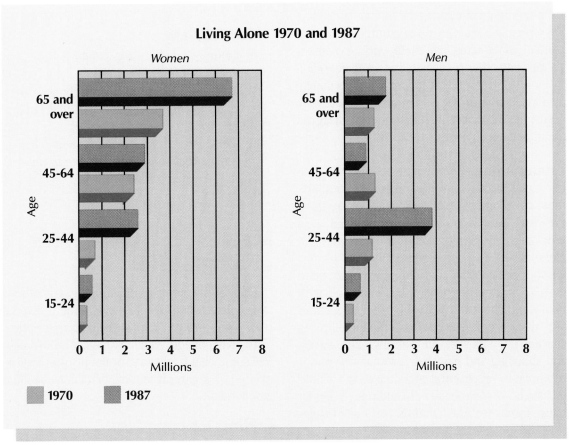

Living Alone 1970 and 1987

Women

Men

Millions

Millions

■ 1970   ■ 1987

Source: U.S. Bureau of the Census

Although older women are the largest group of people living alone, the rate of increase has been fastest among young adults.

live away from their parents, most unmarried persons under age 25 still live at home. In the past, nearly all unmarried adults lived in the households where they had grown up. Most housing in the United States is designed and built for families. Since young single people are not likely to be economically secure, most will probably continue to remain in their parents' homes.

Living with parents has advantages and disadvantages. It is probably cheaper than other arrangements, even when the young adult pays rent. The home environment also provides a certain amount of comfort and familiarity.

Among the disadvantages, however, are the restrictions on freedom and the lack of opportunity to feel independent. There is also the potential for conflicts with other family members. This problem is especially true for young adults who are struggling to gain independence and a sense of self.

Living with Roommates Many single people share housing with one or more roommates. If people are compatible—they get along well together—this type of living arrangement can be satisfying. Roommates gain the freedom and independence of living away from family restrictions, and at the same time they do not face the disadvantages of living alone. Roommates can help with expenses, chores, and other responsibilities, and give each other needed emotional support. Yet, each may also lose some privacy. Further, conflicts may result if the roommates seriously disagree about certain subjects.

Living Alone Some single people choose to live alone, usually in rental units such as apartments or rooms. The advantages of living alone are clear: people can be independent and learn how to handle responsibility. People who live alone are free to come and go as they please, without the need to consider parents or roommates. On the other hand, they get no help with household chores or with the other aspects of life that are easier when responsibility is shared. They must do all their own housework and shopping and pay their own bills. Without roommates or parental assistance, the single life can be very expensive. In addition, living by oneself may at times result in feelings of isolation and loneliness.

Safety Tip

To avoid being a victim of crime:

- Let someone know where you are going.

- Walk with a friend.

- When alone, walk in the street, facing oncoming traffic.

- Walk in well-lighted places. Avoid shortcuts through parks, tunnels, parking lots, and alleys.

- Carry identification, and change for a phone call.

- Carry a shriek alarm or a whistle.

For Review

1. Why are there more single people in their early twenties?
2. How do older single people change the focus of their lives after the death of a spouse?
3. What are some of the special challenges that single people have to meet in the area of housing?

Meeting the Challenges of Single Life

One of life's most challenging transitions takes place when people leave home to live on their own — to work, to enter military service, or to go to college. At such times, it is normal to feel somewhat frightened or doubtful, as well as excited or happy. It is a major task to become independent.

Feeling Independent

Research shows that fear of loneliness is a major problem for single people. Being alone, however, is not the same as loneliness. Loneliness is feeling sad or disturbed about being alone, and can occur even in a crowd. It is caused by negative feelings that arise when a person thinks that he or she should not be alone or that there is something wrong with being alone.

To overcome loneliness, people can pursue activities that take their attention away from themselves, or they can stop and examine their feelings. Loneliness often turns out to be a sense of loss: a desire for a particular companion or an urge to be in some other place. Once examined, these feelings are easier to understand. Often more positive feelings replace them, such as constructive thoughts about setting up a social life and scheduling time.

Eating in Solitary Splendor

"I enjoy being alone, but I hate to eat by myself." We have all heard this complaint. Maybe you feel that way. Mealtime is, traditionally, a social occasion where conversation adds to the enjoyment of the meal. However, increasing numbers of people are living alone and often eat by themselves. They are now discovering how to enjoy solo meals.

There are a number of points in favor of dining at home by yourself. You can choose the foods you like without having to consider others' likes and dislikes. You can eat at your own pace. You do not have to listen to other people's problems or less than riveting conversation. No one is there to criticize you or the way you eat. You do not have to dress up. If you want to watch TV during your meal, you get to choose the program. You can read a good story or catch up on the news. It is all up to you.

A little self-discipline is necessary, however. It is important to plan menus that are tasty, nutritious and varied. They need not be complicated, however. For example, a simple main dish — scrambled eggs, a chop or a fish fillet — with a salad of your favorite vegetables, some whole-grain bread, and a simple dessert, such as fresh fruit or ice cream and fruit, is easy to prepare, healthy, and delicious.

If you live alone, you will find it worthwhile to learn to cook. The fast-food and frozen-food industries are capitalizing on the singles market by producing a wide variety of servings for one. These packaged meals are all right now and then, but freshly prepared food is cheaper and has more vitamins, fewer unhealthy food additives, and better texture.

There are many good cookbooks for single people. Also, many communities offer cooking classes for people who eat alone. Once you have mastered the art of cooking simple dishes, you may want to experiment with more elaborate recipes.

Plan your food shopping to fit your schedule and your budget. Many single people find it convenient to shop at a supermarket once a week for frozen foods, canned goods, and household items such as detergents and paper towels. They then pick up perishable foods like milk and fresh vegetables more often at stores closer to home. Avoid impulse shopping, but pamper yourself sometimes. Buy fresh herbs and condiments that add excitement to simple dishes, and splurge occasionally on an expensive food you especially like. After all, you only need enough for one.

Some day when you are in the mood to cook, prepare a large stew or a big pan of soup. Freeze it in single-serving containers. You can warm up a serving on a night when you are too tired or busy to prepare a main dish.

It is surprising how many people who once hated the thought of cooking and eating alone find themselves looking forward to their next opportunity to dine in solitude.

It is important to eat well-balanced meals whether you are eating alone or with a large group.

Single people decide how to utilize leisure time. They can find satisfaction in sharing special moments alone or with friends.

Single people are able to arrange their time any way they prefer. They have the opportunity to learn how to be responsible for their own lives. They also experience a growing sense of satisfaction in learning to handle life's problems on their own.

Finding Sources of Support

In learning to be independent, people develop self-sufficiency. Nevertheless, people also need to know how and when to call on others for help. Psychologists have found that in order to function well, all people need emotional support of some kind.

It may be difficult at first to find supportive people after leaving home. Family and friends may live far away. However, people living on their own have the privilege of choosing the kinds of support they need from a variety of people and groups.

Friends True friends will listen to others, sympathize with them, and understand their problems. Friends can provide emotional support. They can help out during difficult times and share good feelings when things are going well. Friends can become as important as members of the family unit.

Single people generally spend much time and energy making friends and keeping up friendships. There are numerous functions of meaningful friendships.

Through community and religious organizations single people have an opportunity to meet others and develop friendships.

- Sharing experiences
- Listening to each other's feelings, needs, goals, and dreams
- Giving each other honest feedback
- Supporting each other through times of stress
- Sharing recreational activities

Where does one find friends? This is a common question for those who live alone, especially if they are in a new community. Fortunately, most communities make it possible for single people to meet potential friends.

Social and Religious Groups While some single people manage to meet each other on their own, a number of social institutions make it easier for single people to get together. People can meet other compatible people at cultural affairs such as concerts, plays, and art festivals. Parties and dances given by friends are also favorite meeting places. Further sources are hobby groups and adult education courses. For many single people, the opportunities for meeting others are limited only by their own interests and inclinations.

Single people can find a great deal of support in religious organizations. Many have developed programs especially for single people. These programs can meet spiritual needs at the same time that they are fulfilling social and emotional needs. Besides providing a place to worship, a religious group may also offer opportunities for establishing long-lasting friendships.

Professional Services Single people, along with persons who are not single, can draw support from many community agencies and professionals in their area. Psychologists, psychiatrists, social workers, and counselors are among the many people in the "mental health professions" who can provide guidance and support in times of need. Fees are often reduced for students or retired people, as well.

For Review

1. How can a single person overcome loneliness?
2. What are three functions of a quality friendship?
3. How does a social group serve as a support system for the single person?

16 Chapter Review

Summary

Today, more people are single than ever before. Many young single people have postponed marriage and are pursuing careers or education. Most older people who are single have been divorced or widowed, while some have never married. Studies show that being single does not prevent a person from leading a productive and satisfying life.

Being single presents a certain number of challenges and problems such as discrimination in employment, credit, and housing, and difficulty in establishing friendships.

Most single people need support systems if they are to overcome loneliness and find fulfillment. Sources of support may include friends, social organizations, religious groups, and professionals in private or community services. People who master the challenges of single life are likely to have feelings of independence and self-sufficiency.

Chapter Questions

1. In what ways are common stereotypes of divorced individuals unrealistic?
2. Explain why the belief that older single people lead "half-lives" may be inaccurate.
3. How do you think single people can change negative stereotypes that others have about them in the workplace?
4. What do you think are the advantages and disadvantages of living in an apartment complex for singles?
5. Which home maintenance tasks would be most difficult for you if you lived alone?
6. If young single people must live with their parents, what steps can they take to ensure that their independence and sense of self will continue to develop?
7. What are some of the hazards of traveling alone? How can a single person ensure his or her safety?
8. What are the advantages and disadvantages of living with roommates?
9. In your opinion, which of the housing options discussed in this chapter best meets the emotional needs of young single people in their early 20's? Why?
10. How can single people meet each other?

Skill Activities

 1. Math Determine how much it would cost to live on your own in a one-bedroom apartment in your community. To begin, study newspaper and real estate listings to find the average monthly rents of apartments in your area. Call utility companies to determine estimated monthly costs for fuel, water, electricity, and telephone services. Also, approximate the costs of transportation, food, clothing, and entertainment per month. Total these expenses to find the amount you would need to pay each month. Next, calculate the "start-up" costs of renting an apartment which include a security deposit and other initial renting expenses, furniture, and other household items. After you have itemized and totaled the amount needed to start and maintain an apartment on your own, find ways that a single person could reduce this monthly total. Write these suggestions in a paragraph as a conclusion to your study.

 2. **Human Relations** If you had an apartment and needed a roommate, how would you select one? With four or five students, write a skit that deals with interviewing potential roommates. One student can play the role of a person who needs a roommate. The other students can play the roles of people who are looking for a place to share with a roommate. The following questions can be used: Do you smoke? Do you have pets? Do you have a job? If so, what are the hours? What are your hobbies and interests? How much rent can you afford? What are your social and emotional expectations of a roommate? Feel free to create additional questions. Finally, present your skit to the class.

 3. **Critical Thinking** Investigate the way television programs present single people. View only those programs in which one or more of the main characters are single. While you are watching, analyze the ways in which single people are presented. What are their personal characteristics, values, goals, and dreams for the future? How would you describe their lifestyles? What role does a job or career play in their lives? What are their relationships with friends and family like? As you watch, note your observations.

After viewing four different programs, organize your information. Then, in a brief written report, discuss how single people were presented. How were the presentations of single people similar? How were they different? In what ways were single people presented realistically and/or unrealistically?

 4. **Human Relations** What are some of the problems that might arise among roommates? Some roommates set up house rules to prevent problems. Imagine that you are sharing a house with three roommates. Consider these questions: What are the housekeeping tasks and how will the work be shared? What system will be used for paying bills? Will food shopping and meal preparation be shared tasks? What will be the policy for parties? Write your answers to these questions in a brief report.

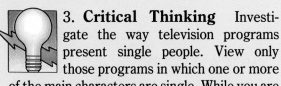 5. **Communication** Imagine that you are a young single person who recently has been transferred to live and work in your community. You want to overcome your loneliness by becoming involved in a variety of community activities, but you don't know of any. With a partner, research the services and activities available to single people in your community. Include recreational activities, religious groups, social organizations, cultural programs and events, hobby groups, and adult education courses. After researching, compiling, and categorizing your list, create an attractive brochure in which you describe these services and activities.

17 Keeping Healthy

As you read, think about:

- how your way of life can affect health.
- what factors can lead to addictive behavior.
- how you can handle stress effectively.
- how regular exercise improves overall health and well-being.
- what qualities are displayed by a person with good mental health.

Good health is perhaps the most important family resource. Without good health, the other resources—time, energy, skills, information, and money—are not really worth very much.

Many people today believe that health is made up of interrelated parts, that the body, mind, and emotions interact to make a whole person. Each aspect is related; none can be separated from the others or examined apart from the rest. People who are under severe mental stress are usually more prone than others to physical illness, while people with a strong will for life often overcome serious illness. This chapter looks at some of the factors that have a strong effect on individual and family health: drugs, smoking, alcohol, stress, disease prevention, exercise, and mental attitudes. As you read, ask yourself how a family can acquire or improve good health habits in order to achieve the best possible life.

VOCABULARY

multifactored
degenerative disease
stress
stressor
immunologic system
addiction
atrophy
cardiovascular fitness
aerobic exercise

Keeping fit is just one part of the formula for good health.

Health Factors

In the late nineteenth century, each illness was thought to be due to a single germ. As the practice of immunization increased, and as sanitation, housing, and nutrition improved, many of the most devastating diseases were brought under control. Nevertheless, an interesting question remained. Why did some people get diseases like typhoid and polio while others, perhaps in the same family or community, stayed well? According to medical researchers, many persons who were harboring disease germs must have failed to come down with symptoms. Modern research has determined that many germs present in people's bodies remain inactive until a failure of resistance brings them to active life. The factor causing loss of resistance tips the scales, and a person becomes susceptible to disease.

Today, health is considered **multifactored,** which means that the state of being ill or of being well is not related merely to one cause. Many factors can contribute to illness. Poor diet, poor hygiene, and lack of rest are common factors. Addiction to drugs, medications, and smoking, or alcohol can be involved. Pollutants in the environment can also cause illness. Several kinds of stress such as worry, loss of love, or adjustments to life changes can affect health. So too can genetic factors that predispose a person to certain diseases, for example, diabetes or one of several types of heart disease. Today, much illness and 75 percent of all deaths are caused by **degenerative disease,** or the breaking down of the body due to a combination of behavioral, environmental, and genetic factors.

Health experts have found that the way a family lives helps determine how susceptible its members will be to most illnesses. The experts offer formulas for good family health. The Johns Hopkins Medical School Good Health Checklist is an example of such a formula:

- exercise
- seven to eight hours of sleep per night
- no smoking
- proper weight
- three meals daily, including an adequate breakfast

Stress

Stress, or any challenge that puts demand on the body or the mind, is part of everyone's life. Stress can have positive or negative, mental or physical, causes. For example, both the excitement of winning an award and the act of running for a bus may produce symptoms of stress.

Dr. Hans Selye, a world authority on stress, believes that the body goes through a three-stage stress syndrome when confronted by any **stressor.** Stressors include heat, cold, pressure, noise, infection, and trauma (shock).

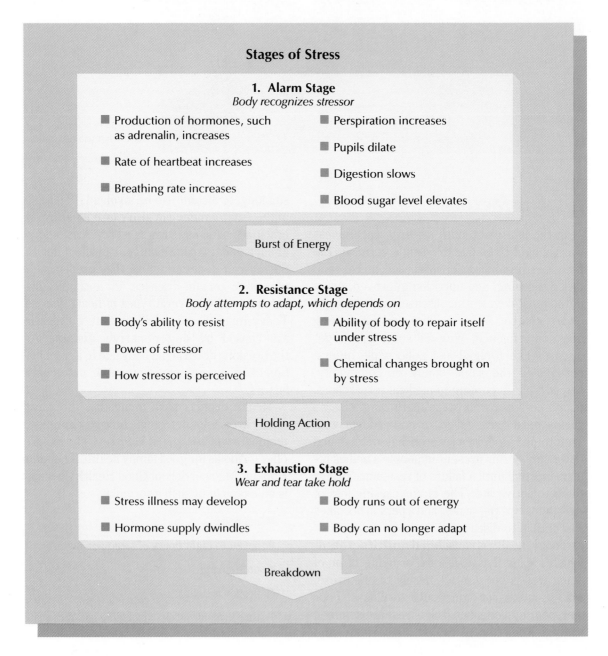

Stages of Stress

1. Alarm Stage
Body recognizes stressor

- Production of hormones, such as adrenalin, increases
- Rate of heartbeat increases
- Breathing rate increases
- Perspiration increases
- Pupils dilate
- Digestion slows
- Blood sugar level elevates

Burst of Energy

2. Resistance Stage
Body attempts to adapt, which depends on

- Body's ability to resist
- Power of stressor
- How stressor is perceived
- Ability of body to repair itself under stress
- Chemical changes brought on by stress

Holding Action

3. Exhaustion Stage
Wear and tear take hold

- Stress illness may develop
- Hormone supply dwindles
- Body runs out of energy
- Body can no longer adapt

Breakdown

Stress Can Be Good For You

"I'm keyed up!"

"I'm psyched!"

"I've never felt so alive!"

However you say it, you know the feeling. It's how you feel just before skiing down a steep slope, trying out for the class play, or dating someone new. It's how you feel when you sit down for a test or job interview.

Athletes and performers know that when they are not "psyched" they tend to give a lukewarm performance. They know that they need to gear up mentally and physically to draw from themselves the very best they have to give. This condition is *stress*.

Normally, people think of stress as harmful and thus as something to be avoided. Although too much stress can damage the body, there is also a positive side to stress.

Dr. Paul J. Rosch, president of the American Institute of Stress, believes that "stress is simply the response of the body to any demand for change." According to Dr. Rosch, the response can include helpful emotions such as love, happiness, and faith. This "positive stress" promotes not only health, he says, but "vibrant good health."

Many people who enjoy vibrant good health deliberately put themselves in stressful situations. For example, a symphony conductor faces stress each time he or she leads a difficult piece of music before a large audience. Stress is positive, says Dr. Rosch, when people enjoy what they do and feel pride in their accomplishments.

Dr. Rosch compares "positive stress" people with those he calls the "worried well." Although "worried well" people have nothing wrong physically, they fret constantly. They generate their own harmful stress by negative actions and attitudes. In contrast to the "worried well," "positive stress" people have a certain kind of enthusiasm.

One reason for the difference, says Dr. Rosch, is that the "worried well" do not set appropriate goals for themselves. They may drift into schools or jobs without deciding exactly where they want to be or belong.

"Young people should set achievable goals —not so high they cannot reach them, and not so low that there is no challenge. It helps to take stock of your assets, pick appropriate goals, and move purposefully with enthusiasm. That," says Dr. Rosch, "is using stress effectively."

All humans are stress seekers to some extent. Certainly, we could live without harmful stress—if we eliminated all challenges, all problems, all surprises, and all risks. However, we would also lose the positive aspect of stress that occurs when people meet challenges, conquer them, and exult in being alive.

Athletes often experience a positive type of stress before an important race or competition.

Everyone encounters stressful situations. Learning how to cope effectively with stress is a challenge.

Stress Factors

Researchers dealing with stress have developed a theory of *input overload.* Input overload means that so many stimuli — sounds, sights, smells, and events — are coming from the environment that it is impossible to adjust to one stimulus before the next one appears. For some people, this overload results in a feeling of helplessness. They may respond by retreating into themselves or even by becoming ill.

Input underload can be just as stressful. Underload may be a particular problem for older people who live alone, for people who live in rural areas far removed from other people, and for the lonely, the unemployed, or anyone who may not have regular contact with others. Modern life contains both kinds of stress.

Stress is likely to occur during a period of adjustment as people learn to cope with a new situation. Familiar, secure, and tested ways of responding do not fit changed circumstances. New ways of acting are required, which can result in confusion, discouragement, self-doubt, and fatigue. Being pushed beyond one's limits can bring about health problems. Perhaps the most severe stressors are related to loss of love through death, separation, or divorce.

Different stressors, pleasant and unpleasant, can cause the same kind of stress. However, if a stressor is perceived as unpleasant, it will have a worse physiological effect on a person than a stressor that is thought to be pleasant. The effect depends, too, on how strong the demand is upon the body to adapt or readjust. Many other factors make a person more or less susceptible to stress: genetic makeup, age, quality of diet, and exposure to drugs, smoking, alcohol, and environmental irritants. The same stressor can affect people differently.

Stress-related Illness

Some of the ailments associated with prolonged emotional stress include hypertension (high blood pressure), peptic ulcers, migraine headaches, acne and other skin ailments, obesity, asthma, rheumatoid arthritis, and heart disease. Excess stress may also be a factor in colds, in accidents, and in increasing the cholesterol level in the blood. During stress, the body speeds up its intake of *toxins,* or poisonous substances given off by certain organisms within the body. Stress also may also influence the **immunologic system,** the body's line of defense against disease, thus contributing to the onset of infections and allergies.

Illness and injury are themselves stressors that bring about upsets in schedules, pressure on others, guilt, resentment about guilt, and a drain on energy, time, and money. In addition, it can be stressful to make crucial decisions concerning necessary medical action.

Music, exercise and sports
are three possible outlets
for relieving stress.

Stress Management

Each person seems to have a unique stress profile based on the social environment, the changes that occur in the person's life, and the person's strengths or weaknesses. Some people see stress as a challenge, while others try to avoid it at all cost.

Every person should have a special stress reliever that helps him or her to cope. One time-tested way for people to relieve stress is to take time out from a problem to catch their breath and regain their balance. They can then approach the problem from a new perspective and with the ability to see things in a new light.

For Review

1. What are some of the factors that lead to illness?
2. Discuss how input overload and input underload lead to stress.
3. What do you do to relieve stress?

Addictive Behavior

Habits make addicts. Some habits start out casually, but after repetition begin to control a person's behavior. When this happens, the person is said to be addicted. **Addiction** is a physical and sometimes psychological dependency on a substance. The body craves the physical effects that are a result of using, for example, a certain drug. At the same time, in psychological terms, the addiction has become a substitute for other forms of satisfaction. Observable physical effects such as pain, headaches, muscle cramps, or digestive upsets occur when the drug is withdrawn. Psychological symptoms—irritability, depression, anger—usually occur as well. A positive respect for oneself is fundamental to good health. When self-esteem is low, undesirable habits can be formed because people are then more easily swayed by others to make choices they might not make otherwise.

The reasons people develop addictions are as varied as the people involved. Some common causes follow. They usually operate in combination rather than in isolation.

- low self-esteem
- peer pressure
- rebellion
- a deprived or tension-filled background
- poor role models
- no one to talk to about personal problems
- ignorance of the effects of excess
- lack of awareness of other ways to cope with stress or to relieve boredom

These reasons do not apply equally to each addictive habit, but some apply to most of them.

Addictive behavior, whether it involves alcohol, illegal substances, or nicotine does not help a person achieve a real sense of well-being. As you learned in Chapter 4, the use of all drugs, including alcohol and nicotine, can become physically and psychologically destructive.

Public Health

Attitudes toward health and health care have changed in recent years. Professionals in the health care field and the general public as well recognize peoples' responsibility for their own health. Health care providers see good nutrition, weight control, stress management, physical fitness through exercise, and good mental health as important ways to stay healthy. They encourage people to see themselves as partners in health maintenance. For example, some people have learned to take their own blood pressure in order to monitor it. People are also becoming aware of themselves as health care consumers and have become better informed about the kinds of health services they receive.

These new attitudes do not mean that conventional public health measures are no longer

Safety Tip

To be prepared for first-aid needs at home, keep the following equipment on hand:

- Several packages of gauze squares, 2″ and 4″ sizes
- A roll of 3″ wide gauze
- A roll of adhesive tape
- A chemical ice pack (keep one in your car as well)
- Tongue depressors for finger splints (use tape to hold in place)
- Hydrogen peroxide for cleaning deep cuts or puncture wounds (soap and water are fine for most injuries)

Leading Causes of Death: Deaths per Life Cycle Stages, 1986 (in thousands)

Cause	Children 1-14	Adolescents, Young Adults 15-24	Adults 25-44	Adults 45-64	Adults over 65	Total Deaths
Disease of heart	1.7	1.1	16.1	127.3	619.1	765.5
Malignant neoplasms (Cancer)	1.8	2.1	20.6	136.6	308.1	469.4
Accidents, motor vehicle and other	8.1	20.0	27.2	14.7	25.1	95.3
Cerebro-vascular diseases	.2	0.3	3.4	16.4	129.3	149.6
Chronic obstructive pulmonary diseases	.2	0.2	0.7	12.7	62.7	76.6
Pneumonia, influenza	1.0	0.3	1.9	5.7	60.9	69.8
Suicide	.3	5.1	11.7	7.5	6.3	30.9
Chronic liver disease, cirrhosis	–	0.1	4.4	11.8	10.0	26.2
Diabetes mellitus	–	0.1	1.8	8.0	27.2	37.2

– = Fewer than 50 ▨ Indicates No.1 cause of death

Source: U.S. National Center for Health Statistics, Vital Statistics of the United States, 1986, annual. Adapted from: Stat Abstract, table 118, pg. 79 ('89 ed.).

necessary. Health habits remain important as preventive measures, as do checkups and immunizations.

Disease Prevention

Some diseases that threatened populations in the past have been controlled by public health measures such as sanitation and immunization. Persistent immunization programs were largely responsible for stamping out smallpox successfully, for example. Recently, however, public health officials have expressed concern that many people seem to think they are safe from contagious diseases. Nearly one-third of the children in the United States have not been immunized against polio, for example, and against various other childhood diseases.

People sometimes do not take childhood diseases seriously enough, even though some are dangerous. Whooping cough can cause infant deaths. Diphtheria can kill, also, and mumps can cause deafness. As mentioned in

Chapter 7, rubella, when contracted by pregnant women, can cause birth defects. The chart on page 185 lists recommended ages for the immunization of children against diseases.

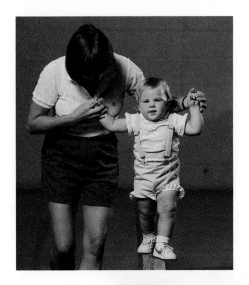

Health Care Medical examinations can detect many health problems before they become serious. Periodic physical checkups for children and pregnant women could be a very effective way to improve public health in the United States.

It has been estimated that 9 million children do not now receive basic health care. For many of their parents, the cost of medical care is a major problem.

The Public Health Service in each community maintains clinics where mothers can take their infants for regular, free checkups. The Public Health Service also provides free immunizations. In addition, Medicaid programs by law include the care of children as well as of the elderly.

Prevention of health problems through periodic checkups is a good idea for adults, too. Some communities have mobile clinics, which provide X-rays and other tests. Mobile clinics are especially useful for parents with young children, the elderly, and the disabled, all of whom have difficulty getting around.

Regular six-month dental checkups are recommended for children. Baby teeth, like permanent teeth, require good care. Older children

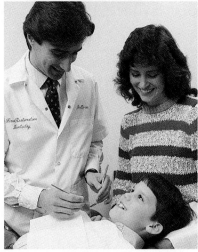

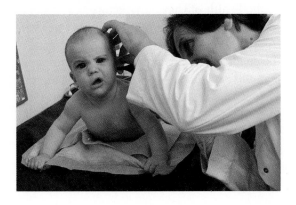

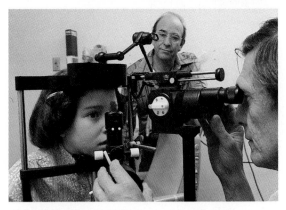

Teaching good health habits and scheduling regular medical checkups are important parental responsibilities.

and adults should visit a dentist a minimum of once a year, depending on their dental history.

Vision problems, too, are an important area of health care. When discovered early, many vision problems can be corrected before a child starts going to school. This measure will make learning and school adjustment much easier. (Schools usually give beginning students vision tests.)

Undetected hearing problems also can affect a child's adjustment as well as the child's ability to learn. Doctors can test hearing during infancy, the time when children begin learning language. Once the stage for learning language "naturally" has passed, acquiring language skills becomes more difficult.

Health Habits Health habits learned from parents are likely to stay with a person for life. Parents can establish regular times for meals, for brushing teeth, for sleep, for elimination, and for outdoor play and exercise. When parents structure routines, children are likely to accept them. Bad habits formed in childhood could lead to heart disease, stroke, and cancer later in life. It is essential that parents set good examples of self care.

Accident Prevention

The fourth leading cause of death among the total population of the United States is accidents. Among children and young adults ages 1 to 34, accidents are the leading cause of death. In addition, one-half of all accidental deaths in all age groups are due to motor vehicle accidents. Other specific causes of accidental death are drowning, fire, and accidents resulting from recreational activities. Many accidents occur toward the end of the day when people are hungry, tired, and therefore less vigilant. Extra precautions then are especially important.

The greatest killer of children is accidents. Three times more children die from accidents as from cancer, the next greatest cause of death

To prevent accidental poisoning, all medications should be kept out of the reach of small children.

Safety Tip

To prevent poisoning in young children:

■ Keep potentially hazardous items in safe places. These include plants (philodendron, dieffenbachia, pointsettia, begonia); household cleaners (polishes, drain cleaner, bleach, ammonia); medicines (aspirin, prescription drugs, vitamins); cosmetics; insecticides; gasoline; kerosene; paints.

■ Use safety packaging for hazardous items. Resecure correctly after use and lock up in a safe place.

■ Keep hazardous products in original containers. Do not store with food.

■ Never say that medicine is candy. Always give correct dosages.

in childhood. Public health officials estimate that attention to various safety measures could substantially reduce these statistics.

Swallowing toxic substances is a frequent cause of death among children. Drugs, pesticides, and cleaning agents are common in most homes. The best guarantee of safety for children and adults alike is to keep all poisons under lock and key.

Lead poisoning is a hazard, especially for small children. When they put chips of paint in their mouths, they may ingest lead, which was once used in exterior and interior paint in older houses. Lead can also be inhaled from automobile exhaust fumes. In cases where lead poisoning does not itself cause death, it can still damage the central nervous system and cause mental retardation.

For Review

1. What is addiction?
2. Describe some of the ways in which public health has been improved in recent years.
3. What is the greatest killer of children?

Exercise

In 1979, the Surgeon General's Office of the Public Health Service issued a report on the nation's health that listed health goals for different age groups in the United States. Reduction of heart attacks and strokes — stress-related diseases — is a primary goal for adults. Exercise is one of the chief recommendations as a way to achieve this goal.

Exercising is an excellent way to handle the stresses of modern living. Deliberate exercise is needed today. The human body was designed to be active, and for thousands of years human survival required physical exertion. Since modern technology has provided machines that do much of the heavy labor in the work world, more and more people now perform jobs in which they do not move around much. When the body is not used, muscles **atrophy,** or fail to develop, digestion becomes sluggish, and excess fat accumulates. The pulse rate goes up and the body becomes tense. Moreover, circulation slows down, breathing becomes more shallow, and sleep is more fitful.

When a body is active, the opposite happens: the whole body is strengthened, and endurance increases. Muscles and joints become more flexible. Lung capacity expands through deeper breathing. Circulation in turn becomes more efficient, and pulse rate goes down. Healthy changes in hormone production take place, and the likelihood of illness decreases. Tensions are worked off, so sleep is more restful.

Types of Exercise Experts recommend that people who are planning to get more exercise should fit their activity to their temperament. If they do not enjoy an activity, they probably will not follow their exercise program. If you are thinking of getting more exercise, ask yourself the following questions:

- Do I prefer to be with others or by myself?
- Do I like being inside or outdoors?
- What is a convenient time for me to exercise and what activities are available at that time?
- Is a fee involved?
- Can I afford it?
- Do I like competitive activities?
- What activity can I learn now that I can enjoy all my life?

Individual and team sports afford opportunities for exercise. However, many activities besides sports can provide daily exercise, too. Walking, running, climbing, stretching, and bending are a few.

People may derive numerous benefits from a life that includes enough exercise. Hair, skin, and body look better. Reaction time quickens and reflexes are better. People feel sharper and more alert. Perhaps an even more important benefit is the feeling of well-being that accompanies these physical effects.

Cardiovascular Fitness Twenty minutes of vigorous exercise three times a week helps achieve better heart and lung function, a drop in blood pressure, and improved oxygen flow. The condition achieved by this type of exercise is called **cardiovascular fitness.**

To achieve cardiovascular fitness, one's heartbeat must temporarily be pushed to about 120 beats per minute, putting moderate stress on the heart but strengthening it at the same time. Some theorists believe that exercise increases the formation of new blood vessels to the heart, the width of the vessels, the number of capillaries, and the amount of oxygen that reaches the heart.

As the heart muscle is strengthened, the rate of "at-rest" heartbeat is lowered. Athletes average a resting heartbeat of 50 beats per minute. The average person has a rate of 72 beats per minute. A heart with a low but firm and steady heartbeat works less, rests more, and may take longer to wear out.

Any physical activity that increases the amount of oxygen the body can process in a given time is called **aerobic exercise.** Brisk walking (3 to 4 miles per hour), swimming, cross-country skiing, and bicycling (10 to 14 miles per hour) are examples of this kind of exercise. Following an aerobic exercise program may be a good route to cardiovascular fitness and a healthier heart.

Mental Health

Good mental health is as important to a person as is good physical health. In addition to general feelings of well-being and self-esteem, mentally healthy people have other characteristics in common:

- They accept themselves and others and make the best of their abilities.

- They adjust well to changing circumstances.

- They like and expect to be liked by people.

- They have warm, lasting relationships with others.

- They cope effectively with life's problems and demands.

- They assume responsibility for their own actions.

Most individuals do not meet all these standards all the time. A wholesome personality and effective functioning are matters of degree.

Self-esteem strengthens a wholesome personality. Researcher Michael Rutter of the London Institute of Psychiatry investigated reasons why some children remain emotionally healthy under difficult circumstances while others do not. He concluded that self-esteem is a critical factor in overcoming difficulties. Yet both teachers and parents often ignore or passively accept good behavior, commenting only on poor or unacceptable behavior. Adults need to recognize children's positive qualities in order to reinforce self-esteem, a key factor in mental health.

When mental health problems develop, parents, relatives, or friends may be called upon for help. Crisis situations may require the assistance of a skilled mental health professional.

For Review

1. What are some of the negative effects of not getting proper exercise?
2. What is cardiovascular fitness?
3. Name three characteristics of a mentally healthy person.

17 Chapter Review

Summary

Many health experts believe that a person's well-being is determined by the interaction of the body, mind, and emotions. Most health problems have complex causes. A combination of genetic, behavioral, and environmental factors, for example, contributes to the formation of degenerative disease.

While some stress is necessary and unavoidable in everyday life, excessive stress can contribute to illness and injury. As a result, people must find ways to alleviate pressures before they become overwhelming.

Many causes contribute to the development of addictive behavior. In general, an individual with low self-esteem is more likely to develop an addiction than a person with a strong sense of self-worth.

People can ensure that they will remain healthy through good nutrition, weight control, stress management, physical fitness, and mental health. Adequate medical care and conscientious attention to accident prevention can also maintain one's health and longevity.

Vocabulary

Complete the following sentences with one of the vocabulary words below.

addiction
aerobic exercise
atrophy
cardiovascular fitness
degenerative disease
immunologic system
multifactored
stress
stressor

1. Any challenge from the environment that places a demand on a person's body or mind is called _____ .
2. Ill health is considered to be _____ because many parts may contribute to it, including inadequate nutrition, poor hygiene, and a lack of exercise or rest.
3. _____ occurs when an individual develops a physical and/or a psychological dependence on a substance.
4. Regular vigorous exercise improves heart and lung function, enabling the body to achieve _____ .
5. The majority of deaths from illness today are caused by _____ , which involves the deterioration of the body resulting from genetic, environmental, and behavioral factors.
6. The stimulus from the environment that creates stress in an individual is called a (an) _____ .
7. Physical activity that increases the amount of oxygen the body can process is called _____ .
8. Excessive stress can negatively influence the _____ , which may result in the body's decreased ability to resist diseases.
9. When the body is not used or there is insufficient nutrition, body organs or tissues may _____ .

Chapter Questions

1. Why are the majority of deaths today caused by degenerative disease instead of infectious diseases?
2. What guidelines have health experts established for the maintenance of good health?
3. What is input underload?
4. Give an example in which one person perceives a single stressor (heat, cold, or other) as unpleasant, while another perceives it as pleasant.
5. How do you cope with stress?
6. Describe the physical and psychological symptoms of an addict's withdrawal from an addictive substance.
7. Which of the causes of addictive behavior do you think are most prevalent among teenagers with drug dependency problems? Why is this so?
8. What should be done to warn parents about the need for immunization?
9. Why are medical examinations important to health maintenance?
10. Why should parents help their children to establish good health habits?
11. Why is it healthy to exercise?
12. How can an individual achieve cardiovascular fitness?

Skill Activities

1. **Reading** Research the development of the vaccine for one or more of the following diseases: polio, diphtheria, tetanus, whooping cough, smallpox, measles, mumps, and rubella. Use encyclopedias, reference books, and other library resources to collect your information. After consulting at least two different sources, discuss what you have learned in a brief written report. Remember to include a discussion of each vaccine's impact on public health at the time it was developed.

2. **Communication** Investigate the different types of aerobic exercise that are popular today. Consult a variety of books and magazines on physical fitness in your school or local library to find this information. Then, design a poster in which you display the varieties of aerobic exercise that are available. For each aerobic activity you portray, describe how a person can begin participating in this exercise. What equipment is needed? What financial investment is required? How much time is necessary? What special precautions should be taken? What books or magazines give more information? Include illustrations, charts, or graphs to accompany the information you present.

3. **Critical Thinking** With a group of other students, discuss how the deaths of children resulting from accidents can be reduced. As you talk about what can be done to achieve this goal, develop a list of recommendations that communities, schools, and families can implement to improve safety. Present your plan to the rest of your class. Ask for their comments and suggestions on how your recommendations can be improved.

18 Enjoying Good Nutrition

As you read, think about:

- what factors influence food choices.
- what foods provide the six necessary nutrients.
- how you can improve your diet to promote health and fitness.
- how family living patterns influence what and how you eat.

VOCABULARY

obesity	cholesterol
nutrition	fiber
nutrients	endosperm
metabolic processes	germ
empty calories	anorexia nervosa
dental caries	bulimia

People everywhere realize the importance of food. Food supplies essential ingredients for the growth and repair of body tissues. Also, eating can be a pleasurable experience, involving the senses of sight, smell, and taste. Equally important, the sharing of food may be a reassuring social experience for those who sit down and eat together. Dr. Bruno Bettelheim, a child psychiatrist, states that eating and being fed are connected with one's basic attitudes toward food itself.

This chapter discusses food habits and preferences, nutrients, and calories. It also shows how to choose foods to gain maximum satisfaction, good health, and a feeling of well-being.

A New England clam bake and a Texas-style barbecue are examples of traditional regional foods.

Food Choices

Americans today have a wide variety of foods from which to choose. Canned, frozen, and other processed foods make many items always "in season." Foods can be quickly transported over great distances without spoiling.

Further, many people are interested in trying new foods as well as different methods of preparing familiar foods.

In the past, food choices were more limited, and there were more pronounced differences in what people ate in the various regions of the United States. Regional dishes were a source of local pride, and included such foods as Southern fried chicken and pecan pie. New England seafood and baked beans, Midwest beef, and West Coast fresh fruit salad. While location and seasonal variations have less to do with what people eat today, both factors still influence food choices.

Advertising in the mass media, such as newspapers, magazines, and radio and television, greatly influences food choices. TV sponsors use a variety of methods to create desires for food products. They show foods in pleasant surroundings, being eaten by good-looking people who are obviously enjoying themselves as they repeat the name of a product over and over. Thus, advertisers affect the national diet by association, repetition, and reinforcement.

Cultural Factors

In the United States, certain foods are associated with holidays: turkey with Thanksgiving, chocolates with Valentine's Day, pumpkins with Halloween, and barbecued meats with Fourth-of-July picnics. Holiday traditions allow people to renew a sense of solidarity with their family and friends each year.

Ethnic factors also may help determine what you choose to eat. Where your ancestors came from and how strongly they felt about their ancestral ties influence food choices for generations. For example, Italian cooking includes pasta, tomato sauce, veal, and eggplant. Oriental cooking often uses rice and quick-cooked

Your ethnic background can influence the foods you eat. At a family gathering members enjoy a feast of traditional Hispanic foods.

meats and vegetables. Hispanic dishes frequently include tortillas and beans. Each ethnic group also has foods reserved for holidays or feast days. Sharing special foods is one way to display a group identity.

Foods may have special meaning within a particular family: a special stew made at a campout where everyone laughed a lot, a midnight supper that ushers in the New Year, a snow pudding that only Grandmother can make. In one family, everyone anticipates and relishes the father's homemade breads and ingenious salads. Perhaps you have a family tradition of this sort. Someday, you may wish to continue this tradition in a family of your own.

Economic Factors

When food prices are high, it is more difficult to buy nutritious food while getting the best value for the money spent. However, limited funds do not necessarily mean that the food people purchase must be of low quality or of little nutritive value.

A survey of families living in the Northeastern region of the United States during the past decade revealed that the families who got the most from their food dollars — both in value and in nutrition — were those with the lowest incomes. These families bought fewer convenience foods and packaged foods and fewer items of low nutritional value, such as soft drinks, than did families with higher incomes. The food they bought included poultry, eggs, meats such as kidney and liver, beans, potatoes, flour, and cereals. While lower-income families had fewer food choices, they actually made better choices.

People with higher incomes can afford "luxury foods," but they are not guaranteed a nutritionally balanced diet. Many of the tasty foods that people enjoy often contain the most fats. Diets that include many fatty foods have been related to health problems such as **obesity,** or gross overweight, and heart trouble. When people have more money to spend on food, they often choose to increase protein by buying expensive beef products, like steak. Many eat fewer fresh vegetables and fruits, which supply other essential nutrients.

Food and Nutrition

The body needs certain foods in order to survive. This is not a matter of personal preference or of economic necessity; it is a physical need. **Nutrition** is the study of the elements in foods the body needs and the ways in which the body uses them.

Nutrients

Nutrients are the elements in food that enable the body to maintain life and to function properly. There are six key nutrients: protein is used for growth and for the replacement of

Some Essential Nutrients

Nutrient	Some Body Uses	Some Food Sources
Water	Part of all cells and body fluids; carries nutrients	Water; lettuce, radishes, celery, watermelon, oranges
Protein (contains 20 "building blocks": amino acids)	Regulates and promotes cell growth, repair; main part of tissues; supplies energy	*Animal:* meat, poultry, fish, eggs, milk; *plant:* dry beans, nuts
Carbohydrates (sugars, starches, fiber)	Energy source; needed by brain; aids use of fat; spares protein for body building	*Sugars:* honey, syrups, sweets, fruits; *starches:* grains, potatoes; *fiber:* celery, bran
Fats	Essential fatty acids; carries fat-soluble vitamins; body insulator	*Saturated:* animal fat, butter, hydrogenated products; *unsaturated:* vegetable oils
Vitamins		
Vitamin A (fat-soluble)	Aids vision in dim light; keeps body linings healthy	Liver; deep yellow/dark green vegetables; potatoes
Thiamin/vitamin B, (water-soluble)	Energy use; cell repair; appetite; healthy nerves	Seeds; pork; peanuts, soy beans; wheat germ; liver
Riboflavin/vitamin B_2 (water-soluble)	Energy use; growth; healthy skin, eyes, nerves	Milk, cheese; liver, heart; wheat germ; leafy greens
Niacin (water-soluble)	Aids digestion	Liver, meat, poultry, fish
Vitamin B_6 (water-soluble)	Helps amino acids develop	Liver; whole wheat; bananas
Vitamin B_{12} (water-soluble)	Needed for cell functions, making of red blood cells	Only in foods of animal origin: meat, poultry, milk
Folacin (water-soluble)	Helps form body cells	Wheat germ; liver, kidney
Vitamin C (water-soluble)	Helps form collagen, bones; protects against infection	Citrus fruits, strawberries; raw cabbage, baked potatoes
Vitamin D (fat-soluble)	Aids calcium absorption to build bones and teeth	Fortified milk; butter; fish liver oils; egg yolk
Vitamin E (fat-soluble)	Helps prevent cell damage	Vegetable oils, margarine
Minerals		
Calcium	Helps build strong bones and teeth; helps blood clot	Milk/milk products; dark green, leafy vegetables
Phosphorus	Aids calcium absorption	Meat, poultry, fish, eggs
Magnesium	Aids calcium, phosphorus use	Whole grains, soybeans
Iron	Combines with protein to make hemoglobin	Liver, kidney; red meats; enriched grain products
Iodine	Helps regulate metabolism	Seafood; iodized salt
Zinc	Promotes healing, growth	Seafood, meat, poultry

worn-out cells. Protein, carbohydrates, and fats supply energy to enable people to move about, to work and play, and to keep their organs and body systems functioning properly. Water, vitamins, and minerals help regulate the body processes.

People need balanced amounts of nutrients in their diet because all six nutrients interact — that is, they work together in order to be most effective.

- Water assists in food digestion.

- The body absorbs calcium better when moderate amounts of protein are present.

- Calcium and phosphorous are used more effectively when the body has enough vitamin D.

- Fat molecules carry vitamins A, D, E, and K.

- An adequate intake of energy-producing fat and carbohydrate spares protein, needed for building cells, from being burned for energy.

Since all nutrients contribute to a person's health, the body lacks something it needs when one nutrient is omitted or short-changed. To get the full range of nutrients from meals, people must choose from a variety of foods and not eat the same kinds of foods all the time.

Choosing from among a variety of foods has a further benefit; even some "good" foods have bad aspects. Peanut butter, for example, is an excellent source of protein and a tasty snack. However, it is high in fat and salt. Spinach, a good source of vitamin A, has a high concentration of oxalic acid. If eaten too often, the spinach can interfere with an infant's calcium absorption. An exclusive diet of calcium-rich milk, which is also low in iron, could lead to anemia, or iron-deficient blood.

What people eat is the most important factor in nutrition, since foods have different nutritive values. However, the way food is prepared also can add to its value or subtract from it. Eating behavior is important, too. A person's digestion may suffer from hurried eating or from eating when he or she is tense or tired. In such situations, the body will not absorb nutrients well. Finally, the nutritive value of what people eat is influenced by how well their diet is balanced.

Food Groups

To help people choose foods that balance their nutritional needs, researchers have suggested guides for good eating habits. It is important for people to be aware of the nutritive value of the foods they eat. In the latest edition of *Guide to Good Eating* published by The National Dairy Council, the Council points out that four food groups make up a simple guide to a healthful diet. These food groups include: *Vegetables and Fruits, Breads and Cereals, Milk and Cheese and Meat, Fish, Poultry and Beans.* A fifth group, called *Fats and Sweets,* shows foods that are high in calories and low in nutritional value.

Varying the choices within each food group and following the recommended number of daily servings can help ensure a nutritionally balanced diet.

It is also important to be aware of higher and lower nutritive values when preparing and eating a balanced meal. A hot dog, white rice, green beans, lettuce, and canned peaches make up a nutritious and balanced meal. However, a meal of turkey, baked potato, broccoli, carrot slaw, and a fresh peach has both balance and higher *nutritive* value. Fruits and vegetables are also more nutritious raw than cooked.

Calories

In addition to receiving a balanced supply of nutrients, the body needs the proper number of calories to function at its best. A calorie is a unit that measures energy in food. The body needs energy for **metabolic processes,** or all the physical and chemical changes it undergoes for growth, for physical activity, and for maintaining proper body temperature.

Food Groups

Vegetables and Fruits

Four servings daily

One serving = about 1/2 cup

Each day include one vitamin C source such as a citrus fruit (orange, grapefruit, tangerine), a melon, or berries. Include vitamin A and iron sources such as deep yellow or dark green vegetables (broccoli, spinach, carrots, sweet potatoes). Frequently include fiber sources such as unpeeled fruits and vegetables (apples, pears, celery).

Besides possible sources of vitamins A and C and fiber, vegetables are low in fat and contain no cholesterol.

Breads and Cereals

Four servings daily of whole-grain, enriched, or fortified products

One serving = 1 slice bread; 1/2-3/4 cup cooked cereal, cornmeal, rice, or macaroni; 1 ounce ready-to-eat cereal

This group supplies B vitamins and iron, and some protein. Whole-grain products also supply fiber.

Milk and Cheese

Four servings daily*

One serving = 1 8-ounce cup milk (any form); 1 cup yogurt; 2-inch cube Cheddar or Swiss cheese; 1½ cups ice cream or ice milk

This group provides calcium and protein, as well as vitamins A and D in fortified products. Some dairy products also contain fats.

Meat, Fish, Poultry, Beans

Two servings daily

One serving = 2-3 ounces lean, cooked meat (beef, veal, lamb, pork), poultry, or fish without bones; 1/2-3/4 cup cooked dried beans or peas, soybeans, lentils; 1 egg; 2 tablespoons peanut butter; 1/4-1/2 cup nuts or seeds

This group can supply protein and minerals such as phosphorus and iron. Only animal foods contain vitamin B_{12} and cholesterol, although fish and most shellfish have relatively small amounts of cholesterol.

Fats and Sweets

No daily servings suggested. If calorie needs permit more food in the daily diet than the recommended servings, choose "extras" from the calorie- and nutrient-rich foods of the other four food groups.

Foods in this group include cooking oils, butter, margarine, mayonnaise, and salad dressings; candy, sugar, jams, jellies, and syrups; soft drinks and other highly sugared beverages; products made with refined but unenriched flour.

This group is high in calories and low in nutrients except for vegetable oils, which supply vitamin E and essential fatty acids.

Recommended for a teenager; two servings for an adult, three servings for a child.

Healthy Vegetarian Combinations

In a vegetarian diet, animal foods such as meat, fish, or eggs are replaced with plant foods such as grains, beans, or nuts. Vegetarians must replace the "complete protein" of animal foods, which provides all eight essential amino acids that the body needs. "Incomplete protein" plant foods can be eaten in balanced combinations to supply complete protein. In fact, they can supply all the same nutrients as animal foods except vitamin B_{12}, which must be supplemented. A few nutritious plant food combinations follow:

- Rice and beans
- Rice/rice products and milk
- Wheat products and milk/milk products
- Wheat products and beans
- Beans and milk
- Peanuts, wheat products, and milk

- Bean curd on rice; rice and peas; rice and soybean casserole
- Rice cereal and milk; rice pudding
- Macaroni and cheese; cheese sandwich; pancakes made with milk; lasagna
- Corn chips and bean dip
- Lentil soup and glass of milk
- Peanut butter sandwich, glass of milk

Some foods contain more calories than others. Carbohydrates and protein supply four calories per gram; fat yields nine per gram. When people eat foods containing too many calories, the extra energy they consume, if not burned off with exercise, becomes fat, which is stored in the tissues.

Caloric intake should be related to the amount of energy a person needs. People use the most calories when they expend the most energy. It is common for people to eat a large dinner and to sit down and watch television or go to sleep. It would be much wiser for people to plan meals around the times of day they need the most energy. One guide suggests eating a large breakfast, a moderate lunch, and a light dinner to fuel the body throughout the day. Perhaps there are people whose energy needs would be better met by six small meals a day.

Many factors affect the number of calories a person needs daily. For instance, a large person requires more food than a small person. Someone who expends more energy in physical work, in exercise, or in athletic activity needs more calories than someone doing light work or resting. Children, adolescents, pregnant women, or nursing mothers all need more calories and nutrients because their bodies are changing and growing.

Climate and temperature also influence caloric needs. In cold climates, exposure to low temperatures may require that the body take in more energy to maintain a constant temperature. In hot climates, a person may need fewer calories since work usually proceeds at a slower pace. In very hot weather, however, the body sweats, losing essential water and salt that must be replaced. Again, more energy is required to maintain proper body temperature.

In selecting foods that provide energy, it is important to consider nutrients as well. Calories from highly-sugared foods (such as soft drinks, candy, and many bakery products), from high-fat foods (such as potato chips), or from imitation foods (such as coffee whiteners) are called **empty calories** because they provide few, if any, nutrients. Both calories and nutrients are necessary parts of a diet.

For Review

1. How does advertising affect the food choices you make?
2. What are the six essential nutrients?
3. What is the fifth food group?

Recommended Diets

Dietary goals are based on human population studies, research that connects dietary factors with certain diseases, and guidelines set by the National Food and Nutrition Board. On the basis of current scientific evidence, most nutritionists would agree that the best approach to nutrition is to eat a wide variety of foods of high nutrient value from among all food groups. Nutritionists specifically recommend that people eat less sugar, less fat, less salt, and more fiber.

In 1977, the Select Committee on Nutrition and Human Needs of the United States Senate issued *Dietary Goals for the United States.* The publication was prepared by the Committee's staff, in consultation with nutrition and health experts. It included suggestions on nutrition

Being aware of foods that make up a healthy diet can help people improve their eating habits.

and general guidelines for the American family on selecting food.

- Eat more fruits and vegetables and whole grains.
- Eat less meat and more poultry and fish.
- Substitute low-fat milk and dairy products for high-fat milk and dairy products.
- Eat less refined and processed sugar and foods high in such sugar.
- Eat fewer foods high in fat. Partially replace foods high in saturated fat with foods that have polyunsaturated fat.
- Eat less salt and fewer foods high in salt.
- Eat fewer eggs, less butterfat, and fewer high-cholesterol foods.

Not all nutritionists agree with each other about the effects of diet. However, most believe that a balanced diet goes a long way toward keeping people healthy.

Less Sugar

Sugar, as found in soft drinks, candy, cake, and many desserts, is a simple carbohydrate that serves mainly to give the body a "lift." It enters the bloodstream quickly, resulting in an instant rise in blood sugar and energy. However, the lift does not last very long. When the blood sugar level falls, there is a "letdown" with renewed feelings of hunger and a need for more energy.

Complex carbohydrates, found in fruit, vegetables, whole grains, and milk products, serve the same purpose as sugar, but are more effective. These foods take longer to metabolize in the body and thus provide steady, dependable energy for a longer period of time. Moreover, they do not provide empty calories; they have nutrient value as well.

One way to avoid excess sugar is to read the labels on food packages and containers. The ingredients are listed in decreasing order of the amount contained in the food itself or added during its processing. Corn syrup or sweeteners, honey, and molasses are all sugars. Look for words with *ose* as an ending: sucrose (table sugar), fructose (fruit sugar), lactose (milk sugar), glucose, dextrose, and maltose. See if sugar is the first or second ingredient listed. A large percentage of most fruit punches, presweetened cereals, and gelatins is sugar.

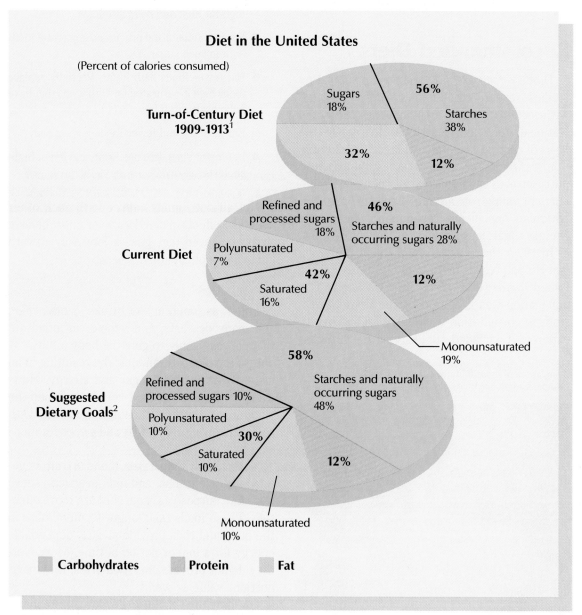

Diet in the United States

(Percent of calories consumed)

Turn-of-Century Diet 1909-1913[1]

Sugars 18%
56%
Starches 38%
32%
12%

Current Diet

Refined and processed sugars 18%
46%
Starches and naturally occurring sugars 28%
Polyunsaturated 7%
42%
Saturated 16%
12%
Monounsaturated 19%

Suggested Dietary Goals[2]

58%
Refined and processed sugars 10%
Starches and naturally occurring sugars 48%
Polyunsaturated 10%
30%
Saturated 10%
12%
Monounsaturated 10%

Carbohydrates   Protein   Fat

[1]*U.S. Department of Agriculture*
[2]*Developed by the McGovern Committee*

Fruit is a good substitute for a snack high in refined sugar.

Sugar may be the additive Americans consume in the largest amounts. High sugar consumption has been related to **dental caries,** or tooth decay. Frequent eating of sticky sugars not followed by brushing the teeth is a major cause of cavities. Scientists estimate that 90 percent of the children in the United States today have some tooth decay. Almost one-half of American people no longer have their own teeth by age 55!

Less Fat

Fats contain twice as many calories per gram as do proteins or carbohydrates. When you eat excess calories, they are stored in the body as fat. Much fat in the diet comes from "hidden" sources, such as fats in meats, in pastries, in deep-fried foods, and in snacks. Hidden fats, especially, may add calories that contribute to being overweight.

Obesity is a major health problem that usually can be prevented by diet management. An estimated 20 percent of this country's adult population is sufficiently overweight to endanger their health and even their projected lifespan. Statistics indicate that for various reasons, low-income women, high-income men, and adolescent girls seem to be most affected by obesity. Some studies now indicate that eating too much fat also may have a bearing on cancer of the breast and colon and on diabetes.

Saturated fats, such as those found in butter, lard, whole milk, hard cheese, and meat (especially beef and lamb or mutton), are usually solid at room temperature. Many nutritionists believe that consuming saturated fats raises the level of **cholesterol** in one's blood. Cholesterol is a fatlike substance manufactured by the body that normally occurs in the bloodstream and is important to the central nervous system. However, reseachers have also linked excess cholesterol to heart disease. It is still a matter of dispute as to how much cholesterol in the diet constitutes an excess. Some scientists believe that the body manufactures excess cholesterol during times of stress.

Vegetable foods in general are low in saturated fat. However, coconut oil and palm oil,

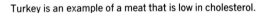

Turkey is an example of a meat that is low in cholesterol.

found in powdered coffee whiteners, some artificial ice cream, and many cookies, contain large amounts of saturated fat. Also high in such fat are avocados, olives and nuts. (Read the labels; "hydrogenated" refers to normally unsaturated vegetable oils that are processed to become saturated, or solid, at room temperature.)

Unsaturated fats are found in poultry, fish, and most vegetable oils and margarines. Although not all nutritionists agree, some research indicates that unsaturated fats do not increase the cholesterol level in the blood.

Fat, and especially cholesterol, intake has become a very complex issue that scientists must continue to study. Until more information is available, the best precaution may be to avoid excessive consumption of any one food or food group.

Less Salt

Nutritionists agree that salt is linked to high blood pressure in certain people. The usual intake of sodium, a chemical component of salt, far exceeds the needs of most people.

Scientists estimate that Americans eat from a little over one teaspoon (5 g) to almost five teaspoons (25 g) of salt per day, with two to three teaspoons (10 to 15 g) considered an average intake. Present knowledge suggests that people probably need less than one-fifth of a teaspoon (1 g) per day. It has also been suggested that salt intake be limited to one teaspoon (5 g) per day.

Increased snacking has raised the consumption of potato chips, pretzels, crackers, and salted nuts to an all-time high. Some foods that seem to be low in salt actually contain large amounts of it. For example, corn flakes contain 1000 mg salt per 100 g and graham crackers contain 670 mg salt per 100 g. Salt often is added during the processing and canning of food. For example, cured ham has 20 times as much salt as does raw pork, and canned peas contain 130 times as much salt as do fresh peas.

It is important to read the labels of the foods you purchase to find out if they contain any of the following ingredients:

Sodium bicarbonate (baking soda)
Sodium chloride (table salt)
Monosodium glutamate
Disodium phosphate
Sodium alginate
Sodium benzoate
Sodium hydroxide
Sodium propionate
Sodium sulfite
Sodium saccharin

It is easier to detect a food's natural flavors when no additional salt is added. The following foods are high in salt:

- Foods prepared in brine, such as pickles, olives, and sauerkraut.

- Salty or smoked meat, such as corned or chipped beef, frankfurters, ham, luncheon meats, salt pork, sausage, bologna, and smoked tongue.

- Canned and instant soups.

- Bouillon cubes, seasoned salt, soy and barbecue sauces, catsup, mustard, and horseradish.

- Cheese, especially processed cheese.

- Salty or smoked fish such as anchovies, caviar, dried cod, sardines, and smoked salmon.

More Fiber

Fiber is the dietary item often referred to as roughage. It is plant material not digested in the gastrointestinal tract. The main advantage of fiber is that it aids in the process of elimination. Fiber also provides bulk to satisfy the appetite. Fiber in the diet often helps people lose weight, causing them to feel filled up sooner and thus eat less. Scientists have found that kinds of fiber

What are some of the benefits of eating foods that are high in fiber?

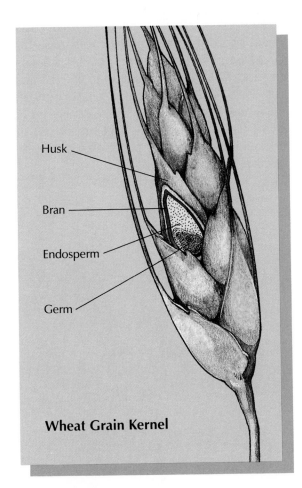

Husk

Bran

Endosperm

Germ

Wheat Grain Kernel

found in foods such as rolled oats or legumes can reduce the blood's cholesterol level.

Fiber is found in whole-grain breads, pancakes, muffins, and cereals, including bran. Whole grain is what it says: the whole of the grain. It retains the bran layer containing fiber and vitamins. Brown rice retains the bran layer, too, and therefore has more fiber. This layer is removed in the processing and refining that produces white rice. Besides whole grains, dried peas and beans, nuts, fruits, and vegetables—especially those with edible seeds and peelings—are good sources of fiber.

Bran, the outer coat of grain, contains fiber and B vitamins. During milling and processing, bran is removed along with the B vitamins it contains. The inner part of grain is called the **endosperm.** Composed mostly of starch and proteins, it is used to make white flour. The **germ** is the part inside the kernel of grain from which a new plant can grow. It contains minerals, B vitamins, oil, and fat. When grain is milled and processed to make white flour and breakfast cereals, the germ is removed.

Federal law states that processed grains must be restored or enriched to replace lost vitamins and minerals. Some of the lost nutrients may or may not be replaced. For example, up to 80 percent of the zinc in whole-grain cereal is lost in milling. Other nutrients such as iron may be added to make the product more nutritious, but the fiber is not replaced. Whole-wheat bread has 1.6 g of fiber, as compared to .2 g for enriched white bread.

For Review

1. What foods give the body a lift but do not contain refined sugar?
2. Give an example of foods that are low in saturated fat.
3. What is the greatest hazard of eating too much salt?

Food Management

In periods of economic decline, most families try to stretch their food dollars. Some people may save money by buying cases of canned goods. Others might form food cooperatives, where people buy wholesale food jointly and distribute it among themselves, or they might raise their own vegetables or check farmer's markets and roadside stands for good buys. Some people investigate wholesale outlets such as bakeries, dairies, and restaurant suppliers to locate low-priced food. Another money-saving device is to buy store brands or generic brands of various food products.

A wise food consumer, however, does more than bargain hunting in the process of food shopping. Management skills also are necessary: decision making, goal setting, planning, and evaluating. To plan inexpensive, nutritious meals requires knowledge about nutrition; one must know which foods contain the most nutrients as well as how to get the best buys.

Planning

Research shows that people should plan before spending their food dollars. Shoppers who go to grocery stores without having decided what they need tend to buy items they really do not need or want. This tendency is most likely to occur when a person shops on an empty stomach.

Shoppers should plan meals around needs. They should use a food guide to help in choosing nutritious menus from a variety of foods. Variety is important not only to balance nutrients but also to increase the appeal of the food. One should choose foods that vary in size, shape, color, and texture, as well as in flavor.

Shoppers should make a list of what they need, based on menus and recipes before they go to the store. A shopping list also should include any staples, or food supplies usually kept on hand, that are running low. To make food shopping easier, the list should be organized according to store layout. A quick review of advertised specials and food coupons on hand may also affect a shopping list. Using food coupons is only a money-saving measure if you were planning to buy a specific food item before you found the coupon.

Shopping

Research has shown that food advertising is not always reliable. A person can usually determine whether an item is really a "special purchase" by knowing its regular price.

Comparison shopping, or checking the prices of various brands of a product, ensures that a person will pay the best price. One should look at unit pricing, too, if it is indicated on a shelf or package. This tells the amount the item costs per standard measure, such as per ounce or gram. In this way, a person can compare different sizes and brands of an item to find the one that costs the least per unit. Price per serving should also be considered when selecting cuts of meat, fish or poultry. A boneless breast of chicken costs more per pound than a regular chicken breast, for example.

Taking time to compare store brands with name brands enables you to get equal value for less money.

Food Labels Can Fool You

Almost everybody today is aware of the importance of eating healthy food. Most supermarket shoppers are on the lookout for foods that are low in sugar, fat, and sodium, and high in fiber and vitamins. They are attracted by food labels that use such phrases as "low in sugar," "light and wholesome," and "all natural ingredients."

Before they toss such packages into their carts, they would do well to examine the smaller type on the labels.

The words *wholesome* and *natural* can mean anything. These terms are not defined by the FTC (the Federal Trade Commission that regulates advertising claims) or the Food and Drug Administration. The word *light* suggests the food is low in calories, but the word may refer to color or consistency.

The phrase "low in sugar" also can be misleading. The FDC requires that most food containers list all ingredients by quantity, with the largest amount listed first. You may find in the small print that while there is little or no sugar used, there may be a great deal of corn syrup, which contains just as many calories as sugar.

It is surprising how many products contain a large percentage of sugar of one kind or another. Sugar makes up as much as one-third of all the ingredients in many boxed cereals. You also might not suspect that almost twenty percent of many fruit-flavored yogurts, salad dressings, and ketchup is sugar. Products list different forms of sugar separately. You may find that these separate kinds—such as sucrose (regular granulated sugar), fructose, dextrose, corn and maple syrup, and honey— add up to a large percentage.

Fat comes in many forms; some people confuse fat and cholesterol. Cholesterol is not listed as an ingredient. You need to know the difference in kinds of oil. Some vegetable oils such as olive oil contain little or no cholesterol, but they can raise cholesterol in the blood of the consumer. Other vegetable oils like corn and safflower oil reduce cholesterol in the blood. However, they are still high in calories.

Many labels now give the size of a single serving and the number of calories per serving. They also tell you the amount of protein, carbohydrate, fat, and sodium per serving. In addition, they list the percentage of the U.S. recommended daily allowance for each of a number of vitamins and minerals.

The aim of the designers of food labels is to sell the product. Fortunately, people are becoming better informed about nutrition and are more aware of the difference between empty claims and helpful facts. As food packagers begin to realize this change in public awareness, they are offering fewer empty descriptions and more real information. It still pays, however, to take the time to study the small print on food labels.

Before food product labels were required to comply with governmental regulations, labels could make outrageous claims.

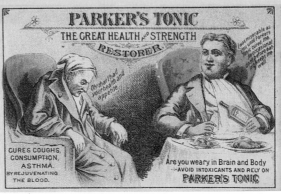

Since there are different types of grocery stores, try to shop at one that best suits your needs.

One of the best ways to find nutrient sources, count calories, or buy quality food is to read labels. According to law, food labels must show *product name, net weight* (without weight of package), *list of ingredients* (in decreasing order of content), and *name and address of manufacturer.* Most packages also carry a *nutrition information panel.* This gives the size and number of servings in the product, and calorie and nutrient content per serving. Also on the panel, the United States Recommended Daily Allowance *(U.S.RDA)* tells, in percentages, how one serving meets daily nutritional needs. Perishable foods are marked with an open *code date* that shows whether the contents are still edible.

People should consider their cooking needs while shopping. For example, they could ask themselves whether fresh, canned, or frozen foods would be best for them. Government grades and standards indicate whether the food is of the appropriate quality for one's needs. For example, the appearance of top quality grade AA eggs is important when a person intends to pan fry them, but the poor appearance of Grade B eggs is unimportant when someone wants an omelet or scrambled eggs. The nutritional value of both grades is the same, but the price of the Grade B eggs is less.

Practical Tip

To avoid eating empty calories, try to have on hand the following foods:

- Fresh fruit
- Raw vegetables
- Raisins
- Shelled nuts
- Pumpkin and sunflower seeds
- Yogurt
- Fruit or vegetable breads
- Popcorn

Family Living Patterns and Eating Habits

When ways of life change, eating patterns change. Today, the faster pace of American life has made eating "on the run" more common. Some families try to counteract this trend by promoting a regular family mealtime a few times a week.

Your life style as well as your self-image affect your eating habits. In an attempt to regulate weight, many young people turn to diet practices that are life-threatening.

Snacking

Television and snacking go together. Many TV commercials advertise snack foods, reminding viewers to eat. More importantly, a family spends less time at the dining table when there is a TV in the home. Cooking may no longer provide a source of enjoyment and pride for some people because of the increasing availability of processed foods. Some people may also choose foods that are fast and convenient in

Pizza is an example of a convenience food that has nutritive value.

order to have more time for other activities. As a result, more snack foods appear on home menus. Since many snack foods have a high sugar, fat, and salt content, they contain many empty calories and do not really satisfy the appetite. A person is likely to feel hungry again soon and to crave more snacks.

It is more advisable to snack on foods that supply necessary nutrients and satisfy the desire for something tasty. Fresh fruits, vegetables, nuts, seeds, and whole grains do this. They also provide bulk, which keeps a person filled up for a considerable period of time.

No matter how often people snack, it is what they eat that counts. You should remember to plan snacks as part of your total caloric allotment for the day. Otherwise, you may not be aware of the amount you eat. You should also remember that since certain foods are necessary for a balanced diet, they can be included as snacks when missed at regular meals.

Fast Foods

The popularity of fast-food restaurants reflects the adjustment many families have made to a faster pace of life. Dual-earner families, in particular, have less time for grocery shopping, food preparation, and cleanup. Usually they also can afford to eat out occasionally. Another attraction of fast-food restaurants is that they are cheaper than many other restaurants. On the average, a fast-food meal for one is less than one-half the price of a full restaurant meal. Service is simple and fast, and choosing foods involves a minimum of decision making.

Researchers have done studies to find out whether most fast food is nourishing. A meal including a hamburger, french fries, and a soft drink has been found to contain less than one-third of the government's daily recommended allowance for eight nutrients. The substitution of milk for a soft drink raises the amount of calcium, protein, riboflavin, and niacin to acceptable levels. A milkshake made with real

How many times a week do you eat at a fast-food restaurant?

dairy products also is more nutritious than a soft drink. Nevertheless, it is high in calories and sugar, and the combination of ingredients in the meal is still low in vitamins A and C. If coleslaw or a tossed salad is added to the meal, vitamins A and C and some fiber are also added.

Fast-food meals are generally high in fat and salt. Many fast-food milkshakes are not made with dairy products. French fries, especially, are high in fat, salt, and calories. Chili is lower in calories, but high in salt. Pizza, with tomato sauce, green peppers, and cheese, is more nutritious than most fast foods, but also high in calories and salt. A *Consumer Reports* survey concluded that fast foods are acceptable nutritionally only if people eat them infrequently and as *part* of a well-balanced diet.

Eating Disorders

Some young people have a desire to be very thin, but have difficulty reaching this goal. If they become overly concerned with weight loss, they may develop an eating disorder. Two weight-related problems that often affect adolescents have received much attention in recent years. The young people who fall victim to these conditions are trying to lose weight, but are using dangerous methods to do so. These victims need both psychological and medical help. It is vital that they receive treatment quickly, since both conditions can be life-threatening.

Anorexia Nervosa (an-uh-REK-see-uh ner-VO-suh) is a disorder that may appear to be simply crash dieting. The difference, however, is that anorexics do not stop dieting, even when they have become unhealthfully thin. They develop distorted images of their bodies and believe they are still fat. Since they cannot see how weak and ill they are becoming, anorexics can actually starve themselves to death.

Bulimia (byoo-LIM-ee-uh) is similar to anorexia nervosa in that its victims also want to lose weight. Bulimics, though, also want to eat a great deal. To do both, bulimics binge (eat as much as they can, perhaps four or five times what most people would eat during a meal). Then they force themselves to vomit to purge themselves of all the calories they have just consumed. Once they make a habit of binging and purging, they may become unable to digest food. They, too, can starve to death.

It is important to realize that anorexia nervosa and bulimia are not just diets. They are potentially fatal illnesses. Survival depends on prompt medical attention.

Mealtime is a good time for family members to communicate with each other.

Food Preparation and Service

Does more mechanical food preparation and service have a bearing on behavior? A recent study showed that prison inmates fed frozen TV-type meals were more irritable and argued more during meals than when they were served chef-prepared foods on plates. Preparation and service had been dehumanizing, and the prisoners acted accordingly.

Other studies on the effects that food service and preparation have on behavior have yielded findings such as the following: Patients in a mental hospital where fresh flowers were on the dining tables became more relaxed and talked more with each other. Schools with family-style lunch programs, where platters of food are passed around to everyone, report less food waste as well as the creation of a friendlier atmosphere for eating. When elderly people lunch with school children, the meal atmosphere has been judged calmer than usual. Finally, it has been found that in families whose members eat in shifts, the experience of a sit-down, family-style meal can be satisfying for the children.

Although a general trend toward increased snacking and fast-food consumption has developed in recent years, a counter trend is emerging. Some people are moving away from mechanical, hasty food consumption and toward more leisurely dining. They seek out unusual foods and enjoy preparing and eating them. They look upon mealtimes as "special events," both at home and in public dining places, for the purpose of bringing the family together.

For Review

1. How can you reduce the cost of weekly food shopping?
2. Name three healthy alternatives to sweet snacks.
3. Describe the nutritional content of two different kinds of fast foods.

18 Chapter Review

Summary

People's food choices vary according to their cultural backgrounds, food availability, economic factors, and advertising.

To function properly and maintain health, the body needs certain amounts of six key nutrients: proteins, carbohydrates, fats, water, vitamins, and minerals. By selecting a variety of foods, like those in the four food groups, people can obtain the necessary balance of nutrients. Most nutritionists believe that people should limit their intake of sugar, fats, and salt, and increase the amount of fiber in their diets to improve health and prevent certain diseases.

Food management skills and nutrition and consumer knowledge can help people plan low-cost nutritious meals. Today's life styles have contributed to the increase in unhealthy eating habits. Snacking and fast-food consumption are considered to be acceptable eating habits. Some teens suffer from eating disorders that are a result of personal and family problems.

Vocabulary

Match each of the following vocabulary words with one of the definitions that follow.

anorexia nervosa
bulimia
cholesterol
dental caries
empty calories
endosperm
fiber
germ
metabolic processes
nutrients
nutrition
obesity

1. _____ tooth decay
2. _____ elements in food that enable the body to function properly
3. _____ condition of being excessively overweight
4. _____ physical and chemical changes in the body that affect growth, physical activity, and temperature
5. _____ inner part of grain made mostly of starch and proteins
6. _____ eating disorder characterized by binging and purging
7. _____ fat-like substance produced by the body, an excess amount may cause heart disease
8. _____ dietary item in whole grains, nuts, legumes, fruits, and vegetables that provides bulk to satisfy the appetite and helps digestion
9. _____ contained in foods that provide few or no nutrients
10. _____ study of the elements in foods that are necessary for the body to function properly
11. _____ structure inside the kernel of grain that contains minerals, B vitamins, oil, and fat
12. _____ potentially life-threatening eating disorder that causes a person to become extremely thin

Chapter Questions

1. Describe the cultural factors that influence your food choices.
2. Why is a balanced diet important?
3. How can the four food groups help a person to establish a healthy diet?
4. What is a calorie?
5. How do complex carbohydrates differ from sugar?
6. Why should a person eat a diet low in saturated fats?
7. How can people reduce their salt intake?
8. Discuss three reasons why eating whole grains is beneficial.
9. How should a food shopper prepare for grocery shopping?
10. Which parts of the nutritional information on food labels would help a shopper who is watching calories and salt intake?
11. Why do bulimics and anorexics need prompt medical attention?

Skill Activities

1. **Math** To begin a study of comparison shopping, plan a well-balanced meal that includes a variety of foods from the four food groups. Make a list of all the ingredients needed to make this meal. Then, visit four different stores from among the following: supermarkets, roadside stands, convenience stores, discount markets, and small grocery stores. Record the price of each item on your list in each store you visit. Compare the prices of items on your list from store to store.

Considering price and quality, which are the best places to buy meat? Dairy products? Vegetables and fruits? Breads? Other grocery items? What shopping strategies would you advise a food shopper to use when food shopping in your community?

2. **Science** With a group of students, plan a nutritious buffet of snacks to present to your class. To find recipes and ideas for snack foods that provide essential nutrients, refer to the "Food Groups" chart on page 319 and other information given in this chapter. Also consult home economics, nutrition, or food management textbooks, and books and magazines in your local library. Remember to balance your snack selections among the four food groups. On the day you serve the snacks, arrange the foods attractively. Attach a sign to each snack to indicate its food group and major nutrients.

3. **Critical Thinking** Keep a food diary in which you list everything you eat at meals and snacks for one week. At the end of the week, evaluate your diet. Which of the four food groups are you often missing? At what meals or snacks are you consuming empty-calorie foods? How can you adjust your diet and eating habits to achieve better nutrition? Make a list of five specific changes that would improve your diet. For example, if a person's diet contains few fruits or vegetables, he or she can eat an apple for lunch instead of potato chips, and eat a potato at dinner instead of a second helping of dessert.

Glossary

abstinence   The act of voluntarily going without certain pleasures; not having sexual relations.

addiction   The condition of being physically or psychologically dependent, especially on a drug.

adoption   The legal process of becoming a parent to another person's child.

aerobic exercise   Physical activity that conditions the heart and lungs by increasing the efficiency of oxygen intake.

alcoholic   A person who habitually drinks excessive amounts of alcoholic liquor.

alcoholism   The disease condition of habitually drinking excessive amounts of alcoholic liquor.

ambivalence   The experience of having two opposing emotions, such as happiness and sadness, at the same time.

amniotic sac   The protective membrane containing a watery liquid in which the fetus develops.

amphetemine   A drug or other substance used to decrease appetite and overcome fatigue and depression; a stimulant.

anorexia nervosa   An eating disorder characterized by excessive dieting and the fear of being overweight.

antisocial behavior   The actions of an individual that interfere with or pose a threat to society.

atrophy   The wasting away of body organs or tissues resulting from insufficient nutrition or disuse.

autonomy   The independent existence, functioning or development of an individual.

barbiturate   A drug or other substance used to induce sleep or reduce anxiety; a depressant.

betrothal   A promise to marry; an engagement.

body language   A facial expression, gesture, or bodily movement that communicates a nonverbal message.

bonding   The development of a powerful emotional attachment that occurs between parents and their infant.

budget   A plan for managing income and expenses during a period of time.

bulimia   An eating disorder characterized by consumption of large amounts of food (binging), followed by induced vomiting (purging).

cardiovascular fitness   The healthy state in which heart and lungs function effectively.

child abuse   The harmful treatment of a child, which may involve physical or emotional injury or neglect.

cholesterol   A fatlike substance found in the bloodstream that can collect on the inner walls of arteries and cause them to harden.

chromosome   The microscopic structure within a cell's nucleus that carries genetic information.

cilia   Tiny hairlike projections lining the bronchial tubes.

complement   That which completes or makes whole.

condominium   Common rule; an apartment building or townhouse in which each unit is owned rather than rented.

congregate housing   An arrangement in which individuals have their own private living space and share some facilities and responsibilities.

continuum   A line. The ends represent opposing extremes; lesser degrees of the extremes are represented between the ends.

contraception   The intentional prevention of pregnancy.

cooperative   Acting or working together; an apartment unit in a building or complex that residents own jointly.

degenerative disease   Illness characterized by a breakdown or physical deterioration of the body.

dental caries   Tooth decay.

depressant   A drug or other substance that slows the body's reactions, muscles and vital processes.

dissolution   A breaking up; termination of a formal or legal bond.

dual-earner family   A family in which both husband and wife hold paying jobs.

ecosystem   A combination of environments that form an interacting system of activities and functions, becoming a unit in itself.

embryo   The developing unborn child up to two months after conception.

empathy   The ability to show concern for another's problems by experiencing the same situation or feelings.

empty calories   A description of foods that provide few, if any, nutrients.

empty nest   The experience of parents who must start living alone again as a couple when children leave home.

endorphin   A chemical secreted in the brain that has a pain-relieving effect; a lack of it is believed to contribute to alcoholism.

endosperm   The innermost part of a seed that contains stored food and supplies nourishment for the developing embryo.

equity   Fairness; value of property beyond the total amount owed.

essence   The qualities that give something its unique identity.

extended family   Parents, children and other relatives sometimes operating as an integrated family.

family day care   Care provided for a child in another family's home.

family life cycle   The stages a family goes through in the course of its lifetime.

feedback   A response.

fetus   In humans, the developing unborn child in the uterus following the embryo stage, from the end of the second month of pregnancy until birth.

fiber   The roughage or plant material in the diet not digested in the gastrointestinal tract.

fixed expense   In a budget, payments one must make regularly.

flexible expense   In a budget, costs that may vary from month to month.

fontanel   The soft space in an infant's skull that allows for compression of the bones during delivery, thus facilitating the birth process. The bones grow together and close this space by the time a child is two.

foster care   The arrangement in which a child is raised by people other than his natural or adoptive parents.

frame of reference   A set of rules, principles or values that are the basis for the formation of attitudes.

gene   The unit in a chromosome that controls the transmission of a specific hereditary trait.

genetics   The scientific study of the processes involved in the transmission of traits from an organism to its offspring.

germ   A microscopic animal or plant, especially one causing disease; the part of a grain kernel that can sprout to form a new plant.

hallucinogen   A drug or other substance that alters perceptions.

headhunter   A person or agency that recruits people for jobs.

heredity The transmission of traits from one generation to the next.

heterogeneous A description of a group that is composed of unlike elements or parts.

homogeneous A description of a group that is composed of similar elements or parts.

hospice Professional support services for terminally ill patients who remain in their homes.

hotline A telephone service that provides information and support in an emergency or crisis.

hypothesis An educated guess, made to explain facts or serve as a basis for future investigation.

immunologic system The body's ability to resist or overcome disease.

infatuation Strong, exaggerated feelings of fondness for another person, usually based on physical attraction.

integrity The state of being complete; in Erickson's stages of development, the contentment of an older adult with the past and acceptance of life's inevitable end.

internalize To make a part of one's own way of thinking; the process of taking on parents' beliefs, ideas, and views.

joint custody The equal legal responsibility of divorced parents for their children.

juvenile delinquency Repeated failure to follow the law by people who are not legally adults.

lease A contract allowing the use of property for a fixed period in exchange for prearranged payments.

life cycle The series of changes throughout an individual's life, from birth to death.

listener feedback The response or answer that the receiver of the message gives.

manufactured housing Prefabricated home construction that involves the building of sections of a home in a factory and the assembly of the pieces at the housing site.

marital role The traits and tasks that a husband or wife assumes.

metabolic process Physical and chemical changes that are concerned with the activity, nourishment and growth of an organism.

mind-altering substance A chemical that distorts perception.

modeling Patterning one's ideas, values, and behavior after someone else.

mortgage A legal pledge of property given to a creditor as security in case a loan is not repaid.

motor ability The muscle control and coordination needed to perform various skills.

multifactored Having more than one cause.

myth A legend or comfortable illusion.

nuclear family The basic social unit, including parents and their children, living in one household.

nurturing Bringing up; physical expression of loving care.

nutrients Nourishing substance; elements in food that enable the body to maintain life and function properly.

nutrition Food; the study of the elements found in foods that the body needs and the ways in which the body uses them.

obesity The condition of being grossly overweight.

officiant A member of the clergy or a civic official who conducts the marriage ceremony.

peer A person who is the same in age, rank or ability.

peer interaction The association of persons who are similar in age, rank, or ability.

peer pressure The force one feels from others one's own age to act similarly.

placenta An exchange organ in the uterus through which pass nutrients and oxygen from the mother's body and waste products from the fetus.

prenatal Occuring or taking place before birth.

preparatory grief A stage terminally ill people go through before death.

prioritize To arrange items in order of importance.

rebellion The behavior that is exhibited in opposition to authority.

reciprocal Existing on both sides; the complementary or completing part.

reflex A simple involuntary response to a stimulus.

resource A person or thing available for support or help.

restrictiveness Rigid control to keep within certain limits.

role making The process of designating tasks and responsibilities for each individual in a relationship.

rubella An infectious virus; German measles.

self-actualization According to Maslow, full development of one's potential, achieved by striving to be the best one can be.

sensory ability The capacity to respond to outside stimuli by sight, taste, touch, sound and smell.

sex-role stereotyping The social pressure to perform certain behaviors considered appropriate only for men or only for women.

socialization The process by which children learn behavior that is acceptable to the family and society.

standard A flag; an expected level of quality, value or achievement.

stepfamily The unit created by the marriage of a single parent.

stimulant A drug or other substance that temporarily increases the activity of the body or one of its systems or parts.

stress Emphasis; a demanding force on the body or mind.

stressor The source causing a demanding force on the body or mind.

sweat equity The work a potential owner does on his or her future home to reduce the building costs.

temperament A person's frame of mind or natural disposition.

toddler A child who is learning to walk; generally, a child between the ages of 15 and 24 months.

toxemia A condition occuring when kidneys malfunction and fluid builds up in the body.

trade-off A giving up of one belief or advantage to gain another regarded as more desirable.

ultimate Most remote or distant; the most fulfilled sense of self.

umbilical cord The tough cordlike structure extending from the navel of a fetus to the placenta, that contains blood vessels that supply nourishment to the fetus and remove its waste.

unromantic love The love for a parent, sibling, relative or friend.

uterus The thick-walled hollow muscular organ in a woman where the fetus develops; the womb.

verbal communication The use of spoken or written words, signs, or sounds to express ideas or emotions.

violence The illegal or unjust use of physical force to injure people or damage property.

zygote A cell created when sperm and egg join; a fertilized egg.

Index

338   Index

Acknowledgments

Technical Art: Boston Graphics
Illustrations: Roget Ink; 14, 17, 325. Allen Schrag (blackline work); 134, 135, 150, 158. Michael Granger (color overlay); 150, 158.

Photo Credits
i Carol Palmer © 1987. ii(T) Courtesy Peg Sawyer. ii(TR, B) Ellis Herwig/The Picture Cube. ii(BL) Ellis Herwig/Stock Boston. iii(L) Erika Stone. iii(R) Carol Palmer © 1987. v(T) John Lawlor/The Stock Market of NY. v(B) Harry Wilks/Stock Boston. vi(T) Coco McCoy/Rainbow. vi(M) Gabe Palmer/The Stock Market of NY. vi(B) Roy Morsch/The Stock Market of NY. vii(T) Erika Stone. vii(M) Jose Carrillo. vii(B) Miro Vintoniv/Stock Boston. viii(T) Bohdan Hrynewych/Stock Boston. viii(M) D.F. Lawlor/The Picture Cube. viii(B) J. Berndt/The Picture Cube. ix(T) Philip Jon Bailey/The Picture Cube. ix(M) John Bowden/Uniphoto. ix(B) Nancy J. Pierce/Photo Researchers, Inc. x(T) Linda Albrizio/The Stock Market of NY. x(M) Dan McCoy/Rainbow. x(B) Michal Heron © 1985/Woodfin Camp & Assoc. 0–1 Carol Palmer © 1987. 2 Dennis Barnes. 3 Peter J. Menzel/Stock Boston. 4 Ellis Herwig/Stock Boston. 5(T) Janet S. Mendes/The Picture Cube. 5(B) Ellis Herwig/The Picture Cube. 6 Erika Stone. 7 Susan Lapides. 9 David M. Grossman. 10 John Lei/Stock Boston. 11(T) Ellis Herwig/The Picture Cube. 11(B) Dan McCoy/Rainbow. 12 Sepp Seitz © 1980/Woodfin Camp & Assoc. 13 Erika Stone. 15 Elizabeth Crews/Stock Boston. 16 Melissa Grimes-Guy/Photo Researchers. 18(T) John Running/Stock Boston. 18(M, B) Erika Stone. 19(T) Peter Menzel/Stock Boston. 19(M) Charles Feil/Stock Boston. 19(B) R. Friedman/The Picture Cube. 22 Rick Smolan/Stock Boston. 23 Susan Lapides. 24 Erika Stone. 25 Erika Stone. 26 Jeffrey Myers/The Stock Market of NY. 28 Blair Seitz/Photo Researchers. 29(T) Jacques Charlas/Stock Boston. 29(B) John Lawlor/The Stock Market of NY. 30 Jack Sullivan/Photo Researchers. 31 Carol Palmer © 1987. 32 Susan Lapides. 33 John Lei/Stock Boston. 35 Michal Heron. 37 Charles Leavitt/The Picture Cube. 40 Michael Manheim/The Stock Market of NY. 41(T) Harry Wilks/Stock Boston. 41(M) Gabe Palmer/The Stock Market of NY. 41(B) John Running/Stock Boston. 42 Jose Carrillo. 43(T) Erika Stone. 43(L) Willie L. Hill/Stock Boston. 43(R) Erika Stone. 43(B) Camilla Smith/Rainbow. 44 Dan Walsh/The Picture Cube. 45 Jeffry W. Myers/Stock Boston. 47 Scala/Art Resource, NY. 49(R) Rick Smolan/Stock Boston. 49(L) Bill Gallery/Stock Boston. 51 Joel Gordon © 1978. 54 Erika Stone. 55 Richard Steedman/The Stock Market of NY. 56 Coco McCoy/Rainbow. 57(T) Mac Donald/The Picture Cube. 57(B) Ellis Herwig/Stock Boston. 58(T) John Running/Stock Boston. 58(B) Peter Vandermark/Stock Boston. 60 David M. Grossman. 63 Courtesy National Council on Alcoholism and The Ad Council. 65(T) Courtesy S.A.D.D., "Students Against Driving Drunk". 65(B) Stephen Ferry/Gamma-Liason. 66(T) Ziggy Kaluzny/Gamma-Liaison. 66(B) Susan Lapides. 67 John Lei/Stock Boston. 68(T) Susan Lapides. 68(B) Patrick Ward/Stock Boston. 69 Mike Mazzaschi/Stock Boston. 71(T) Erika Stone. 71(B) Willie L. Hill/Stock Boston. 73 Jeff Albertson/Stock Boston. 76–77 John Feingersh/Stock Boston. 78 Van Bucher/Photo Researchers. 79(T) Gabe Palmer/The Stock Market of NY. 79(M) Johathan Barkan/The Picture Cube. 79(B) Jose Carrillo. 80 Camilla Smith/Rainbow. 81 Joel Gordon © 1979. 82 Richard Kozak/Insight Archives. 83(T) Gabe Palmer/The Stock Market of NY. 83(R) Barbara Kirk/The Stock Market of NY. 83(L) James Lester/Photo Researchers. 83(B) Dan McCoy/Rainbow. 84 Carol Palmer © 1987. 87 John Lei/Stock Boston. 89(T) M. Ben David/Woodfin Camp & Assoc. 89(L) David Barnes © 1980/The Stock Market of NY. 89(R) Jeffry W. Myers/Stock Boston. 91 Susan Lapides. 94 Alain Walch/The Stock Market of NY. 95 Roy Morsch/The Stock Market of NY. 96 Jose Carrillo. 97 Carol Palmer © 1987. 98 Gabe Palmer/The Stock Market of NY. 99 Jose Carrillo. 101 Erika Stone. 102 John Lei/Stock Boston. 104 Erika Stone. 105 Ted Cordingley. 108 Erika Stone. 109 Erika Stone. 110(T) Solomon Butcher/Nebraska State Historical Society. 110(M) Culver Pictures, Inc. 110(B) UPI/Bettmann Newsphotos. 111 Joel Gordon © 1979. 112 Ted Abell/Stock Boston. 113 Erika Stone. 114 The Image Works/Alan Carey. 115 Philip Jon Bailey/Stock Boston. 117 Paula M. Lerner/The Picture Cube. 118 Jerry Howard/Positive Images. 121(T) Joel Gordon © 1985. 121(BL) Erika Stone. 121(BR) Will McIntyre/Photo Researchers. 122(T) Stuart Cohen/Stock Boston. 122(M, B) Carol Palmer © 1987. 123(T) Ellis Herwig/The Picture Cube. 123(M) Matthew Maythons/Stock Boston. 123(B) Janet S. Mendes/The Picture Cube. 126 Barbara Kirk/The Stock Market of NY. 128 Erika Stone. 129 Erika Stone. 130 Erika Stone. 131 Jose Carrillo. 132 Charles Gupton/Stock Boston. 133 Ellis Herwig/Stock Boston. 136 Erika Stone. 137(T) Andrew Brilliant/The Picture Cube. 137(B) John Curtis. 138 Joel Gordon © 1983. 139 Courtesy Hale House. 141(T) Dan McCoy/Rainbow. 141(B) Russ Kinne/Photo Researchers. 143 Suzanne Szasz. 145(T) Herb Snitzer/Stock Boston. 145(B) Larry Mulvehill/Photo Researchers. 148 Erika Stone. 149 Dan McCoy/Rainbow. 151 Jose Carrillo. 152 Suzanne Szasz/Photo Researchers. 153(L) Erika Stone. 153(R) Jose Carrillo. 154 Michal Heron © 1982/Woodfin Camp & Assoc. 155 Michal Heron. 156 Daniel Brody/Stock Boston. 157(TR) Anna Kaufman Moon/Stock Boston. 157(TL) Gabor Demjen/Stock Boston. 157(BL) John Coletti/Stock Boston.

157(B) Jeffry W. Myers/Stock Boston. 160 Peter Vandermark/Stock Boston. 161(TR) Randall Hyman/Stock Boston. 161(TL) John Lei/Stock Boston. 161(BR) Jonathan Barkan/The Picture Cube. 161(BL) Diane M. Lowe/Stock Boston. 163 Carol Palmer © 1987. 164 Diane M. Lowe/Stock Boston. 165(TR, TL) Miro Vintoniv/Stock Boston. 165(BR) Terry Eller/Stock Boston. 165(BL) Joseph Schuyler/Stock Boston. 166 Courtesy Peg Sawyer. 170 Erika Stone. 171(T) Bill Gillette/Stock Boston. 172(T) J. Berndt/Stock Boston. 172(B) Jose Carrillo. 173 Stuart Cohen/Stock Boston. 174(L) Julie O'Neil/The Picture Cube. 174(R) Mike Mazzachi/Stock Boston. 175(T) Betsy Cole/The Picture Cube. 175(B) David Woo/Stock Boston. 177 James H. Simon/The Picture Cube. 178(T) Dave Schaefer/The Picture Cube. 178(B) Donald Dietz/Stock Boston. 179 John Lei/Stock Boston. 181 Erika Stone. 183(TL) Frank Siteman/The Picture Cube. 183(TR) Ellis Herwig/The Picture Cube. 183(BL) Bohdan Hrynewych/Stock Boston. 183(BR) Erika Stone. 185 Owen Franken/Stock Boston. 186(R) Carol Palmer © 1987. 186(L), 187(R) David Woo/Stock Boston. 187(L) Bonnie Griffith/The Picture Cube. 190 Michal Heron/Woodfin Camp & Assoc. 191(T) Ellis Herwig/The Picture Cube. 191(B) Joel Gordon © 1976. 195(T) James H. Simon/The Picture Cube. 195(B) Liane Enkelis/Stock Boston. 196 Charles Gupton/Stock Boston. 197 Richard Steedman, © 1982/The Stock Market of NY. 198, 199 Richard Kozak/Insight Archives. 200 Mikki Ansin/The Picture Cube. 201 Frank Siteman/The Picture Cube. 202 J.D. Sloan/The Picture Cube. 203 D.F. Lawlor/The Picture Cube. 204(T) Bob Daemmrich/Stock Boston. 204(M) John Running/Stock Boston. 204(B) Jonathan L. Barkan/The Picture Cube. 205 Michal Heron. 206(L) Blair Seitz/Photo Researchers. 206(R) R.P. Kingston/The Picture Cube. 207 Mieke Maas/IMAGE. 208 Patty Chock/Stock Boston. 209 Chet Seymour/The Picture Cube. 212 Dan McCoy/Rainbow. 213 J. Berndt/The Picture Cube. 214 Frank Siteman/The Picture Cube. 215(R) Focus On Sports. 215(L) E. Williamson/The Picture Cube. 217 Erika Stone. 218 Owen Franken/Stock Boston. 220 Ted Cordingley. 221(B) Eric Roth/The Picture Cube. 221(T) Sarah Putnam/The Picture Cube. 223 Courtesy Covenant House. 224(T) Dave Schaefer/The Picture Cube. 224(B) Sarah Putnam/The Picture Cube. 225 Houtchens-Kitchens/The Picture Cube. 228 Roy Morsch/The Stock Market of NY. 230 Camilla Smith/Rainbow. 231 Camilla Smith/Rainbow. 232(L) Ellis Herwig/The Picture Cube. 232(R) Milton Feinberg/Stock Boston. 233 Richard Pasley/Stock Boston. 234 Rob Nelson/Stock Boston. 235(L) Dan McCoy/Rainbow. 235(R) Philip Jon Bailey/The Picture Cube. 235(M) Frank Siteman/The Picture Cube. 237(T, M) Michal Heron. 237(R) Richard Hutchings/Photo Researchers, Inc. 238(L) Philip Jon Bailey/The Picture Cube. 238(TR) Michal Heron. 238(BR) Dan McCoy/Rainbow. 239(T) Richard Wood/The Picture Cube. 239(B) Jeff Albertson/The Picture Cube. 240(L) Therese Frare/The Picture Cube. 240(R) Seth Resnick/Stock Boston. 241 Donna Moore/Stock Boston. 243 Dan McCoy/Rainbow. 245(R) Carol Palmer © 1987. 245(L) Carol Palmer © 1987. 248 Michal Heron © 1984/Woodfin Camp & Assoc. 249(T) Jose Azel © 1984, Contact Press Images/Woodfin Camp & Assoc. 249(M) Carol Palmer © 1987. 249(B) Martha Bates/Stock Boston. 251 Mike Mazzaschi/Stock Boston. 252 Michal Heron © 1981/Woodfin Camp & Assoc. 253 Michal Heron © 1984/Woodfin Camp & Assoc. 254 Michal Heron © 1981/Woodfin Camp & Assoc. 255 John Running/Stock Boston. 257(T) Richard Steedman/The Stock Market of NY. 257(B) Fredrik D. Bodin © 1979/Stock Boston. 258 Jose Carrillo. 259 Lester Sloan © 1986/Woodfin Camp & Assoc. 262 Andrew Brilliant. 263 Peter Vandermark/Stock Boston. 264(L) Cary Wolinsky/Stock Boston. 264(R) David Austen/Stock Boston. 265 Terry Eiler/Stock Boston. 266(T) J.T. Miller © 1985/The Stock Market of NY. 266(B) Andrew Brilliant/Stock Boston. 267 Culver Pictures, Inc. 269 Dan McCoy/Rainbow. 270(T) Erika Stone. 270(B) Carol Palmer/The Picture Cube. 271 Bruce Davidson, Magnum Photos, Inc. 272 Carol Palmer © 1987. 273(T) J. Berndt/The Picture Cube. 273(B) Dan McCoy/Rainbow. 274(L) Peter Southwick/Stock Boston. 274(TR) Eric Neurath/Stock Boston. 274(BR) Peter Menzel/Stock Boston. 275(TL) Peter Vandermark/Stock Boston. 275(TR) James H. Simon/The Picture Cube. 275(BL) Charles Kennard/Stock Boston. 275(BR) Jim Hamilton/The Picture Cube. 276(L) Owen Franken/Stock Boston. 276(R) Owen Franken/Stock Boston. 277(L) J.D. Sloan/The Picture Cube. 277(R) Glenn Kulbako/The Picture Cube. 279 Erik Anderson/Positive Images. 280 John Bowden/Uniphoto. 281 John Coletti/Stock Boston. 283(L) Donald Dietz/Stock Boston. 283(TR) Cary Wolinsky/Stock Boston. 283(BR) John Coletti/Stock Boston. 284 Erik Anderson/Stock Boston. 285 Nancy J. Pierce/Photo Researchers, Inc. 288 Bill Gallery/Stock Boston. 289 Ted Cordingley. 290(L) Paula M. Lerner/The Picture Cube. 290(R) Ted Cordingley. 291 Jerry Howard/Stock Boston. 292 Michal Heron © 1984/Woodfin Camp & Assoc. 295 Paul Conklin. 296(R) Linda Albrizio/The Stock Market of NY. 296(L) Jeff Dunn/Stock Boston. 297 Andrew Brilliant. 300 David Burnett, Contract Press Images/Woodfin Camp & Assoc. 301 John Blaustein/Woodfin Camp & Assoc. 304 Christopher Morrow/Stock Boston. 305(L) Chuck Fishman/Woodfin Camp & Assoc. 305(R) Owen Franken/Stock Boston. 305(B) Bill Gallery/Stock Boston. 308(T) Charles Gupton/Stock Boston. 308(M) Jon Feingersh 1986/Stock Boston. 308(BL) Erika Stone. 308(BR) Michal Heron © 1984/Woodfin Camp & Assoc. 309 Michal Heron © 1981/Woodfin Camp & Assoc. 314 Dennis Barnes. 315(L) Anestis Diakopoulos/Stock Boston. 315(R) Michal Heron © 1985/Woodfin Camp & Assoc. 316 Stephanie Maze © 1985/Woodfin Camp & Assoc. 319(all) John Curtis. 321 Jeffry W. Myers, © 1985/Stock Boston. 323(T) Richard Hutchings/Photo Researchers. 323(B) National Turkey Federation. 325 John Curtis. 326 Charles Gupton/Stock Boston. 327 The Bettmann Archive, Inc. 328 Leif Skoogfors © 1985/Woodfin Camp & Assoc. 329 Roy Morsch/The Stock Market of NY. 330 Mike Mazzaschi/Stock Boston. 331 Michal Heron/Woodfin Camp & Assoc.

Text Citations: 3 Excerpt from "The Summer of Truth," copyright © 1955 by Lucile Vaughan Payne. First published in *Seventeen Magazine*. Reprinted by permission of McIntosh and Otis, Inc. 11, 15 Maslow quotes as cited in Paul Good, *The Individual* (New York: Time-Life, 1974). 31, 253 Feature and quote from *I Lost Everything in the Post-Natal Depression*, by Erma Bombeck. Copyright © 1970, 1971, 1972, 1973 by Field Enterprises, Inc. Reprinted by permission of Doubleday & Co., Inc. 46 Excerpt from Stuart Emery, *Actualizations: You Don't Have to Rehearse to Be Yourself* (New York: Doubleday, 1978). 63 Questions adapted from "Too Young?" Reprinted with permission of Alcoholics Anonymous World Services, Inc. 81 Quote from Editors of *Bride's Magazine, Bride's Book of Etiquette* (New York: Grosset and Dunlap, 1976). 96 Quote from *Marriage and Family Development*, Fifth Edition, by Evelyn Millis Duval (J.P. Lippincott Company). Copyright © 1957, 1962, 1967, 1971, 1977, by Harper & Row, Publishers, Inc. 139 Quotations reprinted with permission from "Mama Hale and Her Little Angels" by Claire Safran, Reader's Digest, September 1984. © by The Readers' Digest Assn. Inc. 177 Green quote from M. Green, *Fathering* (New York: McGraw-Hill, 1976), p. 150. Biller quote from *New York Times Magazine*, June 17, 1979, p. 50. 182 Information adapted from W.C. Becker, "Consequences of Different Kinds of Parental Discipline," in M.L. Hoffman and L.W. Hoffman, eds., *Review of Child Development Research*, 1 (1964), p. 175. 199 *Chicago Sun-Times* quote © *Chicago Sun-Times*, 1975. Excerpted with permission from Pat O'Brien's article, "The Stepparents." 244 Bolles quote from Richard Nelson Bolles, *What Color Is Your Parachute? A Job Hunters Manual* (Berkeley, Calif.: Ten Speed Press, 1980). 302 Feature quote from Ogden Tanner, *Stress* (New York: Time-Life Human Behavior Series, 1976), p. 29.

The authors and editors have made every effort to trace the ownership of all copyrighted selections found in this book and to make full acknowledgement for their use.